MODERN GREECE

MODERN GREECE

Facets of Underdevelopment

NICOS P. MOUZELIS

HM HOLMES & MEIER PUBLISHERS, INC.
New York

First published in the United Kingdom 1978 by
THE MACMILLAN PRESS LTD
London and Basingstoke

First published in the United States of America 1978 by
HOLMES & MEIER PUBLISHERS, INC
101 Fifth Avenue
New York, N.Y. 10003

Library of Congress Cataloging in Publication Data

Mouzelis, Nicos P
  Modern Greece.

  Includes bibliographical references and index.
  1. Greece, Modern — Economic conditions. 2. Econom-
ic development — Social aspects. 3. Greece, Modern —
Social conditions. I. Title.
HC295.M63 1977   330.9′495′07   77-17314
ISBN 0-8419-0357-3

Printed in Great Britain

Contents

Acknowledgements

I would like to thank the following persons who, either through reading parts of the manuscript or through discussing various problems with me, have greatly helped my work: Mike Attalides, Anthony Barnett, Richard J. Crampton, George Grimpas, George Dertilis, Nikiphoros Diamandouros, Jane Dimaki, Nicos Garganas, Rousos Kouudouros, Victor Papacosmas, Spilios Papaspiliopoulos, Leslie Sklair, Melina Serafetinidi, Constantine Tsoukalas, Thanos Veremis, Costas Vergopoulos, Tasos Yiannitsis, and Yanis Yianoulopoulos.

I would also like to mention here a number of unpublished Ph.D. theses which I found particularly helpful in my work. Among these, Melina Serafetinidi's work (*The Breakdown of Parliamentary Institutions in Greece*, unfinished Ph.D. thesis, London School of Economics) played an important role in shaping some of my ideas on the structural basis of the 1967 coup (Chapter 7); Thanos Veremis' thesis (*The Greek Army in Politics*, Ph.D., Trinity College, Oxford, 1974) provided much basic information for my analysis of political developments during the inter-war period (Chapter 6); the following works were very useful for the elaboration of specific points in various parts of this book:

George Dertilis, *Social Change and Military Intervention in politics: Greece 1881–1928*, Ph.D., University of Sheffield, 1976; Nikiphoros Diamandouros, *Political Modernization, Social Conflict and Cultural Cleavage in the formation and the Modern Greek State 1871–1878*, Ph.D., Columbia University, 1972; Victor Papacosmas, *The Greek Military Revolt of 1909*, Ph.D., Indiana University, 1970; Constantine Tsoukalas, *Dependance et Réproduction: le rôle de l'appareil scolaire dans une formation trans-territoriale*, Ph.D., Sorbonne, 1976.

Finally I must express my gratitude to Ellen Sutton for her invaluable editorial and secretarial help, and to Doriana Collins for her translation of some Bulgarian texts.

N.P.M.

February 1977

Introduction

This collection of essays is an attempt to assess various theories concerning the development problems of third-world countries, by examining their relevance and utility for the analysis of a concrete case study — that of Greece. I started working on these articles several years ago when I embarked on a long-term and as yet unfinished project of studying peasant movements in Greece and Bulgaria during the inter-war period. Examination of the Greek inter-war society soon showed that to understand it properly a more comprehensive view of the development of the modern Greek economy and polity was needed. I also felt that, notwithstanding the relative scarcity of serious economic-historical research on modern Greece, the application of sociological theory to such material as did exist already could (even without systematic groundwork on primary sources) shed some new light on the country's historical development and could provide guidelines for a fresh look at some crucial problems of the Greek social formation. Also, focusing on a country which, in a variety of ways, had experienced for centuries the disrupting effects of Western imperialism would be a useful way of investigating in concrete terms the various theories on underdevelopment — theories which occupy a prominent place in today's sociological literature.

The present volume, which lays the foundations for a more intensive study of Greek and Bulgarian inter-war social structures, is the result of an attempt to get better acquainted with the historical development of the Greek class structure by using conceptual tools derived from the vivid debates on the problems which poor countries are now facing in their efforts to overcome their poverty and dependence.

Part I of the book consists of a single chapter which gives an overall analysis of the development of Greek capitalism from the Ottoman period until today. This rather long chapter provides the connecting links between the essays that follow. It spells out some basic themes which will be taken up and examined in greater detail in subsequent chapters; and more generally it provides for the non-Greek reader an overall framework, with the help of which he can more easily locate specific problems and developments treated in the rest of the book.

Part II has a predominantly theoretical orientation, in the sense that the main emphasis is on the conceptual frameworks and the ensuing problems of development theories. Here empirical materials from the Greek case are brought in to illustrate a number of theoretical points. Thus Chapter 2 is an attempt to depict the state of development literature today by focusing on the highly influential neo-Marxist school, and the various criticisms recently formulated against its main theses.

Chapter 3 assesses the social science literature on modern Greek development/underdevelopment in the context of a comparison between Marxist and functionalist analyses of class.

Finally, Chapter 4, starting with a review of two important books by a Greek Marxist economist — one on the general relationship between capitalism and agriculture, the other on the development of Greek agriculture — assesses the relevance of Althusserian Marxism to the study of agricultural developments in Greece.

The general theme which links Chapters 2, 3 and 4, and which constitutes the theoretical basis of the whole book, is that only a conceptual framework with class analysis at its centre can successfully deal with development problems; and that from this point of view the most influential paradigms in both non-Marxist and Marxist social sciences today (i.e. Parsonian functionalism and Althusserian Marxism respectively) are highly inadequate guides for the study of the obstacles that most poor countries are facing in their efforts to overcome their economic backwardness.

In Part III the focus shifts from the theoretical to a more empirical level of analysis. With the help of conceptual tools clarified in Part II, this section examines certain key problems which arise out of a closer look at the relationship between the historical trajectory of the Greek economy and its politico-ideological superstructure. Chapter 5 opens with a problem which is crucial for understanding the political structure of modern Greece and its decisive difference from that of her Balkan neighbours before the Second World War: the problem of why Greece, in striking contrast to Bulgaria and all other Balkan countries, did not develop an important peasant party during the inter-war period.

Chapters 6 and 7 deal with another important problem area in the study of modern Greece, that of the role and position of the army within the Greek social formation, and the relation of the military to economic and political developments during the twentieth century. Specifically, Chapter 6, focusing more on the political superstructure, sets out to identify the major structural differences between pre-war and post-war military interventions in Greek politics — as well as to explain such differences in terms of the changing class structure. Given this general framework, Chapter 7 proposes a theory which links the rise and fall of the Greek junta to the post-war model of capital accumulation in Greece.

Finally, Chapter 8 identifies, and tries to offer some tentative explanations of the excessive formalism which rules not only in political debates but in all spheres of Greek life. This leads back to the concept of underdevelopment (discussed in Chapter 2), and to a further assessment of its political and cultural dimensions.

As these essays were written over a long period of time, they are not of a methodologically uniform character. For instance, the mode-of-production concept plays an important role in the more recently written essays on the development of Greek capitalism (Chapter 1) and on the Greek dictatorship (Chapter 7), whereas it does not in Chapter 5, which compares the Greek and Bulgarian peasantries. However, I believe that all chapters show a consistent attempt to place the concept of class at the centre of the analysis; and to do this in a way which avoids the treatment of classes as anthropomorphic entities doing and regulating all social issues — or, at the other extreme, as mere 'bearers of structures' or, even worse, statistical categories useful for a static study of social stratification.

Some of the essays presented here have already been published (Chapters 3, 4, 5, 7). In such cases the original text has been modified so as to avoid excessive overlapping and to ensure continuity and conceptual consistency. (It is for this latter reason also that many cross-references are given to indicate the major linkages between the essays.) However, so as not to destroy the self-containment of each essay, I have kept the above changes within reasonable limits, which means that in some cases I could not avoid repeating the same point more than once. Also, the notes have been arranged in such a way that the reader need not refer to previous chapters to find the title and other particulars of an author's work. Finally, in order to make the main exposition less cumbersome, extensive use has been made of notes at the back of the book (especially for Chapters 1 and 2), not only for bibliographical references but also for developing a variety of indirectly relevant points.

Part I
The Historical Framework

1 The Development of Greek Capitalism: An Overall View

Despite the risks of overgeneralisation and schematisation implied in such an enterprise, it was considered necessary to give in this introductory chapter a general picture of the development of the Greek social formation from Ottoman times until the present. To overcome the complexity of the task, the main emphasis will be on the changing articulation of modes of production, from the period when Greece was a province of the Ottoman empire and the capitalist mode of production played only a peripheral role in its social formation, to the inter-war and post-war periods when capitalism became dominant.[1] Within this perspective, the focus is more specifically on the *changing relations of production*, rather than on the evolving technologies or the politico-ideological developments. Because of this emphasis, the periodisation adopted here is somewhat different from that found in political histories of Greece, or in those works which trace purely technological developments.

1   THE OTTOMAN PERIOD

Some of the basic features of modern Greece having been delineated while the country was still under Ottoman rule, it is necessary to give a brief review of developments during that period.

A   The Ottoman State and the development of agriculture

The fifteenth century is usually considered the Golden Age of the Ottoman empire. It was then that rapid territorial expansion went hand in hand with increasing centralisation of the State authority and the effective functioning of the major religious and politico-economic institutions of

3

the huge multinational empire.

It is generally accepted that the Ottoman patrimonial system of power was organised in such a way as to prevent the creation of a strong landed aristocracy which might have presented a challenge to the absolute authority of the Sultan. Contrary to the situation in both Western and Eastern Europe, all land belonged, at least in theory, to Allah and his representative on earth, the Sultan. Leaving aside the *de facto* existence of private lands,[2] during this early period at least the cultivated land was organised under the *timar* system of landholding. This was nearer in kind to the Carolingian benefice than to the medieval fief. In contrast to European feudal lords, timar holders (the *spahis*) had no ownership rights over the land. They simply had a non-hereditary right to part of the produce, in exchange for which they were obliged to provide both administrative and military services to the Porte. The direct producers, on the other hand, whether Christians or Muslims, had hereditary usage of their land, subject to the obligation to cultivate it regularly. And despite the heavier taxation burden for the non-Muslim subjects, by most accounts the total surplus exacted from the peasants by the State (through taxation) and the timariots (through rent payments in kind or money) was lighter than in the rest of Europe.[3] In other words, the sultanic State, in its concern to minimise any challenge from local potentates during the time of its ascent, favoured and supported the peasantry by putting very strict limits to the type and degree of control which the spahis could exercise over the direct producers. It is for this reason that *corvée* dues, for instance, played only a minor role in the timar system, and serfdom was not as widespread as in the rest of Europe.[4]

Of course, in making such comparisons one must always keep in mind the radical differences between the structures of the sultanic and the Western monarchical States. For the latter, a very fine balance of power between the monarchy and the aristocracy had been fully established as early as the fifteenth and sixteenth centuries; this compromise constituted the most distinctive feature of European absolutism,[5] and was related to the constitutionalist and pluralistic regimes of post-*ancien régime* Europe. If the Western nobility failed to resist the rise and expansion of the monarchical administration, a sizeable part of it was very successful in safeguarding and promoting its interests by occupying key posts within the monarchical State.[6]

Such a compromise was never achieved in the Ottoman case. When the State was strong, as in the fifteenth century, the aristocracy was completely subjugated to the Sultan's despotic rule. Not only were its rights on the land severely curtailed, but its control of the State apparatus was minimised by the appointment to key administrative posts of non-aristocratic elements totally subservient to the Sultan (slaves, eunuchs, Christians etc.). Thus the weakening of the sultanic authority (after the middle of the sixteenth century) did not result in a strengthening of aristocratic influence *within* the State, but in the more or less total autonomy of local pashas, and hence in the ultimate disintegration of the imperial policy.[7] All this means that, in comparison with the West, there was an absence of organic articulation between the State and the economically dominant classes (timariots, merchants), a structural feature which weakened the 'rule of law' and led to a generalised insecurity and arbitrariness — an arbitrariness emanating from the top when the State was strong, and from below, i.e. from the local potentates, when the State was weak.

In the sixteenth century, after the end of the wave of conquests, the Ottoman State entered a long phase of gradual decline, at a time when the Western European monarchical State was being consolidated and the Continent experienced an unprecedented period of economic expansion,[8] an expansion marked by technological innovations, the transatlantic discoveries, the development of long-term trade, the influx of precious metal, the general rise of prices, the growth of populations and urban centres, etc. It was during this time that, to use Wallerstein's term, a world economy was born through the institutionalisation of an international division of labour — a development which contributed gradually to the differentiation of Europe into core, peripheral and semi-peripheral States.[9] Although the significance of this early 'world economy' is probably exaggerated by Wallerstein, there is no doubt that the European economic expansion of the 'long' sixteenth century had serious repercussions on the Ottoman economy and polity. For it was during this period that the major European States, in their efforts to improve their economies and to secure cheap raw materials and food for their growing populations, started to extract a variety of trading privileges from the declining Ottoman State. The famous *capitulatory privileges* (i.e. trade concessions granted by the Sultan to various foreign powers)[10] which began in the sixteenth century and went on growing with the gradual disintegration of the Ottoman State, were quite effective in imposing extremely favourable trade terms for the West and in orienting the whole Ottoman economy to the developmental requirements of Western Europe.[11]

Under the impact of these developments and with the spectacular rise of international grain prices, Turkish landlords started to introduce cultivations of new crops (maize, cotton) and to increase the production of cereals.[12] In the absence of any significant technological improvements in Ottoman agriculture during this period, the increase of production was to a great extent due to the cultivation of new lands and to the growing exploitation of the Christian and Muslim peasantries.[13] This was made possible by the central State no longer being capable of protecting the peasants against the rapaciousness of their lords. The latter, lured by huge potential profits from grain exports, began to increase their privileges at the expense of the direct producers. Thus timar holdings gradually became hereditary, rents and other dues increased, and the traditional rights of the peasantry working the land were weakened or forfeited altogether. It was in vain that various reformers, especially Sultan Suleiman the Magnificent, tried to stop this deteriorating situation through a more centralised control of timar distribution and through the stipulation of strict rules on timar inheritance and transfer.[14] The increasing commercialisation of agriculture and the decreasing authority of the Porte unavoidably led to the emergence of big landed property and the gradual passage from the timar to the *chiflik* system of landholding.[15]

Under the chiflik system, the triangular balance between the State, the peasants and the local lords was upset in favour of the latter. The chiflik holder became the *de facto* hereditary owner of the land at the expense of both the State's and the peasants' rights. Initially the chiflik system had emerged as an institutional device for putting unused areas of land under cultivation. But gradually, with the weakening of the State controls, the system expanded to cover previously timar lands and later came to dominate most agricultural production.[16] Already in the seventeenth century, when the Ottoman empire felt the severe and prolonged European crisis in the wake of the sixteenth-century expansion, one of its results was the further strengthening of the chiflik system. Just as in the rest of Europe, this crisis brought a movement of 'back to the land', accompanied by an intensification of peasant exploitation and by increased polarisation of rich and poor.[17] If in England this exploitation took the form of an acceleration of the enclosure movement, and in France the strengthening of feudal dues, in the Ottoman empire – and in Eastern Europe too – it resulted in the peasantry being cut off from any State protection and being reduced to the wretched state of *de facto* serfdom.[18] Hence the spectacular development of brigandage, of mass village desertions, and of peasant revolts, which were to increase during the eighteenth century.[19]

It must be emphasised here, however, that despite the strengthening of private property and the intensive commercialisation of agriculture, the chiflik system did not lead to the development of a capitalist agriculture, i.e. to the creation of a rural proletariat. Those who lost their small landholdings did not become 'free' labourers; they were obliged to cultivate the same land under sharecropping arrangements. During the whole of Ottoman rule, wage remuneration played only a peripheral role in the Greek countryside.[20] And, contrary to the situation in some Western cases,[21] the Ottoman land rent did not lead to the development of agrarian capitalism.[22] Up to this time, capital either remained in the sphere of distribution, or only made some hesitant but ultimately unsuccessful advances in the direction of artisanal-industrial production.

B   *The development of commerce and industry*

The Ottoman conquest of the Balkans in the fifteenth century put an end to the political and economic chaos which the continuous quarrels between Byzantines, Venetians, Genovese and Slavs had been creating in the peninsula. The establishment of the *Pax Ottomanica*, the early lenient policy of the State *vis-à-vis* the conquered peasantries, and its attempt to repopulate the deserted towns and the various centres along the major commercial routes,[23] contributed to the development of trade and to a general improvement of the economy.

During this period it was the Venetian merchants who played the dominant role in eastern Mediterranean commerce. Through a good part of the sixteenth century, during the great West-European economic expansion, the Italians continued to be the exclusive providers of textiles and other manufactured goods to the Porte, and were the foremost exporters of the empire's agricultural produce to the West. But towards the end of the sixteenth century, French and later English and Dutch merchant capital put an end to the Venetian trade hegemony. The 1569 agreement between the Sultan and King Francis I, which obliged all foreign ships (except the Venetian) to trade under the protection of the French flag, enabled the French merchants to control a sizeable part of the Ottoman import-export trade.[24] A quarter of a century later the English, despite strong French opposition, also succeeded in extracting similar privileges from the Porte, whereas the Dutch obtained their capitulatory privileges only in the middle of the seventeenth century.[25]

Greek merchants, though not yet so important in the sixteenth century, were nevertheless already quite actively involved, not only in internal trade but also in the burgeoning commerce of the Black Sea and the Adriatic. With the tremendous rise in Western demand for grain and other foodstuffs during this period, the Greeks[26] were very soon able to control a considerable portion of the cereal provisioning trade. It was in vain that the Ottoman authorities tried to regulate this trade to ensure the provisioning of the big Ottoman cities, especially Constantinople where the population at that time was coming up to 700,000. Under the lure of huge export profits, Greek merchants disregarded the regulations of the weak Ottoman State and specialised in the illegal export of cereals, gaining vast fortunes in the process.[27]

Another illegal source for the formation of Greek merchant capital was piracy. During the late sixteenth century, with the gradual decline of Venetian commerce and the temporary weakening of the French position in the Levant (due mainly to religious wars), piracy took on considerable dimensions. Greek seamen did not miss their chance to engage in this very lucrative activity — an activity which soon became an integral part of the Ottoman economy. Indeed, especially in the Aegean islands, stable agreements developed between pirates and merchants who, frequently having obtained the consent of the local administration with bribes, were buying looted goods at very low prices and re-exporting or selling them back inside the empire.[28]

Thus the end of the sixteenth and the beginning of the seventeenth century, when Greek merchants together with the French, the English and the Dutch were gradually displacing the Italians in the eastern Mediterranean trade,[29] can be seen as the phase of 'primitive accumulation' of Greek capital. However, during this early period, Greek capital was clearly playing a secondary role and was subservient to the activities of the Western European merchants. This was true not only in the general sense that its growth was limited and its structure shaped by the growth of Western economies; but also in the sense that it mostly thrived as the result of illegal activities. Greek merchants, lacking the opportunities and political autonomy that Western merchants enjoyed through the capitulatory privileges, as well as the material means of transportation by sea, were still only occupying a secondary and, at that, rather precarious position in the Levantine trade.

This situation changed dramatically in the eighteenth century. The wars between England and France disorganised their trading networks in the Mediterranean and presented a unique opportunity for the Greeks to fill the vacuum. An even more decisive boost was given to them by the Kuchuk Kairnarji agreement of 1774 which the victorious Russians imposed on the Sultan. By this treaty Russia not only acquired trading privileges similar to if not greater than those previously enjoyed by the French and English, but also established a legal framework which was favourable to the Christian subjects of the empire in a number of ways. Thus Kuchuk Kairnarji was the basis for subsequent agreements[30] which, for instance, enabled Greek merchants to fly the Russian flag — a privilege which allowed them to engage in maritime trade without fear of the arbitrary and extortionate taxation policies of the Porte.

Apart from these more or less conjunctural events, another important development which helped Greek commerce was the dominant position acquired by the Phanariote Greeks, especially in the eighteenth century, within the Ottoman administration. The Phanariotes could almost be defined as a *'noblesse de robe'* of the Ottoman empire. Most claimed to be direct descendants of Byzantine aristocratic families, but a considerable number of them had accumulated their wealth as traders in the Aegean, the Danubian principalities and Russia before they settled in Constantinople and extended their activities to the political and administrative field. Their organisational skills, their knowledge of languages, their education and urban sophistication made them the indispensable advisers and technical experts of the Porte. They managed not only to occupy and maintain for generations key positions in the Ottoman administration (such as Dragoman of the Porte, and Dragoman of the Fleet) but a handful of them, through their political influence, played a crucial role in banking and finance. Moreover, they acquired the right to appoint from among their members the governors of the Danubian principalities, and had a strong influence in the highly powerful Greek Orthodox Church. This formidable urban patriciate, a strange combination of financial and administrative elite, by simply protecting and promoting their own interests, through their considerable political power contributed to the rise of the Greek-orthodox merchant in the Balkans.[31]

Another major factor explaining the importance of the Greek merchant under Turkish rule was the Greek Orthodox Church. Since the Turks were practicing an indirect-rule system of government, the Orthodox Church constituted the main link between the Sultan and his Greek subjects. In that sense the Church, although subjected to strict central control, not only had a high degree of autonomy in religious and cultural matters, but also acquired a large number of political functions. Indeed, together with local Greek notables, the Church was responsible for the running of all municipal affairs. Moreover, the power of the Patriarchate was not limited to the Greeks alone: to a lesser extent it extended over all the Orthodox subjects of the empire — at least up to the date when the non-Greek Orthodox nationalities fought for the establishment of national churches.[32]

The subjugation of the Church by the Ottoman administration explains to a great extent the venality of its highest offices. The device of putting ecclesiastical positions on auction was a convenient way for the Sultan to increase his revenue. Since such positions were extremely expensive, the high clergy was dependent on the financial support of wealthy merchant families. Usually the transaction took the form of loans advanced to members of the clergy, on the understanding that once the office had been secured, the debt would be repaid from the considerable income attached to the post. As a result of this situation, many Phanariote families could, for instance, nominate bishops and even influence the choice of Patriarch. With this, in very rough outline, being the relationship between the Greek bourgeoisie and the Orthodox Church, it is understandable that the latter was advancing Greek economic interests through its spiritual and political influence, both in relation to the Porte and to Balkan trade competitors. In addition, this secularisation of the Church helped Greek commerce by institutionalising an extremely lenient attitude in such matters as usury, and the accumulation of wealth by whatever means.[33]

In these highly favourable circumstances, and with the new expansion of European trade after a long economic crisis of the seventeenth century, Greek merchants were able to extend their operations beyond Italy to France, Germany, Austria, Hungary and Russia. This extension meant the creation of numerous Greek merchant establishments abroad, and the growth of Greek diaspora communities in the major European urban centres (Vienna, Marseilles, Trieste, Odessa, Budapest etc.). Thus the Greeks came gradually to play a very important role, especially in external sea and land trade. For instance, by the end of the eighteenth century Greek merchants had virtually monopolised the illegal wheat trade of the western part of the Ottoman empire,[34] and were the important middlemen in exports of oil, corn, silk and other agricultural produce.[35]

Given these spectacular developments in the distribution sphere, it is not surprising that Greek capital started entering the sphere of production. Thus the middle of the eighteenth century saw an important concentration of capital mainly in the shipbuilding and textile sectors. Whereas at the beginning of the century Greek merchants were still dependent on foreign shipowners for their commercial operations (a dependence which drastically limited both their room for manoeuvre and their profits), the years after 1730 brought the appearance of many Greek-owned merchant ships and the development of shipbuilding first in western Greece (in Messolonghi and Galaxidi) and later in some of the Aegean islands (Mykonos, Crete, Thassos, Hydra, Spetsai, Psara etc.). The initial capital for these shipbuilding ventures seems to have come from Peloponnesian and northern Epirote merchants in the former case, and from Smyrna and Chios in the latter.[36] According to the calculations of the French, who were watching the growth of the Greek merchant marine with dismay and despondency, in the 1760s there were already 200 to 250 Albanian and Greek ships engaged in the Ionian maritime transport, and in 1780 the island of Hydra alone had 100 merchant ships in the Aegean.[37] It is also worth mentioning that up to 1808 the three main Aegean islands of Hydra, Spetsai and Psara built an average of six or seven ships per year each.[38] The French Revolution and the Napoleonic wars gave an even greater boost to Greek shipping. Greek seamen, defying Napoleon's Continental blockade, were making huge profits at a time when French commerce had virtually stopped in the eastern Mediterranean.[39] Just before the onset of the severe economic crisis in the industry, which started in 1813, the Greek merchant marine had 625 ships with a total tonnage of 153,580. These ships were furnished with 5878 cannons, and manned by 37,526 seamen.[40]

If shipbuilding was the major industrial activity in western Greece and in some of the islands, the North concurrently saw a very important development of handicraft industries, both in the major urban centres (Salonica, Kastoria, Ioannina) and in the more remote and relatively autonomous mountain areas of Thessaly, Epirus and Macedonia. Ambelakia, on Mount Ossa in Thessaly, is the most famous example of this type of growth. The Ambelakia cooperative was an association of a number of villages specialising in the production and export of high-quality yarn. At the peak of its expansion it had a capital of 20 million French francs and employed between 40,000 and 50,000 people.[41] Overall, it has been calculated that around the beginning of the nineteenth century, artisanal industries were responsible for 30 per cent of the gross national product of Ottoman Greece.[42] And although 30 per cent seems a rather inflated figure, there is no doubt that in the second part of the eighteenth century there was very significant capital accumulation in the sphere of production — a growth which a Greek historian has labelled the early 'take-off' period of the Greek economy.[43]

To what extent can these significant developments in shipbuilding and textiles be called capitalist? As far as Ambelakia is concerned, where those participating in the cooperative usually had a share, even if a very small one, in the capital and profits of the enterprise, most Greek historians consider it a non-capitalist venture, the first modern production cooperative in the world.[44]

Nevertheless, the growth of Ambelakia and other similar production organisations leaves no doubt that there was a marked polarisation between the few rich merchants who owned most of the capital and therefore controlled the decision-making process, and the mass of artisans and workers whose share in the distribution of profits did not amount to more than a wage.[45] And although by taking into account some cooperative and guild elements,[46] one cannot, strictly speaking, call this a capitalist enterprise, I think that Ambelakia can be better understood if it is compared to the organisational forms and the development of the sixteenth-century handicraft industry in Europe. If the English putting-out system, for instance, has been rightly considered as the early phase of capitalist development in industry,[47] the Greek eighteenth-century textile and shipbuilding enterprises can be seen as its equivalent in the Balkans. In both cases a fraction of merchant capital, previously only involved in distribution, did enter production and manage to a great extent to break both the restrictive character of the traditional urban guilds and the fragmentation of output by the individual domestic producer. Both the English and the Greek merchant capital (the one in the sixteenth and the other in the eighteenth century), by achieving serious concentration of production,[48] drastically reduced the autonomy of the direct producer and contributed to his virtual proletarianisation. If this proletarianisation was not as obvious in the Greek case and did not go as far as the cottage industry in England, this was due mainly to the strength of communal institutions in pre-revolutionary Greece;[49] it was also due to the fact that, in contrast to the development of the West-European putting-out system, in Greece this proto-capitalist industrial beginning did not have time to develop into the strictly capitalist system of factory production. It was cut short by the English Industrial Revolution which brought about the elimination, all over the world, of unprotected industries based on pre-factory modes of technology and work organisation.

It was precisely at this point in time that Western imperialism took a new form. In its mercantilist phase it had effected the disarticulation/ underdevelopment of the Ottoman territories through the so-called capitulations, i.e. through the extraction of trade privileges resulting in the one-sided growth of export agriculture (a development which to some extent hindered the growth of an internal market and oriented the Ottoman economy towards the developmental needs of western Europe). Although, as already mentioned, these early distortions resulting from unfavourable terms of trade were real enough, one should not exaggerate their contribution to the overall decline of the empire,[50] given the small part that trade played in the pre-capitalist Ottoman economy. It was much later, in the eighteenth and nineteenth centuries, that Western imperialism had a devastating impact on the Ottoman economy. Indeed, with the growth of industrial capitalism and the resulting wholesale destruction of all industries which the weak Ottoman State was unwilling or unable to protect,[51] Western imperialism inaugurated a new phase in the under-development of the world. For it is at this stage that the distinction between 'central' and 'peripheral' areas becomes much more clearly defined.[52]

As far as the Greek territories are concerned, the new industrial might of England started to make itself felt at the beginning of the nineteenth century. The unavoidable economic crisis in the textile and shipbuilding industries took on acute dimensions during the second decade of the nineteenth century – a few years before the beginning of the Greek War of Independence. As export profits started falling and production dropped, the ruined small artisans and seamen joined the ranks of the discontented over-exploited peasants, and contributed significantly to the development of the revolutionary effervescence which was to lead to the 1821 uprising.[53]

2   THE GREEK WAR OF INDEPENDENCE

Before the revolutionary period (1821–8) the bulk of the uneducated peasantry, given the limited spread of Greek nationalist ideas in the countryside, did not have any very clear political goals. Most of them were interested less in political independence than in a return of the 'good old days' when a strong Ottoman government could safeguard their traditional rights and could check the rapaciousness of landlords and officials.[54] It is from this perspective that one should assess the contribution of the Greek bourgeoisie and intelligentsia to the development of the national consciousness and the revolutionary spirit which led to the overthrow of the Turkish oppressor. For while the Greek peasants and ruined artisans constituted the energy source for the revolution, it was sections of the merchant class and the Western-trained intelligentsia who managed to direct this energy into nationalist channels.[55] A fraction of the diaspora Greek bourgeoisie especially helped the popular revolt, not only by providing it with leadership and material resources, but also by disseminating French revolutionary ideas and, more generally, Western science and culture in a society hitherto dominated by the anti-Enlightenment, anti-Western orientation of the Greek Orthodox Church.[56] Together with intellectuals, teachers, and other professionals educated abroad, the bourgeoisie acted as the catalyst which started the whole revolutionary process and gave it direction.

The Church, the Phanariotes, and the Greek landowners were ambivalent towards the revolution. The Church, and especially the high clergy, was at the beginning clearly hostile to any idea of overthrowing the Ottoman rule under which it occupied such a privileged position. The Patriarchate, exercising political and spiritual power over all the Orthodox subjects of the empire whether Greek or non-Greek, quickly realised that the emergence of a new autonomous nation in the Balkans would fragment not only Ottoman power, but its own as well. Moreover, Greek nationalism being influenced by Western Enlightenment provided an additional reason for opposition. In parallel, the Phanariote aristocracy, although initially responsive to Western ideas,[57] was opposed to the Greek nationalist movement. Their privileged position within the Ottoman administration, their close links with the Church, and their cosmopolitan orientation explain their reluctance to join the revolution. The Greek landlords of course, whether involved in trade or not, were initially against any idea of a nationalist revolution — afraid that the exploited peasants would unavoidably demand land reforms. It was only when these groups realised the irreversibility of the revolutionary movement that they threw their weight behind the insurgents and thus contributed to its final success.[58]

Inevitably, as soon as the revolution had gained momentum, the diverging interests of the various groups involved came to the fore and led to internecine fighting which seriously threatened the ultimate success of the insurrection. As for the interests of the peasants and artisans, those were put aside and suppressed quite early on in the game.[59] The inter-Greek struggles during the later phases of the civil war, in so far as they were not based on purely regionalist differences and kinship alliances,[60] were due to a conflict between fractions of the upper classes: between those who wanted to overthrow the Turks simply in order to take their place without any change in the traditional structure of political control, and those who wanted to 'Westernise' Greece by establishing a strong centralised State which would eliminate regional fragmentation and the politico-military autonomy of the local notables. For obvious reasons the 'traditionalist' policy was adopted by the autochthonous landowning-cum-merchant class, whereas the 'modernisation' policy appealed to the intelligentsia and the diaspora bourgeoisie which, having kept its wealth abroad, did not risk very much by pursuing such a 'progressive' strategy. At the end of the protracted civil war the 'Westernisers',[61] despite their weak control of local resources, managed to impose their views on the *form* at least that the future political institutions of modern Greece would take. This was due both to the fact that they alone possessed the legal and administrative skills indispensable for the running of the new-born State and, more significantly, to the fact that they enjoyed greater support from the Western powers.[62] This last point becomes crucial if it is remembered that the insurrectionist effort, jeopardised by the civil war, was finally salvaged only by the active intervention of the Great Powers (England, France, Russia).

In conclusion, the leading role of the bourgeoisie and the Westernised intelligentsia before and during the War of Independence, and their partial victory over the more traditional oligarchy, explains to a great extent why from the very start there was a persistent attempt to organise national life along liberal-bourgeois lines, despite the weak capitalist development and the non-existence of a strong Western-type autochthonous bourgeoisie.[63]

On the other hand, it must be emphasised that the victory of the 'Westernisers' was very relative indeed. If they had succeeded in imposing a Western form of government, they were much less successful in making it function in the same way as in the West. For although the 'traditionalists' accepted the inevitability of a centralised State and army organisation and the relative loss of their local autonomy, it did not take them long to infiltrate the expanding State apparatus and to gear the whole political system to the safeguarding and promotion of their interests.[64] So what they had lost in terms of local political and military influence, at least some of them regained in terms of control over the powerful State apparatus.

3   1830—80: UNDERDEVELOPMENT IN A PRE-CAPITALIST CONTEXT

During the first fifty years of independent national life, Greece was a predominantly agrarian society with very low social overhead capital and a non-existent industry.

A. Where agriculture was concerned, the Turkish landlords fleeing the country did not leave the bulk of the land to be taken over by the few big Greek landlords. Although there were extensive usurpations of land by both landlords and peasants, most of the ex-Turkish estates became 'national lands' under the direct ownership of the Greek State.[65] The latter, contrary to its promises, refused to implement the gratis distribution of these lands to the unpropertied peasants who had fought for Greek independence. Instead of this, the Dotation Law of 1835 gave them the right to purchase small plots of national lands against low annual payments over a 36-year period. Although this law was not very popular and took effect at a snail's pace,[66] the Greek government's refusal to sell the national lands by auction was a very decisive step hindering the emergence of big landed property in the newly-born State.[67] Thus, during the period under examination, the Peloponnese area was dominated by small landholdings.[68] The situation was different in Attica and Euboea where, due to the later incorporation of these territories, special treaties with Turkey safeguarded the large chiflik properties. But even on these big estates no rural proletariat came into existence. Most of the landless peasants working on the chifliks in Attica or the national lands of the Peloponnese were not remunerated for their labours by means of wages but through sharecropping arrangements. In other words, despite the relative commercialisation of Greek agriculture (especially in the Peloponnese where currant cultivation for export was already quite widespread), capitalist enterprises simply did not exist in this sector of the economy.[69] Moreover, the 1871 distribution of national lands by Prime Minister Koumoundouros further reinforced the pattern of the small peasant landholding. In this first land reform, 662,500 acres were distributed in 357,217 individual lots. Since at this time the agricultural population numbered 254,000 families, one may conclude that after 1871 the majority of Greek peasants had acquired some landed property of their own.[70]

B. If capital had not entered agricultural production, neither had it oriented itself in industry. The spread of industrialisation in the rest of Western Europe reinforced the pattern of destruction which, as already mentioned, had begun in the first two decades of the nineteenth century under the impact of the English Industrial Revolution. This process of underdevelopment was greatly facilitated by the Greek State having adopted a non-protectionist, 'liberal' customs policy.[71] Thus, for instance, sporadic attempts to produce certain types of light machinery in Greece did not, finally, succeed in standing up to Western competition.[72] And the shipbuilding industry, which had started to grow again after the revolution,[73] was threatened by a severe crisis towards the middle of the nineteenth century – a crisis very much accentuated by the introduction of the steamboat into maritime transport.[74] It is not, therefore, surprising that, notwithstanding some governmental attempts during Koumoundouros' premiership to develop industry, there were only 199 small and medium-sized industrial establishments in 1874, employing 7342 workers, only half of them being operated by steam.[75] If industrial growth was insignificant, so was the rate of investment in social overhead capital. The Greek government had very little to show in this direction. Between 1828 and 1852, road construction did not exceed 168 kilometres, a state of affairs which could only hinder the development of internal trade and the creation of a unified national market.[76]

Big capital remained in the sphere of distribution and finance. The growth of the import-export trade over the five decades under consideration[77] was a very serious source of capital accumulation both for the diaspora and for the indigenous comprador bourgeoisie. The former, during this period, was mainly attracted by a variety of speculative and financial operations which, in a capital-starved economy, ensured enormous profits with minimal risk. Given the international connections and orientation of the diaspora capital entering Greece, there is no doubt that much of the surplus extracted from the peasants was quite systematically transferred abroad.[78]

In conclusion, despite the integration of the Greek economy into the world capitalist market during the first half-century of independent nationhood, non-capitalist modes of production remained dominant in both industrial and agricultural sectors. In other words, the economically dominant merchant and finance capital (whether indigenous, foreign, or of diaspora origin) avoided the sphere of production and chose to extract surplus labour through a set of market mechanisms and State policies geared to maintain and promote its own interests.

C. In view of this lack of capitalist development, the importation and imposition of political institutions which had been shaped during the growth of Western capitalism could hardly be expected to harmonise with the infrastructural realities of post-independence Greece.

More specifically, the major political conflict during the first three decades of the post-independence period was between the centralising efforts of the monarchy[79] and the centrifugal tendencies of the various local oligarchies which were anxious to maintain the type of autonomy they had enjoyed during the revolutionary years when there was virtually no central government. From this point of view the 1844 and 1862 'democratic revolutions' which curtailed the powers of the Crown and strengthened the political parties cannot be seen as popular victories. They were simply the attempts of the various local oligarchies to undermine the absolutist inclinations of the Bavarian monarchy. For not unlike the Crown-vs-aristocracy conflict in *ancien-régime* Europe, the local notables, once they realised the inevitability of State expansion, tried to compensate for their loss of regional autonomy by controlling the State from *within*. For such control, and given their ability to manipulate the local vote, a malfunctioning parliamentary regime was an ideal instrument.[80] But — and this is very significant — unlike in the Western case, the articulation in Greece between the State and the various interest groups had a less collective, more personalistic character. In the pre-capitalist Greek economy, the linkage between State and 'civil' society was not in terms of classes or rather of secondary organisations representing class interests, but in terms of purely personal clientelistic networks. This was due to the overriding dominance of patronage politics[81] during this period, which excluded all possibility of distinct 'class' politics.

So it is not surprising that the political parties, before as well as after the introduction of universal male suffrage in 1864, were simple *coteries* of 'personalities' heading extended clientelistic networks. In consequence, parliamentary conflict did not centre around issues emerging out of class differences, but out of personalistic struggles over the distribution of spoils. The greater the range of the State administration — and it soon acquired enormous dimensions — the higher the patronage stakes: for if the State lacked any effective policy for the development of the Greek economy, it indirectly provided employment for a lot of those who were leaving the countryside and could not be absorbed into a non-existent Greek industry. It was a natural corollary of this that the Greek State bureaucracy quite early on achieved a size completely out of proportion to the country's resources and population. It has, for example, been calculated that towards the end of the period examined, the number of civil servants per 10,000 of the population was approximately seven times higher in Greece than in the United Kingdom.[82] This precocious administrative growth is very germane to the understanding of the basic structure and dynamics of the Greek social formation. The monstrous administrative expansion, in combination with the imported political institutions not fitting the pre-capitalist infrastructure of nineteenth-century Greece, explains the *relative autonomy of the Greek State* in relation to the class structure. For clientelism not only kept the peasantry, as a class, outside the sphere of active and autonomous politics, it also slowed down or actually prevented the political organisation and the ideological coherence of the economically dominant classes.

The overall picture which emerges from this period, therefore, is of a huge State apparatus controlled by the Crown and by a more or less fragmented political oligarchy at the head of extensive clientelistic networks. Of course, the lack of class-based pressure groups and the enormous size of the State does not mean that the latter enjoyed the sort of autonomy from civil society that one sees in totalitarian political systems. It was not only clientelism that paralysed the State's capacity to implement collective goals, but also the strict limits imposed on internal politics by Greece's political and economic dependence on the Great Powers and, to a lesser extent, on the big diaspora capital.[83]

4 1880–1922: THE TRANSITION PERIOD

In the forty years straddling the turn of the century, Greece underwent a number of fundamental transformations which, although they did not lead to the dominance of the capitalist mode of production, led the Greek economy away from the agrarian stagnation of the previous period and created the necessary preconditions for the growth of industrial capitalism in the 1920s.

A. Some of these changes were of trans-Balkan character and linked with the changing nature of Western imperialism around the end of the nineteenth century. As was mentioned earlier, sixteenth- and seventeenth-century Western capitalism affected the Ottoman economy negatively, mainly through the imposition of exploitative terms of trade (the capitulatory privileges), whereas later, in the second half of the eighteenth century, the industrialisation of England dealt an unprecedented blow to the empire's handicraft industries, thus eliminating any possibility of an autonomous industrial growth. In the course of the period under consideration in this chapter, Western imperialism in the Balkans entered a third and very important stage. The industrialisation of the western part of the Continent during the first half of the nineteenth century brought the end of the English industrial hegemony, and the industrial nations' competition for markets resulted in the unprecedented plundering of weak societies all over the world. And whereas previously the weak and dependent Balkan States had been controlled by military, political and diplomatic means, in the last quarter of the nineteenth century this control took a more directly economic form.[84] Especially during and after the big European economic crisis of the 1870s, Western capital kept pouring into the backward Balkan economies in search of quick and high profits. Foreign capital had penetrated the Balkans before, but this time there was a difference both quantitatively and qualitatively. Not only were foreign investments more substantial,[85] they also had the full backing of their respective governments.[86] Most of this capital took the form of government loans and railway investments. Although railway construction, encouraged by foreign capital, had started after the Crimean War, it was during the last quarter of the nineteenth century that these investments became intensified and had serious repercussions on the Balkan economies.[87]

Alongside this general wave of Western capitalist penetration, the most dramatic change in Greece was undoubtedly the more than doubling of its territory and population — first by the annexation of the wheat-growing area of Thessaly in 1881, and later, as a result of the Balkan Wars and the First World War, by the incorporation of Epirus, Macedonia, part of Thrace, the Aegean islands and Crete. This spectacular expansion, in combination with the development of the railways and the rapid monetisation of the economy,[88] created for the first time a unified and relatively large internal market — a fundamental precondition for the development of agriculture and an indigenous industry.[89]

At the same time, in response to the influx of foreign capital — first under the leadership of Premier Trikoupis and later, during the second decade of the twentieth century, under that of the great bourgeois statesman Venizelos — a serious effort was made to build a basic communication network (bridges, ports, roads, etc.),[90] and create the necessary institutional framework for Greece's capitalist transformation (rationalisation of the State administration, creation of new financial institutions, improvements in the educational system, etc.).

For instance, under Trikoupis, the State abandoned its passive role of 'night watchman', made frantic efforts to attract diaspora and foreign capital, and generally took on a much more active role in the economic field. In the industrial sector, the mild protectionism that had existed before the 1880s was jettisoned in favour of a dramatic raising of tariffs for both industrial and agricultural imports.[91] With Venizelos, protectionism increased even further, and the State took major steps towards the management and control of the economy. Apart from State attempts to get a tighter control over the country's banking system,[92] there were the first attempts at elaborating coherent State policies for the various sectors of the economy, and especially agriculture (establishment of a specialised Ministry of Agriculture, Commerce and Industry, development of agronomical schools, organisation of agricultural insurance schemes, etc.). Finally, in 1917, Venizelos passed a series of decrees on land reform which were to become the legal basis for the break-up of the big estates and the extensive land distribution which followed the influx of refugees from Asia Minor in 1922.[93]

B. Individual examination of the major sectors of the economy, beginning with agriculture, shows that the annexation of the fertile plain of Thessaly and later of the wheat-growing areas of Macedonia and Thrace increased cereal production. However, given the dramatic population growth and the low productivity of the chiflik system prevalent in the newly annexed territories, this increase, big as it was, was not big enough to make Greece self-sufficient in cereals. Moreover, the annexation of the new territories made big landed property an important factor again in the Greek social formation. The Turkish landlords, although protected by special treaties which safeguarded their property, sold their chifliks cheaply to rich Greeks — mainly diaspora Greeks from Constantinople, Smyrna and Alexandria. These newly established Greek chiflik owners, under the Roman Law provisions which had been reinforced in post-independence Greece, enjoyed more rights over the peasants than their Turkish predecessors ever had. Thus the peasants' hereditary right to the cultivation of the land, already weakened with the rise of the chiflik system in the seventeenth century, was now abolished *de jure*. From this time on the chiflik owner had the legal right to expel the peasants from the land at the termination of the sharecropping agreement.[94] These increased powers of the landlord were not, however, used for the technological modernisation of agriculture or the development of capitalist forms of production. During all this period, as numerous peasants were cultivating their small plots of land under a variety of sharecropping agreements,[95] land remained fragmented, technological improvements were slow or non-existent, and large portions of chiflik land remained fallow for years on end.[96] It is not, therefore, surprising that Greek agriculture failed to supply the growing demand for wheat resulting from the population increase after annexation of the new territories.[97] This had the consequence of a dramatic deterioration in the trade balance, a deterioration which was to be further accentuated by the influx of refugees and the acceleration of dependent industrialisation after 1922.

Agriculture was more dynamic in the currant-growing small-freehold area of the Peloponnese. Due to a phylloxera blight which had ruined the French vineyards, the demand for Greek currants rose sharply in the 1880s, and production increased spectacularly, contributing to the relative prosperity of the small cultivator and to the much greater prosperity of the merchants in control of the export trade. But since this sudden growth was due merely to conjunctural circumstances, the eventual fall in French demand meant that currant cultivation entered into a long crisis of overproduction (starting in 1895) from which it never fully recovered. This was the beginning of a gradual shift of emphasis from currants to tobacco, with the latter becoming Greece's main export crop during the inter-war period.[98]

In the secondary sector, increased protectionism and the influx of foreign and diaspora capital did contribute to some industrial growth. Thus by 1921, the number of industrial establishments had reached 2905, and the industrial work-force had multiplied by eight compared with the end of the previous period.[99] As in the other Balkan countries, the leading industrial sectors were those of textiles and food processing, with the main economic centres of this period being Athens and the Piraeus area, Volos, Patras, Kalamata and (after 1913) Salonica.[100] But although this growth seems quite impressive when seen against that of the preceding period, it is less so when it is remembered that most of those 2905 industrial establishments mentioned above were small family businesses with no significant employment of wage labour.[101] Thus, some promising beginnings notwithstanding, one cannot seriously speak of industrial capitalism at this stage of Greek underdevelopment. Most of the foreign and diaspora capital, in so far as it was not employed in purely speculative or financial operations, was used for the purchase of chiflik lands or invested in public works projects — mainly railways. But the massive spending on railway construction hardly helped the manufacturing sector as such. In typically colonial fashion, railway construction in the Balkans was much more geared to the military and economic needs of the western industrial States than to the developmental needs of the Balkan peninsula itself.[102] There were very few organic links between railway growth and the rest of Greek industry, since most of the materials used in these large-scale public works were imported, even those which could easily have been produced locally.[103] Given this situation, as well as the usurious rates at which foreign loans were contracted and the quasi-colonial behaviour of foreign and diaspora capital, it is not surprising that Greece went bankrupt towards the end of the century and was obliged to accept the establishment of an international control commission (manned by the representatives of foreign bond-holders), which for decades had a very important say in the public finances of the modern Greek State.[104]

If foreign and diaspora capital did not effectively contribute to the growth of the manufacturing sector, neither did the indigenous merchant capital choose to play a more constructive role. Despite its huge profits during a decade of almost continuous wars (1912–22), its erstwhile comprador traditions left it extremely reluctant to exchange the certainty of its easy trade profits for the risky and bothersome business of factory production.

Moreover, despite the massive rural unemployment after the curre
crisis, there was no major source of cheap industrial labour. Peasants
preferred to vegetate in the countryside or migrate to the United States
rather than become proletarians.[105] Thus the number of Greeks who left
for the United States every year was greater than the total number of
workers employed in the Greek industry.[106]

To sum up, the territorial and population growth, the influx of foreign
capital, the development of an extensive transport system, the creation of
a unified internal market and the establishment of an institutional
framework facilitating State intervention in the economy, provided some
of the basic preconditions for the development of capitalism in the Greek
social formation — a development which will lead to the dominance of the
capitalist mode of production after 1922. However, the manner in which
these preconditions were created (the impetus originated mainly from the
outside and serving foreign and diaspora interests) presaged the kind of
peripheral, underdeveloped capitalism which in fact did flourish in the
next period — a capitalism radically different from and much less autonomous than that of the West.

C. Concerning, finally, the superstructural developments during this
transition period, the political debate had ceased to be merely a purely
personalistic feud between patronage-mongers and had acquired a more
distinctive flavour of class issues. Although clientelism had not by any
means ceased to operate, and although this still pre-capitalist phase was
hardly capable of fully articulated class politics, there is no doubt that first
the Trikoupis and later the Venizelos policies were inspired by more than
exclusively short-term clientelistic orientations. Both these statesmen were
motivated by a powerful desire to 'Westernise' Greece and made serious
efforts to realise their vision. Moreover, there is no doubt that the 1909
military coup which weakened both the old political oligarchy and the
Crown, as well as the spectacular rise of Venizelos and the electoral
victories of his party, resulted in drastic changes in the composition of the
parliamentary forces.[107] These changes indicate the rise of the middle
classes, and this rise in turn helped Venizelos to contribute in a spectacular
way to the bourgeois transformation of Greek society.

Though this be granted, one must be very careful not to fall into the
kind of evolutionist trap which interprets political events in terms of
conceptual schemes derived from Western European political development.
It has been a great temptation, especially for Greek Marxist historians, to
explain the 1909 coup as a bourgeois/merchant-instigated military intervention; or to see the political conflict between Venizelos and his royalist
opponents as a struggle between the rising bourgeoisie and the declining
feudal landlord classes.[108] Such interpretations are not only much too
schematic, they are also highly misleading because: *first*, in contrast with
the Western experience, the lack of industrialisation during this period

ious antagonisms between landlord interests and those
or industrial bourgeoisie;[109] *second*, the dividing line
nd merchant was not at all clearly drawn (for instance,
a rule had other investments both inside and outside
most important, given the pre-capitalist state of Greek
ticulation between the State apparatus and civil society
much in class as in clientelistic terms.

With the above holding true for all of this period, not only were the
working classes kept firmly outside the sphere of active politics (in the
sense of not being politically organised along class lines), but even the
intra-dominant class conflict which manifested itself both inside and
outside parliament can by no means be seen as a struggle between
merchants and chiflik owners. Although there were occasional parliamentary debates on the tariff protection of the big wheat growers
(reminiscent of the English parliamentary debates on the corn laws) or on
land reform,[110] the issues which really dominated political life were
irredentism and, later, the question of the monarchy.[111] Thus it was only
with the rise to dominance of the capitalist mode of production in the
following period (1922–60), and the emergence of a threatening urban
proletariat, that Greek politics finally acquired a more pronounced class
character.

5 1922–60: CAPITALIST DOMINANCE AND UNDERDEVELOPMENT

A. The year 1922 was the turning-point in the history of modern Greece.
On this fateful date the Asia Minor defeat of the Greek army by Kemal
Atatürk's nationalist forces put a full stop to Greek irredentism, thus
setting more or less definite and permanent boundaries to the modern
Greek State.[112] Moreover, the sudden arrival after the debacle of more
than one million Greek refugees from Asia Minor[113] had fundamental
consequences for the Greek social structure. On the one hand this massive
influx created severe disruptions in a population of only five million; but
on the other hand it changed the ethnic composition of Macedonia (where
many of the refugees went to settle) in favour of the Greek element, and
thus closed the famous 'Macedonian question' once and for all.[114]
Furthermore, in the long term the refugees gave a big and compelling push
to the Greek economy.

B. The desperate need to accommodate this huge mass of uprooted
people had as one of its consequences the acceleration of the land-reform
programme already initiated by Venizelos towards the end of the previous
period.[115] By 1936, a total of 425,000 acres had been distributed to
305,000 families.[116] These significant developments dealt the *coup de
grâce* to big landed property. From then on and quite irreversibly, the
small private landholding was to be the dominant basis for cultivation in

the countryside.

Apart from bringing drastic changes in relations of production, the break-up of the chiflik estates (where large areas of land had been left fallow) resulted in a higher acreage of cultivated land and thus an increase in agricultural production. Whereas in 1915 wheat acreage had been 184,000 acres, by 1931 it had gone up to 339,000. There were even more impressive increases in tobacco-growing areas, which over the same period multiplied approximately sixfold. However, the higher production of wheat and tobacco was still less than proportional to the higher acreage under cultivation.[117] The State, once it had distributed national lands, washed its hands of the matter and left the small peasant-owners to their own fate. It did little in terms of education, credits, or distribution of fertilisers to assist them and improve their methods of work and organisation.[118] But despite these shortcomings and the very low per-capita income[119] of the post-land-reform cultivator, there is no doubt that the break-up of the highly inefficient chiflik properties did contribute to the further commercialisation of Greek agriculture and, indirectly, gave a major boost to the development of industrial capitalism.[120]

C. Not all of the refugees could be accommodated through land distribution. A sizeable number of them settled in the big urban centres, especially in Salonica, Pireaus and Athens, thus providing an abundant and relatively skilled labour force at the disposal of Greek capital. (This available potential was reinforced in 1921 when the USA government's decision to close its doors to new immigrants put an abrupt end to the Greek migratory flow.) Moreover, since a number of the refugees had occupied important positions in the industry, trade and finance of the Greek communities in Asia Minor, they brought with them badly needed entrepreneurial skills,[121] as well as considerable money savings.[122] To this refugee capital should be added the enormous influx of foreign funds, which took the form of government loans, private investments in public works, international aid to the refugees etc. Thus from 1923 to 1930, imported foreign capital amounted to 1162.8 million gold French francs. Considering the short period during which this capital came into Greece, it was an injection of foreign funds unprecedented in modern Greek history.[123] This, of course, meant increasing domination of the Greek economy by foreign interests.[124] On the other hand, there can be no doubt that this second wave of foreign capital (the first was in the 1880s) — finding itself in a context where there was already a serious social overhead capital and a favourable institutional framework, in combination with the availability of refugee labour and entrepreneurial skills — gave the decisive push to the development of Greek capitalism.[125]

All of these circumstances brought about the first major breakthrough in the industrial sector. From 1923 to 1939, the horsepower and the value of industrial production doubled, and its volume tripled.[126] It is this stage, in fact, that may be said to mark the effective entrance of capital into the sphere of production. Before this, not only was the industrial sector as a whole relatively small, but the number of enterprises using wage labour was quite insignificant. The later twenties and thirties saw a notable concentration of capital as well as a closer collaboration between banking and industrial capital — i.e. the emergence of finance capital.[127] This was the time of the multiplication of holding companies, trusts and cartels which, although they did not achieve the dimensions of their Western European counterparts, were very impressive by Balkan standards.[128] At the same time occurred a marked differentiation in banking capital, as some of the functions previously performed by the all-pervasive and powerful National Bank of Greece were spread over several specialised institutions: the Bank of Greece, founded in 1927 and responsible for currency issue and control, the Agricultural Bank (1931), responsible for the management of agricultural credits, and the National Real-Estate Bank (1927).

These developments are clear indications of the gradual rise of finance and industrial capital at a time when big landed property had virtually disappeared, and when merchant capital, in the wake of increasing State control of the import-export trade, and the gradual deterioration of the export markets for currants and tobacco, was at a standstill.[129] In terms of modes of production, capitalism can be said to have become dominant at this point in the Greek social formation. Of course, this dominance did not become markedly visible in the relevant statistics. After all, even today large capitalist enterprises in industry using wage labour constitute only a little island in the sea of small family-based artisanal units.[130] Also, up to the late fifties, the industrial sector as a whole was less important than the agricultural or the tertiary sector,[131] both in terms of labour employed and of its contribution to the GNP. But I think that a look at the way in which the modes of production were articulated in the Greek social formation leaves no doubt about the post-1922 dominance of the capitalist mode. It is from this time onward that the capitalist sector of industry functions as the dynamic pivot of the Greek economy — where 'dynamism' is meant to imply not so much any high rates of growth, as rather the fact that from this time on the systematic transfer of resources from the simple commodity mode of production[132] (prevalent in agriculture *and* handicraft industry) to the 'modern' capitalist industrial sector became a salient feature of the Greek social formation.

The mechanisms through which such a transfer took place were obvious: enormous State subsidies to big industry, scandalous credit facilities, indiscriminate tariff protection enabling highly inefficient industrial firms to achieve quasi-monopolistic positions, the prevalence of indirect taxation which hit the small incomes very hard, etc.[133] The profits of big industrial and finance capital, therefore, as far as they can be measured, reached spectacular dimensions,[134] whereas in the still vast simple-commodity sector in agriculture and industry the small family unit was hardly able to make ends meet.[135] Inevitably, increasing inequalities and the growing marginalisation of those involved in small commodity production — phenomena closely linked with the dominance of the capitalist mode of production in peripheral social formations — became the two major features of the Greek model of capital accumulation.[136]

D. All the above developments came to an abrupt stop with the Second World War and the civil war that followed.[137] The post-civil war governments, in the context of the general European expansion that followed the war years, and with the help of considerable amounts of American aid, managed as early as 1950 to get the Greek economy back to its pre-war level of output.[138] Since then, all the trends already present during the later inter-war period have continued at great speed.[139] Thus in 1959 the volume of industrial production was double that of 1938, and had tripled by 1964. The production of electrical energy, which had amounted to 270,000 kwh in 1938, was almost ten times that by 1961. Agricultural production too increased at a rather fast rate, but the two sectors with the most remarkable growth rates were tourism and the merchant marine. In 1938, approximately 100,000 tourists visited the country annually. This number had increased fivefold in 1961, and twenty-fold towards the end of the sixties. As far as the merchant marine is concerned, in 1945 Greek shipowners started their operations with only a hundred 10,000-ton American Liberty ships. In 1950 they managed to reach their pre-war tonnage, and two decades later they had one of the most important merchant fleets in the world.[140]

On the level of relations of production, there too the inter-war trends were highly accelerated. Capital concentration went on increasing, with finance capital in the lead. Suffice it to say that during the post-war period two giant banking concerns (the Commercial Bank and the National Bank of Greece) handled between them approximately 90 per cent of the country's considerable savings and, of course, participated directly in the ownership and management of an important part of the insurance and industrial sectors.[141] The more powerful of these two giant concerns (the National Bank) being largely State-controlled shows the degree to which the State had moved away from its nineteenth-century 'nightwatchman' position.[142]

E. Concerning political developments during the four decades under consideration, the intra-dominant class type of conflict which had characterised the previous transition period gradually gave way to a 'masses v. the dominant classes' type of conflict.[143] Of course it is true that the bourgeois in-fighting during the whole of the inter-war period between Venizelists and anti-Venizelists over the monarchy issue managed to disorient the peasants and to involve them in a conflict which had very little relevance to their own interests.[144] The same point could be made about the political mobilisation of the Asia Minor refugees. The majority of them saw the royalists as wholly responsible for the 1922 fiasco and gave their massive vote to Venizelos, who had actually been the principal architect of the Asia Minor folly.[145]

But despite the disorienting consequences of the monarchy issue, the development of an industrial proletariat during the last two pre-war decades and the large-scale settling of refugees in Athens and Salonica provided the basis for the creation and development of the Greek Communist Party. Although its following during the later inter-war period was pretty slim, its very presence slowly began to change the style of political debate and the ideological orientation of the dominant classes.[146] Already in 1929 the first anti-communist law, the notorious *idionimo*, was passed which became the legal basis for the persecution of all those whose acts (or even thoughts) were judged to undermine the dominant bourgeois social order.[147] Moreover, the 1936 Metaxas coup, although directly linked with the issue of the monarchy, was quite a different type of military intervention from the earlier inter-war coups. Previous army interventions in politics had been a direct outcome of purely intra-bourgeois differences, mostly over the fate of the monarchy; whereas in 1936 the threat 'from below' played an important (though not supreme) role in the establishment of the Metaxas dictatorship.[148]

Later, when the German occupation had destroyed the various control mechanisms by which the peasants were integrated into bourgeois politics (patronage, State credit system etc.), the field was open for the highly organised Communist Party to mobilise the peasantry against both the Germans and the considerable fraction of the Greek bourgeoisie who, under the threat of the coming social revolution, largely preferred to remain inactive or to join with the German occupying forces against the massive, communist-led resistance movement. From this time on the monarchy issue, although it did not disappear altogether, was relegated to second place.[149] The main issue in Greek politics now became the 'containment of the masses', the problem of safeguarding the bourgeois order from the incursion of the masses into active politics, a process indissolubly linked with rapid capitalist industrialisation.[150]

In conclusion, trying to express the above points in more theoretical terms and following Althusser,[151] it can be argued that with the dominance of the capitalist mode of production in the Greek social formation during the forty-year period since 1922, the economy became not only 'determining in the last instance' but also dominant in relation to the political and ideological spheres. This dominance was, of course, reflected on the political and ideological levels of the social formation. On the political level, the overriding importance of the economy meant: (*a*) that the State ceased to be a mere 'night watchman' and acquired very important economic functions. State intervention in the economy, in so far as it aims not at the destruction but the buttressing of bourgeois interests, does not, of course, imply any weakening of capitalism (or the dominance of the political over the economic instance): on the contrary, it

is one of the fundamental preconditions of fully developed capitalism;[152]
(*b*) that the political conflict, contrary to the previous pre-capitalist
periods, took a more directly class character. This does not mean of course
that clientelism ceased to play an important role in Greek politics, or that
political parties lost entirely their personalistic character and started
operating like their Western counterparts (given the underdeveloped character of Greek capitalism, the 'malfunctioning' of parliamentary institutions
did not cease but took different forms). But the greater involvement of the
masses with politics, a concomitant of capitalist dominance, had consequences which did make the articulation between class locations and
political practices more direct; consequences like the emergence of a
communist party organised along non-clientelistic, ideological principles,
the very gradual decline of clientelism in the large urban centres, the
greater organisational cohesion — on the national level — of bourgeois
parties, etc.[153]

Finally, in the ideological sphere, the dominance of the economic
instance meant that the ideology of the dominant classes became more
'economistic' — in the sense that the 'heroic' panhellenic irredentism of
the *Megali Idea* gave way to the glorification of economic growth, the
'freedom' of enterprise, and the elevation of anti-communism to the
national credo.

6 THE POST-1960 PERIOD

Up to the late fifties, despite the high growth rates of the Greek economy
and the clear dominance of the capitalist mode of production in industry,
Greece still exemplified the classical characteristics of underdevelopment
seen in most formations of peripheral capitalism: a low-productivity
agriculture, a highly inflated and parasitic service sector, and an industrial
sector unable to absorb the redundant agricultural labour force[154] and to
expand into capital goods production. Concerning this last point, even the
high control exercised by the State over the Greek economy (both through
the banking system and through its own massive investments in industry)
did not succeed in directing Greek capital into those key manufacturing
sectors of the economy (metallurgy, chemicals) whose growth has great
transformative power and serious multiplying effects on the rest of the
economy. Greek private capital, following its preference for quick and
easy profits, has continued to orient itself either towards tourism, shipping
and other 'comprador' activities; or, where it did enter the sphere of
industrial production, it has been in the traditional industrial branches of
textiles, food etc. In the late fifties more than half the labour force was
still employed in agriculture, while the contribution of the industrial
sector to the GNP was only around 25 per cent. This last figure is even less
impressive in view of manufacturing being the slowest growing sector in

industry, so that its contribution to total industrial output was in fact decreasing (whereas that of construction, transport and public utilities was growing).[155]

In this situation and with the commitment to 'liberal' economic principles of all post civil-war governments, there was no other solution for the further industrialisation of the country than to mobilise all means for attracting foreign capital. Legislation to this end was initiated in the fifties, but it was in the sixties that foreign capital, taking advantage of the enormous privileges granted it by the Greek State, really began to invade the Greek economy. Thus whereas in 1960 the yearly influx of foreign capital amounted to $11,683,700, it went up to $50,026,290 in 1963, and to $157,606,242 in 1966.[156]

After 1880 and 1922, this was the third massive wave of foreign funds to enter the Greek economy. On the two previous occasions, the major bulk of the capital influx had taken the form of public loans and social overhead investments, and their origin was predominantly English. In the sixties it took the form of direct investments in industry by multinational companies, this time mainly of American origin.[157] Of course, the amount of capital imported in the sixties, if compared to that of 1880 and 1922, is not all that great (especially in view of the declining purchasing power of the dollar). But since most of it found its way into the most crucial industrial sectors where Greek capital was unwilling or unable to go, it had a very significant impact on the overall structure of the Greek economy. Thus 1962 was the first time that the contribution of the industrial sector to the GNP was greater than that of agriculture. Gradually there was a very definite shift in emphasis from the production of consumer goods to that of capital goods, and a concomitant change in the composition of Greek exports as Greece, traditionally an exporter of agricultural produce and unprocessed minerals, began to export consider-able quantities of industrial goods.[158]

There can be no doubt that by the middle sixties the effective industrialisation of the Greek social formation was well under way. However, as I shall try to show in some detail in the next chapter, Greece not only followed an industrialisation path different from that of the West, but was also unable to eradicate the major features of underdevelop-ment which had characterised the 1922–1960 period.

7 CONCLUSION

Looking at the overall development of the Greek social formation and taking into account that the major source of its dynamism was exogenous rather than endogenous, four major phases of Greek underdevelopment stand out, directly related to corresponding phases in the ever-changing western imperialism.

(*a*) The first phase is located in the sixteenth and seventeenth centuries when the Greek territories of the Ottoman empire felt the impact of the rising Western capitalism and the creation of a relatively coherent world market. This first influence was chiefly indirect, in that Western growth was to a limited extent instrumental in shaping the Balkan economies through international trade, by the increasing demand for Balkan agricultural products, and by the imposition of unfavourable terms of trade on the declining Ottoman empire.

(*b*) The shaping and integration of the Balkan economies in accord with the developmental needs of Western Europe assumed a different and more drastic form during the second half of the eighteenth and the beginning of the nineteenth centuries, when the industrialisation of England and later of the Continent destroyed the Balkan handicraft industries and put a full stop to the feeble attempts at an endogenous industrial take-off.

(*c*) Towards the third quarter of the nineteenth century, Western imperialism took yet another and more aggressive form *vis-à-vis* Greece and the other Balkan States. In the previous stage it had eliminated the attempts of indigenous capital to enter the sphere of production, now Western capital tried in a limited way to fulfil this function itself, but of course on terms not beneficial to the host economies. Thus Western capital, in the form of railway investments and government loans, entered the Balkan economies and contributed considerably to the development of social overhead capital — and, at the same time, to the disarticulation and further underdevelopment of these societies. This intrusion prepared the ground for the growth of industrial capitalism, as during the late inter-war period capital began to orient itself towards the sphere of production.

(*d*) Finally, after the Second World War, all Balkan societies except Greece having adopted a radically different course of State-planned industrialisation, Greek industry managed to keep up with her northern neighbours' fast industrial growth by means of direct help from foreign capital — which under the new form of multinational company investments had injected itself into the key sectors of Greek industry. This last phase of Western imperialism is linked with a new phase of Greek underdevelopment which is no longer that of a weak manufacturing sector. Instead, it takes the form of a technologically advanced, highly dynamic, foreign-controlled manufacturing sector not organically linked with the rest of the economy; so that the beneficial effects of its growth are not diffused over the small-commodity agricultural and artisanal sectors but are transferred abroad. A further elaboration on the general meaning of underdevelopment and of the various forms it has taken in post-war Greece will be given in the next chapter and in Chapters 7 and 8.

Part II
Theoretical Perspectives

2 The Debate on the Neo-Marxist Approach to Development

INTRODUCTION

An area where Marxist interpretations and tools of analysis seem gradually to be replacing the Parsonian functionalist paradigm is the sociology of development. In fact, Marxist methodology, in the wider sense of the word, has been so successful in this field of study that few serious students, whether Marxists or not, are very much concerned with the sort of functionalist/neo-evolutionist theories which were fashionable in the fifties and early sixties (for instance the work of Hagen, McLeland, Rostow, Lerner, Smelser, Eisenstadt).[1] At present, interesting debates on such problems take place within Marxism as various theorists start taking a critical look at what has been called the neo-Marxist approach to development. Some of these critics pay attention mainly to the method-ological shortcomings of neo-Marxist writers, others contest their substan-tive findings and conclusions. In this chapter I shall try to analyse and assess both types of critique (paying greater attention to the former)[2] in the light of developments in Greece — a country whose economic trajec-tory portrays characteristics pertinent to the above debates.

1   THE NEO-MARXIST POSITION

A   *The concept of underdevelopment*

A convenient way to examine the various issues involved is to focus attention on the central concept of the neo-Marxist school, that of underdevelopment. In fact, this concept lies at the heart of the debate on the nature and prospects of the economic growth which third-world countries are experiencing today. An understanding of the concept is particularly important in the case of Greece, since the considerable growth of its industrial sector in the sixties has been seen as a clear index that Greece has definitely left the club of underdeveloped nations behind. Is this really so, or is Greece still an underdeveloped country? To answer such a question, and to understand what underdevelopment means, this key concept must be placed in its proper context: in the early theoretical debates between neo-evolutionists and neo-Marxists on the third world's prospects of economic growth.

In the fifties, the dominant theories on development, both economic and sociological, had a clear evolutionist bias. Poor countries, it was argued, once integrated into the world capitalist market, would follow the course of the already industrialised Western societies. Sooner or later the diffusion of Western capital, technology and values would close the gap between rich and poor, agrarian and industrial societies, and 'developing' countries would move up the evolutionary ladder to go through the same stages of development as nineteenth-century Europe had done.[3]

Theories of underdevelopment were a reaction to this type of evolutionism. As it became obvious that the gap between rich and poor countries was not closing but widening, and that the increasing incorporation of the latter into the world capitalist system was creating more problems than it solved, a group of Marxist-orientated writers among others gradually developed a much more pessimistic view on the economic prospects of third-world capitalist countries.[4]

According to this view, poor countries today are following an economic course which is radically different from that of nineteenth-century Western Europe. One obvious difference is that, being late-comers into the development race and having to face a powerful bloc of already industrialised countries, they are integrated into the world capitalist system as mere appendages to the powerful metropolitan economies. Their integration is such that not only is there a systematic transfer of their wealth to the developed countries, but even the resources left them are not, when freed from agriculture, used for the creation of an autonomous industrial base; rather, through a variety of mechanisms, they are channelled into the service sector — thus creating an overinflated, parasitic merchant economy. In this way third-world countries have to accept an international division of labour which casts them in the role of raw-material producers, and forces them to import most of their industrial goods from the West. In such conditions both their internal and external problems are increasingly aggravated: the lack of industrialisation and the general misallocation of resources not only creates severe imbalances and large-scale chronic unemployment at home; it also increases dependence on the industrial countries and destroys any chance for balanced and autonomous growth. Thus the rising GNP in third-world countries is not a sign of growing development at all, but rather of growing underdevelopment.[5]

Underdevelopment, therefore, seen in the context of this early debate, has connotations of both *anti-evolutionism* and *misgrowth*: it implies that the economic growth of third-world countries (*a*) is *different* from that of Western countries, this difference being partly explained by the fact that the latter have exploited the former in the past and continue to exploit them in the present; (*b*) is also *less satisfactory* for the majority of their populations, since despite the growth of the GNP, third-world countries are unable to solve their problems of mass unemployment, poverty and dependence on the metropolitan centres. Therefore the fruits of their economic growth (or rather misgrowth), when not transferred abroad, go to a tiny, overprivileged minority (traditional landlords, comprador merchants etc.). Furthermore, most underdevelopment theories do not limit themselves to stating the differences between Western development and third-world underdevelopment. They go on to explain them in terms of *exploitative relationships* on the level of both the international market (in terms of imperialism, neo-colonialism, unequal exchange)[6] and the national class structure (in terms of the anti-development strategies and interests of the comprador bourgeoisie, the traditional landowning classes etc.).[7] On the basis of such an analysis they usually conclude that third-world countries will never be able to industrialise and solve their problems of chronic unemployment and poverty within capitalism. Only a revolutionary breakaway from it can provide the necessary (although not sufficient) preconditions for effective industrialisation and development.

B   The underlying conceptual framework of neo-Marxist theories

To a great extent, the contrasting diagnoses and prescriptions of the neo-Marxist and the neo-evolutionist perspective derive from the adoption of different conceptual frameworks, different ways of looking at social change and stability. It would be outside the scope of this paper to give a systematic account of these variants.[8] Here, I would simply like to stress one fundamental difference which is relevant to our discussion. This has to do with the place of collective actors or groups in the two perspectives.

In the neo-Marxist perspective, actors,[9] classes, groups or quasi-groups are central to the analysis. The obstacles to development are not, as in the functionalist school, seen in normative terms — as traditional values inhibiting effective entrepreneurial activity; they are seen rather in terms of collective actors, classes whose interests hinder the effective utilisation of resources. More generally, development and underdevelopment are always seen and analysed in terms of choices, policies, or strategies of interest groups operating within a framework of more or less limiting structural constraints. In so far as values and norms are considered at all, it is always in relation to specific actors. There is no discussion in the Durkheimian manner of *society's* norms and values, but of the values or ideologies of the bourgeoisie, the peasantry, etc.[10]

In contrast to the above, in the functionalist/neo-evolutionist perspective actors disappear from the analysis, or at least are mentioned only peripherally. The central stage here is occupied by a set of institutionalised processes, grouped together not according to their relationship to specific actors, but with reference to society's systemic problems or functional requirements.[11] The process of development, therefore, is seen in terms of role or institutional differentiation as societies pass from a simple to a more complex evolutionary stage. The question of *who* is behind such differentiation, *who* profits or loses from such developments, is hardly asked. The problem is easily avoided by speaking anthropomorphically of society and its values as 'doing things', creating obstacles, or facilitating economic growth.[12]

2   SUBSTANTIVE CRITICISMS OF THE NEO-MARXIST SCHOOL

A   *Foreign capital and industrialisation*

With the spectacular development of multinational corporations, it has become gradually obvious, as foreign capital is penetrating third-world countries in a more direct and intensive manner, that in certain countries (Brazil, Spain, Portugal, Greece) foreign capital started doing what the autochthonous, comprador bourgeoisie was unable or unwilling to do: i.e. going into the manufacturing sectors of the economy and contributing to a more or less rapid process of industrialisation.

Greece is a good example of this type of development. In the fifties and early sixties the country was portraying the 'classical' features of underdevelopment: a growing, highly parasitic tertiary sector, a weak and more or less stagnant manufacturing sector with a low labour absorption capacity, and a large but inefficient agricultural sector. Thus, in the late fifties, more than half of the labour force was still employed in agriculture, whereas the contribution of the industrial sector to the GNP was round 25 per cent. This last figure is even less impressive if one considers that manufacturing was the slowest-growing sector of industry, so that its contribution to the total industrial output was decreasing (whereas that of construction, transports and public utilities was growing).[13]

Thus, despite the relatively high post-war rate of growth[14] and the availability of abundant financial resources,[15] the indigenous Greek capital, whether in its mercantile or finance form, was unwilling and/or unable to orient itself towards the manufacturing sector — especially in those key branches (chemicals, metallurgy) which, through their multiplying effects and their great transformative powers, can contribute most to an integrated and relatively autonomous industrial base. To a large extent, following its comprador traditions, it found it more profitable and less risky to operate in the non-manufacturing sector, mostly on borrowed money, and to shift a considerable part of its profits to foreign banks or to shipping.[16] Given this state of affairs, and given the State's long-term commitment to a free-enterprise economy, there was no solution for Greece other than to resort to the help of foreign capital.

Although legislation aimed at attracting foreign investors was initiated in 1953, it was not until the beginning of the sixties that foreign capital (in the form of direct investments) came into the country on a large scale and had a serious impact on the structure of the economy. And although the total amount invested was not so very impressive[17] (by Latin American standards, for instance), as it was mainly directed towards the key manufacturing sectors, its impact on the Greek economy was much greater than its relatively small size would suggest. In fact, especially during and after the years 1962–3, when the metallurgical, chemical and metal construction industries experienced a great boost due to foreign investments, one can speak of a qualitative break in the growth of Greek industry. Not only did the industrial sector start expanding at a much faster rate, but there was an important shift in investment from the light consumer-goods industry to capital goods and durables.[18] Therefore it is in the sixties that one can place the first real advance in the industrialisation of modern Greece.[19]

B   The persistence of underdevelopment

What is the relevance of this industrialisation for underdevelopment theories? For certain writers[20] it clearly shows the bankruptcy of these theories and the vindication of Marx's position, which was both more evolutionist and more optimistic as to the ability of the capitalist mode of production to spread into and industrialise the third world.[21]

The neo-Marxist reaction to this argument is to point out that the recent industrialisation of countries like Brazil or Greece does not in any way challenge the two fundamental tenets of underdevelopment theories: the 'anti-evolutionist' and the 'misgrowth' theses. Because the foreign-induced, dependent industrialisation these countries are experiencing is not only radically different from the type of industrialisation which was experienced by the West, it also aggravates rather than solves the major internal and external problems of these societies (unemployment, lack of national sovereignty). Underdevelopment cannot be characterised merely by lack of industrialisation. Although a weak industrial sector is a common form of underdevelopment, it is by no means the only one. A country's economy can industrialise and still go on growing in a distorted, under-developed manner: i.e. without overcoming the fundamental bottlenecks and imbalances of peripheral capitalism. More specifically, the crucial question according to this position for assessing the course and nature of capital accumulation is not that of industrialisation or non-industrial-isation, but rather the type of articulation that connects the dynamic high-productivity sectors of the economy (whether industrial or not) with those that are technologically backward. If the Western pattern of this articulation is compared with that of third-world industrialisation, some fundamental differences emerge which clearly demonstrate that both the 'anti-evolutionist' and 'misgrowth' theses still hold true.[22]

Western European industrial capitalism, as a very gradual and relatively indigenous process, managed to both spread more widely and link itself organically with the rest of the economy and society. Using a more precise Marxist terminology, we can say that the capitalist mode of production dominant in the industrial sector either destroyed pre-capitalist modes (feudal, small-commodity production), or incorporated them in a 'positive' manner — positive in the sense that small units of production for instance, whether in agriculture or industry, managed to specialise, increase their productivity, and establish *organic complementarity* with big industry. This meant that the effects of technological progress originating in the dynamic sectors quickly spread to the rest of the economy, with beneficial consequences on income distribution, the expansion of internal markets, etc. In contrast to this type of capitalist development, the 'under-developed' type of industrialisation typically takes an *enclave* form — in the sense that here the growing, technologically advanced industrial sector cannot transfer its dynamism and high productivity to the rest of the economy.[23]

If we consider the growth of the Greek economy, for instance, we note the persistence of large sectors both in industry and agriculture where small commodity production remains dominant, and where the links with the 'modern industrial' sector are clearly negative — meaning that these sectors, without being destroyed, are permanently kept in a depressed, vegetative state while their resources, through a variety of mechanisms, are systematically transferred to the technologically advanced sector and abroad.

As far as industry is concerned, one of its striking characteristics is the persistence of a plethora of small family units. The extent to which small firms persist in the Greek manufacturing sector can be seen by the fact that whereas in 1930 93.2 per cent of manufacturing establishments were employing fewer than five persons, by 1958 this percentage had only gone down to 84.9 per cent.[24] Moreover, the industrial census of 1969 registered 124,600 manufacturing establishments in Greece, which means that in relation to the population there are approximately 15 establishments per 1000 persons (compared with three in Chile, 3.8 in Spain, and 0.6 in the United States).[25]

On the other hand, side by side with these small units one finds some very large firms which exercise quasi-monopolistic control of the market. Thus, according to the industrial census of 1971, the 49 biggest firms employed 33 per cent of the industrial labour force and possessed 51.5 per cent of all capital assets. The same study shows that among industrial limited liability firms, the largest 100, employing 70,000 persons (47 per cent of the total labour force in such firms), owned 65 per cent of all capital assets, and their profits amounted to 68 per cent of the total profits. Of course, most of these firms belonged to the technologically advanced, foreign-dominated sectors of industry (chemicals, metallurgy).[26] This structure of the Greek industrial sector and the huge gap in productivity between the very small and the very large firms[27] gives a very clear picture of the 'enclave' character of the foreign-capital dominated dynamic sectors of industry.

The persistence of small-scale inefficient units is demonstrated even more clearly in agriculture. From the time of the agrarian reforms between the wars, which spelt the virtual disappearance of large landed estates, most agricultural establishments have been small family holdings, with very few of them employing outside labour. The drastic reduction in the agricultural population during the fifties and sixties has made very little change in this basic structure, neither as regards any marked concentration of holdings into larger units, nor evidencing capital investments on any notable scale.[28] Greece still lags far behind Western Europe in all aspects of agricultural production and, worse, its agricultural rate of per-capita output is growing more slowly than that of all other sectors of the economy (whereas in Western countries it is rising more quickly).[29]

Of course the big gaps in productivity between simple commodity production (agriculture, small industry) and the capitalist sector (medium and big industry)[30] is reflected in the distribution of income. Despite the scarcity of reliable data on this area, the few existing calculations suggest clearly that not only are wealth and income differentials much greater than those of Western European countries, but that they go on increasing at a rapid rate.[31] This makes sense if one takes into account that to the 'normal' inequalities between labour and capital generated within the capitalist mode of production are added, in this case, the inequalities resulting from the huge productivity differentials between the simple commodity and capitalist sectors.[32]

In other words, as has already been noted in other underdeveloped countries,[33] the Greek model of capital accumulation operates in such a way that, through a variety of direct and indirect mechanisms (prices, taxation etc.), a systematic transfer takes place of resources from the technologically backward to the technologically advanced sectors of industry.[34] In this way the former, without being destroyed, are reduced to a state of permanent stagnation. It is precisely in this sense that the links between small commodity production and industrial capitalism are 'negative' in Greece. In the last analysis, industrial capital, concentrated in the hands of a few foreign and autochthonous investors, grows at the expense of agriculture and small industry (i.e., at the expense of the majority of the population).[35] Finally, the 'negative' links between the modern-industrial and technologically backward sectors are also seen in the low labour absorption of the Greek manufacturing sector.[36] Despite this sector's growing share in the GNP, rise of employment has been extremely slow here and, as industry cannot absorb all those who leave the primary sector, there has been massive emigration to western Europe, and a further inflation of the service and artisanal sectors.

If industrialisation has not solved the problem of making effective use of human resources inside the country, neither has it solved Greece's increasing financial dependence on the international level. Apart from the dominance of foreign capital in the dynamic manufacturing sectors being directly responsible for a drainage of resources abroad, the low value-added ratio of Greek manufacture[37] means that increasing industrialisation brings about a more than proportional increase in imports and a continuous worsening of the balance of payments.[38]

The Greek case, then, seems to demonstrate that, despite the country's recent industrialisation, the basic theses of the neo-Marxists hold true. Greece is following a different economic trajectory from that of Western Europe — one which fails to solve the problem of unemployment and external dependence. Of course, it could be argued against this neo-Marxist pessimism that a look back at the history of western European industrialisation shows problems of unbalanced growth and dependence similar to those which countries like Greece are facing today. Perhaps the present misgrowth aspects of dependent industrialisation are simply transitional phenomena, which will disappear as international capital penetrates the third-world economies more intensively and fully.

I do not find this argument very convincing. Western countries have undoubtedly experienced severe dislocations during their early phases of industrialisation. But given the different timing and the different position of these countries in the international division of labour, such features did not last long and had a completely different impact on their overall economies.

Let us look, for instance, at the problem of foreign dependence. It is true that French development in its initial stages of railway construction was very much helped by the borrowing of funds from abroad. But given France's international power position, this borrowing did not result in chronic indebtedness and therefore dependence on foreign creditors. Through its successful and more or less balanced industrialisation, France was able to meet its debts and become in its turn an important exporter of capital.[39] In the Balkans, on the other hand, foreign loans, because of the terms imposed and the way in which they were used, contributed to the growing dependence and underdevelopment of these social formations. From the moment of their emergence as independent national entities, the Balkan States had all to depend on foreign loans for the development of their armies, the maintenance of their overinflated state bureaucracies, and the running of their economies. This financial dependence was not reduced, as in the case of France, with the growth of their economies; on the contrary, it increased steadily in relation to their economic mis-growth.[40] Towards the end of the nineteenth century, for instance, Greece had to make extremely humiliating concessions to its creditors: owing mainly to the deterioration of the international market for currants (Greece's main export crop at the time) Greece had reached the state of bankruptcy. She was obliged, therefore, to accept an international financial commission on her own territory which not only controlled a specified number of Greek sources of revenue, but also had an important say in the emission of money, the contracting of new loans, and on all fiscal matters. In this way, and for a considerable number of years, the most vital functions of the Greek State and parliament were exercised by a group of foreign bond-holders directly nominated as members of the financial control commission by the foreign powers.[41] And although in subsequent years dependence did not take such extreme forms, the post-war model of capital accumulation in Greece is such that, as already indicated, continuing industrialisation implies *ipso facto* continuing dependence.

It may be objected that there is no reason why a strong State, given the right balance of political forces, could not 'correct' the misgrowth aspects of capitalist industrialisation. Most bourgeois Greek politicians argue that the right State policies could gradually eliminate the disarticulation and dependence aspects of Greek industrialisation through stricter control and guidance of foreign and indigenous capital etc. But stricter control and more rational direction of investments according to the needs of the Greek economy and people, if pursued *seriously*, would immediately destroy the 'favourable' climate for foreign investment in Greece. It would mean a dramatic reduction in the flow of foreign capital (the basic force behind Greece's recent industrialisation), and the flight of indigenous capital abroad. In other words, the very dynamism of Greek industrialisation depends on the maintenance and accentuation of its underdeveloped features.[42]

Although I certainly do not believe in any 'iron laws' of capitalist underdevelopment, the present structure and dynamism of the Greek model of capital accumulation do not leave much room for optimism over the prospects for the country's relatively autonomous and balanced capitalist development.

3   THE METHODOLOGICAL CRITIQUE

A   *Althusserian Marxism versus neo-Marxism*

A more serious attack on underdevelopment theories comes from those who object to the methodological differences between Marx's work (especially *Das Kapital*) and that of neo-Marxists. In fact, for Althusser and his growing number of disciples,[43] most underdevelopment theories

use Marxist concepts in a loose and *ad hoc* manner; they totally lack the
rigour and 'systematicity' of Marx's mature work. These theories, despite
their radical conclusions, are scarcely Marxist at all: their basic conceptual
tools, their problematic, is not far removed from the empiricist orientation
of bourgeois historians, economists and other social scientists.[44] The
critique of the Althusserian school has had and still has a profound impact
on contemporary Marxism, especially in France. In fact, it would not be
an exaggeration to say that, given the emphasis which, as far as metatheory
is concerned, Althusser lays on rigorous and systematic reappraisal,
clarification and further theoretical elaboration of basic Marxist concepts,
his position in Marxism is becoming equivalent to that of Parsons within
non-Marxist sociology. So it is not surprising that in France, that citadel of
Western Marxism, there is scarcely any Marxist who has not been
influenced, whether negatively or positively, by Althusser's work. In other
terms, the considerable influence that Althusser exercises, especially
among the younger generation of social scientists, should not be seen as a
'passing fashion'. The type of work that he and his disciples are doing
has, despite its serious shortcomings, filled a very real gap in Marxist
theory. As far as the study of third-world countries is concerned, the
theorists who have been most influenced by Althusser's critique are mainly
Marxist anthropologists who try to see to what extent a rigorous
application of such Marxist concepts as forces and relations of production,
mode of production, social formation etc. can be useful in analysing the
impact of western capitalism on the so-called primitive societies.[45]

Some of the differences between neo-Marxists and the French anthropological school may conveniently be examined by considering the
former's criticism of dualistic theories of development. By adopting a
functionalist/neo-evolutionist problematic, dualistic theories see third-
world capitalist countries in terms of a dichotomy between a modern
capitalist-sector and a traditional-technologically backward one, with very
few links between. According to such theories, the further development of
capitalism will strengthen the inter-sectoral links as the values and
technology of the modern sector will gradually be diffused to the
traditional one, the whole society moving up the evolutionary ladder
towards full industrialisation and development.[46]

Neo-Marxist critics like Stavenhagen, Furtado and Frank have pointed
out that the big differences in productivity noticeable in underdeveloped
countries between modern and traditional sectors are not due to the lack
of linkages between the two, but to the fact that the existing strong
linkages are such that they reinforce and perpetuate the gap between
them. More specifically, it is not the lack of capitalist development which
can account for the persistence of backwardness, but the fact that the
growth and dynamism of the capitalist sector is founded on the permanent
drainage of resources from the backward one. Thus the two sectors are
linked in such a manner that the growth of the one presupposes the

stagnation of the other.[47] It is this type of 'negative' connection between sectors that Amin calls *disarticulation*,[48] and that I have illustrated by examining the Greek case of industrialisation.

As was pointed out in the previous section, this neo-Marxist criticism of dualistic theories is fundamentally valid; it really pinpoints the core of the underdevelopment problem. Methodologically, however, the concepts used are still very close to that neo-evolutionist problematic which neo-Marxists try to reject. Gunder Frank, for instance, has launched a devastating critique of the modern-traditional dichotomy as used by the functionalists, but has replaced it with a terminology which, used in an *ad hoc* manner, is just as misleading. At least the concepts of modernity and tradition have a long history in sociological literature and their meaning is relatively clear, whereas in reading Frank we are never quite certain of the meaning of his terms. Thus the centre–periphery dichotomy which plays such a crucial role in his analysis, and which is a potentially very fruitful concept, is never worked out clearly. Sometimes the 'centre' refers to collective actors (e.g. the metropolitan or indigenous bourgeoisie), at others it refers to systems (the urban centre).[49] There is a similar vagueness in Frank's use of the concept of capitalism. In his eagerness to show that, contrary to the dualists' thinking, the traditional sector is no less capitalist than the modern one, he broadens the concept of capitalism to such an extent that it comes to refer to any economic system or sector linked to the world capitalist market. As Laclau has rightly pointed out, by focusing on distribution rather than on the structure of production, this definition fails to make the crucial distinction between social formations in which the capitalist mode of production is dominant, and those which, although integrated into the world capitalist system, have other modes of production in dominance.[50] Moreover, his blanket usage of the term capitalism leads away from one of the most important facets of the Marxist problematic: that of the manner of articulation of the various modes of production within a specific social formation, and of the transition from the dominance of one mode of production to that of another.

It is precisely on problems of *articulation* and *transition* that the attention of the French anthropological school is focused. By viewing a society as a social formation, i.e. as a structural totality in which a dominant mode of production is articulated in specific ways with other modes of production, they can deal much more exactly and fruitfully with the problem of the penetration of Western capitalism into third-world countries. It allows them to account for the severe dislocations and dependence of third-world economies, while avoiding the vagueness and ambiguity of such terms as traditional-modern, advanced-backward, or centre-periphery. More specifically, with reference to the study of third-world countries, there are several ways in which the concept of mode of production, as used by the French Marxist anthropologists, is useful.

First, it is based on a more or less rigorous theory of the structure of societies and the broad principles of their persistence and/or transformation. This theory provides guidelines on how to conceptualise the relationships between modes of production and their constituent parts (forces and relations of production), as well as their political and ideological superstructures.[51] Whether or not Althusser's interpretation of historic materialism is accepted, his emphasis on the importance of theory and the necessity to avoid *ad hoc* concepts must be welcomed as a healthy reaction against the narrow-minded empiricism rampant in the Anglo-Saxon social sciences — a tradition of research hiding its lack of theory behind extensive use of jargon and sophisticated statistical techniques.[52]

Second, in contrast to the tradition-modernity typology, the concept under discussion points directly to where the main dimension of development/underdevelopment lies: the economy, the forces and relations of production. This is a very obvious point, but one which is often forgotten, especially by functionalist sociologists who, by accepting the absurd division of labour existing nowadays in the social sciences, limit their focus to the non-economic aspects of development (religion, family, culture, personality structure). The emphasis on the economy, moreover, does not as in other brands of Marxism lead to any crude technological and economic determinism. Althusser's insistence on the relative autonomy of the political and ideological instances warns the student away from a mere reduction of political and cultural structures to their economic bases.[53]

The mode of production concept not only stresses the importance of the economy in general, but also that of *production*. It has already been mentioned in connection with Frank's work how misleading it can be when too exclusive a focus on the sphere of distribution neglects to consider the productive structures. Such a neglect leads invariably to crude and/or misleading generalisations. This is true not only in the context of present-day underdeveloped countries. Lublinskaya for instance, in her work on French absolutism, shows quite convincingly, I think, how prominent economic historians, by neglecting the fundamental differences in the development of the productive forces in various European countries, were led to the erroneous conclusion that there was a general economic crisis in seventeenth-century Europe.[54] Moreover, if one looks from this point of view at another famous debate in European economic history, that on the transition from feudalism to capitalism, it becomes obvious that a lot of misunderstandings and misconceptions about the transition stem from the fact that not enough attention was paid to feudalism as a mode of production.[55]

Third, the Marxist conceptualisation of modes of production cuts across and rejects the present compartmentalisation of the social sciences — a compartmentalisation which, I think, is particularly crippling in the study of underdeveloped countries. The mode of production concept, by its very construction, leads unavoidably to the study of a social totality —

a totality seen as an articulation of various modes of production and their political and ideological instances. Moreover, the idea that a social formation consists of a specific combination of various modes of production is particularly useful because it avoids the naïve evolutionism of vulgar interpretations of Marxism which view historical development as a unilinear succession of modes of production.[56]

Fourth, the mode of production concept provides a much clearer and more rigorous conceptualisation of underdevelopment, as well as pointing the *type of dependence* that third-world countries are experiencing. To return to the Greek example, we have already argued that under-development keeps persisting in Greece, and can be seen in the manner in which the technologically advanced industrial sector is linked with the backward sectors of the economy (small industry, agriculture). The terms 'advanced' and 'backward' are too general, however, whereas the idea of articulation and transition between different modes of production 'allows for much greater variety and complexity in the relation between, and the internal dynamics of the capitalist and pre-capitalist sectors of a social formation'.[57] Thus, taking the Greek case as an example, the imprecision of the 'modern'-'traditional' dichotomy can be overcome if Greek underdevelopment is considered as a *specific type of articulation between two different modes of production: the capitalist mode (CMP) which prevails in 'big' industry, and the simple commodity production (SCP) prevalent in agriculture and 'small' industry.*[58]

Underdevelopment persists because, contrary to the Western pattern, the CMP has neither expanded far enough into the economy (it has failed to destroy the SCP), nor has it organically integrated the SCP into itself. More precisely, by a lack of organic integration I mean (*a*) that the links between the two modes are such that there is a one-sided, systematic transfer of resources from the simple commodity to the capitalist sector;[59] (*b*) that the capitalist sector has more numerous and positive connections with the economies of the 'metropolitan' centres, so that its dynamism and productivity gains are transferred abroad.[60]

It is this articulation between the modes of production which is at the basis of Greece's dependent and peripheral position within the world capitalist system. Greek Marxist writers like Poulantzas and Vergopoulos have argued that for a characterisation of economies such as that of Greece, the terms 'dependent' or 'deformed' capitalism are more meaning-ful than the concept of underdevelopment — especially now that Greece, through its industrialisation and its high per-capita income, must be differentiated from the group of third-world impoverished countries.[61] I think that the terms dependent and peripheral, *if they are used as substitutes for the term underdevelopment*, have the same conceptual vagueness as Frank's terms of centre-periphery. More specifically, the term 'dependent' cannot, on its own, help us distinguish the dependence of third-world countries from that of a declining industrialised, capitalist country such as today's England. England is certainly dependent on the United States, but its dependence is radically different from the dependence of Greece or Latin American countries, for instance. To understand such differences, one has to examine the internal structure of the latter. It is the internal disarticulation (i.e. underdevelopment)[62] of such economies which gives *specific* character to their international dependence.[63] When the above point is left out of account, it is very easy to arrive at Vergopoulos' unacceptable position that the Greek economy, as far as its internal development is concerned, resembles the developed economies of Western Europe, and that it is mainly from the aspect of its dependent, peripheral position in the international capitalist market that it should be compared with the underdeveloped countries of the third world.[64]

Fifth, and most important, the mode of production concept suggests ways in which it is possible to pass from a system to an action analysis:[65] to use Althusserian terminology, from instances to practices,[66] from contradictions or non-correspondences between structures to class conflict. Contrary for instance to the tradition-modernity or centre-periphery terminology, the mode of production concept — in referring to the types of property relations that characterise a system of production — points directly to lines of social cleavage and potential loci for the development of class-consciousness and class conflict. Failure to systematically use the mode of production concept leads either to a total disregard of classes, as in neo-evolutionist theories; or, as in some neo-Marxist theories, to an arbitrary use of class categories — arbitrary in that no systematic effort is made to show how classes are rooted in specific structures of production and how, through their location in production, they relate to the social whole.[67] Hence the proliferation of such *ad hoc* categories as underclasses, *Lumpenbourgeoisie*, marginal classes etc.[68]

Furthermore, if the highly abstract, 'logico-deductive' analysis of any single mode of production leads to the identification of two opposing classes — the one dominant, and the other being dominated — the concept of social formation, as a specific combination of a variety of modes of production leads to a more 'historico-genetic' approach, which then allows for examination of the intricacies of class alliances and struggles in a concrete situation.[69]

B   The problem of class analysis

However, it is precisely at this point, at the passage from a system to an action analysis, i.e. from 'structures' to 'practices', that Althusser's contribution becomes negative. His emphasis on the structural determination of action is such that ultimately collective actors disappear from the analysis altogether, or rather are portrayed as mere products of a complex and hierarchical articulation of systems (structures). Althusser's justified critique of Feuerbach's anthropological subject ('Man' operating in a social vacuum), or Hegel's idealist one leads him ultimately to denying the subject any intentionality in the social process. For him, any emphasis on the autonomy of collective action appears idealistic, psychologistic and 'historicist', it reduces history to a series of conjunctural events, to the deeds of great men. Thus, in reaction to the crude voluntarism of idealist philosophers, social phenomenologists and psychologistic social scientists, Althusser ends up at the other extreme: with a structural determinism which denies the possibility of any autonomous collective action, a superstructuralism which reduces social analysis to the ahistorical identification of a number of invariant elements and the study of their intricate articulations and combinations.[70] In this way classes become the mere 'bearers' of structures. Not only the places of class members, but their collective practices too, are overdetermined by the complex structural reality. The latter appears as a *deus ex machina*, regulating everything and everybody. In an almost Durkheimian fashion, the analysis always moves from structures (systems, instances) to practices (agents, 'bearers of structures'), never the other way round. Classes, as relatively autonomous agents of social transformation, disappear from the analysis.

As this is a very crucial point, I would like to refer briefly to the work of Nicos Poulantzas who, among Marxists influenced by Althusser, has done the most serious and systematic work on the problem of social classes.[71] Although the author, in many respects, differentiates his position from that of Althusser,[72] he remains very close to him as far as the passive portrayal of classes is concerned. Basically Poulantzas, following Althusser, defines social classes as 'a concept which indicates the *effects* of all the structures of a mode of production matrix or of a social formation on the agents who constitute the supports: this concept indicates therefore the effects of the global structure in the sphere of social relations.'[73] This one-sided conception of classes as the 'effects' (rather than the 'causes') of structures is not, of course very different from Althusser's position, who explicitly argues that 'The real subject of all partial history is the *combination* under the dependence of which are the elements and their relationships, that is to say something which *is not a subject*. So it could be said that the chief problem of a scientific history, a theoretical history, is identifying the combination on which depend the elements that are to be analysed.'[74]

In his more recent book on classes, Poulantzas makes a distinction which could have led to a less passive portrayal of classes. This is the distinction between class 'places' and class 'positions'. The former is basically a concept which refers to the 'objective' location of agents in the division of labour, these locations being structurally determined by the relations of production but also by equivalent structures on the superstructural level (i.e. politico-ideological relations of domination—subordination). If class place refers mainly to the idea of the structural determination of classes, 'class position' is a 'strategy concept'. It refers to such things as the political organisation representing a class, the strategies (positions) that it adopts *vis-à-vis* specific issues, the sort of alliances it establishes in a concrete conjuncture etc.: 'What one means by "class consciousness" proper and by an autonomous political organisation — i.e. from the point of view of the working class, a revolutionary proletarian ideology and an autonomous party — refer to *class positions* and to the *conjuncture*, they constitute the conditions for the intervention of classes as *social forces*'[75] (In English, the term 'class position' often implies what Poulantzas terms 'class places', so in order to avoid the confusion I will always use the term in quotes or I will substitute it with the term 'strategy'). The above distinction between places and 'positions' is important because often class places and class 'positions' do not coincide. For instance, in the case of the 'labour aristocracy', as Poulantzas argues, whereas in terms of class places this group of workers belongs to the proletariat, often it adopts bourgeois class 'positions' (i.e. strategies which are incongruent with its objective class interests).[76] However, Poulantzas does not make much use of this fundamental distinction. Given his one-sided structuralist perspective, 'strategy' concepts do not receive any attention whatsoever. Except for a few pages at the end of his book, his whole analysis is about class places. The impact of class 'positions' on class places, i.e. the way in which social forces (e.g. a political movement or party) can have an impact on the relations of production and hence on class places remains totally untheorised.

The same bias against 'strategy' concepts is seen when Poulantzas considers another important and related distinction, that between class places and agents. On this he writes:

'The analysis made here of the relations of production according to the phases of present-day monopoly capitalism, concerns the *place* of capital and its functions. Another is the problem of *agents* who exercise its powers, i.e. those who occupy this place or who depend on it directly. It is evident that the modifications of these relations have as an effect the diversification of the categories of agents who exercise these powers: the famous question of the managers and of the techno-structure are one aspect of this problem. These modifications have thus effects on the institutional organisation of the firm which are manifested as a tendency for the centralisation-decentralisation of decision-making . . . without any doubt these questions are important: *but in the last analysis they are simply an effect of the modification of the relations of production*'.[77]

But why should agents be the 'effect' of the modification of the relations of production and not the other way around? Poulantzas and Althusser see agents as 'effects' of structures, simply because they portray them on the micro-level of analysis, to use functionalist terminology, as individual role players who occupy specific class places. On this level, of course, they are right. Neither the individual manager nor the worker can have any appreciable impact on the relations of production. From the point of view of *individual agents*, it is perfectly true that societal structures, as Durkheim has pointed out, portray the characteristics of unchangeability, externality and constraint. But if one talks about relations of production on the societal level, one should view agents on the same level of analysis. Which means that one should talk not about individual but about collective agents, not about the worker or the manager as an occupant of a place (i.e. as a role player) but about workers and managers as collective agents. In other terms, on this level of analysis agents become what Poulantzas has called *social forces* (a 'strategy' concept) — in which case it is not at all clear why social forces should be the 'effects' of structures. In so far as structures and their modifications do not come from the sky but are the result of collective movements, group strategies, the intended or unintended consequences of pressure groups etc., why should collective agents be portrayed as the passive products of structures, and not structures as the 'effects' of collective agents (social forces)?

In conclusion, without denying the necessity of the type of work that Poulantzas and other Marxists have done on class places,[78] and without denying fundamental differences between that work and the writings of non-Marxist sociologists on class, it is still quite obvious that the Althusserian conception of class is as static as that underlying the social stratification studies of functionalist sociology. In fact, as far as the system-action relationship is concerned, Althusserian Marxism is not very different from Parsonian functionalism. In both these theoretical traditions, collective actors are portrayed as puppets and in consequence are constitutionally incapable of dealing with problems of social change and development. This basic weakness of both systems is hidden by an extremely complicated and obscure terminology which ultimately presents society as a reified structural entity made up of systems and sub-systems which, in an anthropomorphic way, pull all the strings behind the actors' backs. It is not, therefore, surprising that Althusserian Marxism not only does not transcend, but actually perpetuates some of the most untenable excesses of functionalist explanations.

C   *The Problem of Structural Causation*

Before examining in greater detail this fundamental point, I would like to make it clear that Althusser's structural determinism is by no means inherent in the mode of production concept; not only Marx, but many other Marxist writers who are influenced by Althusser and/or use a mode of production analysis, do manage to avoid it.[79] On the other hand, there is no doubt that a marked tendency to reduce collective actors in general and classes in particular to mere products of structures permeates all of Althusser's work and that of his disciples. This tendency emerges not only from what they say explicitly about the 'bearers of structures', but also from the way they construct their major concepts; from the manner, for instance, in which they discuss the central problems of causation and transition.

As an example, let us take a look at Godelier's discussion of structural causality. In contrast to Althusser, Godelier expresses himself quite clearly and provides concrete instances to illustrate his points; it is therefore easier in his work to see the logical implications of some aspects of Althusser's structuralism. In order to show how the economic structure produces effects on other structures or instances, Godelier discusses the social organisation of the Mbuti pygmies, a society of hunters and gatherers in equatorial Congo.[80] Their system of production (mainly hunting in bands, with the women and children driving the game into nets held by the men) generates three fundamental 'constraints' (in Parsonian terminology: 'functional problems or requirements') which 'express the social conditions for the reproduction of the productive process' (Parsonian translation: 'for the maintenance of the system'):[81] (a) the *dispersion constraint*, which refers to the fact that for the system to operate effectively, the band members cannot be above or below a certain number; (b) the '*co-operation constraint*', which emphasises the need for collaboration of all members in the productive process according to their age and sex;[82] and (c) the '*fluidity*' or '*non-closure*' *constraint*, which is the band's need to be in 'permanent flux', i.e. in frequent movement of members from one band to another.

These three constraints form a system which 'is the origin of a certain number of *simultaneous* structural effects on *all* other instances of the Mbuti's social organisation.'[83] For instance, on the political level Mbuti society is characterised by a relative equality among band members and by a remarkable lack of wars and violent conflict among bands. Why are inter-band relations so peaceful, why is war rare in Mbuti society? Because 'war is incompatible with the mode of production constraints (a), (b) and (c) taken separately and in their reciprocal relations.'[84] How can one explain the role of the 'fool' within the band? By the fact that the fool, by means of certain institutionalised techniqes, detonates conflict between tribal members and thus enhances harmonious relations and cooperation, a prerequisite for the reproduction of the system. In this way one finds similar norms of cooperation not only in the productive sphere but in all other instances as well; and this *isomorphism* between instances is 'generated by the fact that they are all different effects of the *same cause* [i.e. the system of the three constraints] which acts simultaneously on all societal levels'.[85]

So here we arrive at the type of naïve teleological functionalist explanation that even 'bourgeois' sociologists have criticised and rejected long ago: the illegitimate transformation of function (constraint, functional requirement) into cause.[86] Taking away the verbiage and structuralist jargon, all that Godelier seems to say with his 'structural causality' is that institutions, roles, structures are what they are because they constitute effects of a fundamental cause: the reproduction needs of the productive system.

It is not surprising that neither Althusserian Marxism nor Parsonian functionalism can provide an adequate theory of social causation. For in so far as collective actors become the mere products of the social system, one has to reify social reality or revert to teleological explanations in order to account for the very existence and change of such a system.[87] At best, aware of and wishing to avoid the risks of teleology and reification but remaining within the system/structure problematic, one can simply *describe but never explain* change and development. Thus, leaving aside Godelier's discussion on causation, what he does show with his example is a certain *compatibility* (a certain correspondence of structures) between the Mbuti system of production and their political and kinship institutions. But his analysis simply describes this compatibility, it does not and cannot explain it.

C   The Problem of Transition

Having discussed the problem of causation, let us take a look in greater detail at the Althusserian position on the problem of transition from one mode of production to another, or rather the problem of explaining how a new mode of production reaches dominant position in a specific social formation. This problem is, of course, a crucial one in the study of development, as many third-world countries are in a transitional stage in the sense that Western capitalism is in the process of destroying or placing into a subordinate position the local non-capitalist modes of production.

As mentioned above, Althusserians criticise the neo-Marxist school for having left the rigour and strict structuralism of *Das Kapital* too far behind in the empiricist, often voluntaristic-historicist orientation of its under-development theories. What they seem to forget is that the questions asked by the neo-Marxists are quite different from those asked in *Das Kapital*, both sets of questions being perfectly legitimate from the Marxist point of view. Marx in his major work tried to produce a *synchronic* study of the capitalist mode of production and its reproduction, whereas neo-Marxist theories try to deal with a special type of transition: the change in dominance of modes of production within the social formations of peripheral capitalism. Given this fundamental difference in theoretical preoccupations, it is not surprising that the methodology applied should be quite different too. As a matter of fact, even in *Das Kapital* the methodology changes radically, becoming less structuralist and more 'historicist', as soon as Marx tries to deal with the famous problem of primitive accumulation, the problem of transition from the feudal to the capitalist mode of production.[88]

Many analysts of Marx's work have pointed out that, whereas in the

main body of *Das Kapital* the method is rigorous, logico-deductive and
holistic in the structuralist sense (actors are portrayed as mere 'bearers' of
the structured totality), in those parts which try to explain how capitalism
has emerged from the womb of feudalism, the methodology changes
radically: here structuralism recedes and actors, social classes, emerge as
autonomous agents of social transformation.[89] Of course, Marx's change
in approach does not degenerate into an *ad hoc* description of historical
events. Theoretical considerations, directly derived from the synchronic
study of capitalism, constantly guide the analysis. Thus Marx examines in
a highly selective way the 'genealogy' of those elements in feudalism
whose development and different articulation at a later period will
constitute the core of the capitalist mode of production: the separation of
the direct producer from his means of production (the emergence of 'free'
labour), and the development of capital in the strict sense (as the employer
of wage labour).

For Althusserians, Marx's analysis of the emergence and development of
these two crucial elements within the decaying structures of feudalism
does not have the rigour and logic that one finds in his study of the
capitalist mode of production proper. For some of them this is a major
weakness of Marx's opus. It shows that even in *Das Kapital* Marx did not
manage to eradicate 'ideological' elements which played such a noticeable
role in his earlier work. Althusserians see it as one of their major
theoretical tasks, therefore, to construct new concepts which would
permit the problem of transition to be treated with the same rigour as
found in the rest of *Das Kapital*. Balibar, for instance, sets himself
precisely that task. He tries to build up theoretical concepts which will
eliminate the 'dualistic' character in Marx's methodology and elevate the
problem of transition from the 'ideological to the scientific mode' of
analysis.[90] But as he tries to do this without abandoning Althusser's
superstructuralism, he ends up with the following tautological and highly
confusing solution: according to Balibar, transition does not imply a lack
of structures or their destruction, it implies structures and laws which
cannot be deduced from the theories of the feudal or capitalist mode of
production. Therefore, since the transition is not random but guided by
structuralist principles, one must construct the concept of a new mode of
production to deal with transitional phenomena. The main characteristic
of this transitional mode of production is the non-correspondence of
structures both within the economy and between the economy and the
other instances (political, ideological).[91]

This rather simplistic solution does not, unfortunately, solve the
transition problem; it simply shifts it elsewhere. Because now we would
have to explain (*a*) how the change takes place from a non-transitional
mode of production (e.g. feudalism) to a transitional one; and (*b*), given
the non-correspondence of structures within the transitional mode of
production, how this non-correspondence leads to social trans-

formation.[92]   Lockwood has rightly pointed out that the non-correspondence of structures, i.e. system contradictions, do not automatically bring about class conflict and change.[93] In order to find out under which conditions system contradictions generate social conflict and under which they do not, one has to shift the analysis from systemic constraints to problems of class consciousness, strategies and tactics, i.e. one has to view classes as relatively autonomous agents which can contribute to both the change and the stability of a social system.

The fact is that the attempts of Balibar and others[94] to solve the problem of transition within a strictly structuralist perspective cannot but fail, because it is impossible to explain change, the transformation of structures, by pointing to yet more structures. It is only possible to deal with change and development by seriously taking into account the truism that men are both the products and producers of their social world, by stressing both the system-actor and the actor-system relationship. From this point of view, Marx changing methodology in his analysis of primitive accumulation may have had to do less with a theoretical failing, and more with the nature of the problem in hand. For there is no doubt that when examining the functioning and reproduction (simple or enlarged) of a mode of production with its dominance already established, the system (structure) → practice relationship is more crucial. In this case the 'social machine' seems to function and reproduce itself irrespective of the intentions and wishes of those who are at its base – and therefore it does make some sense to speak of 'trends' or even 'tendential laws' of the system. But in examining situations where the old structures and modes of production are disintegrating and the new ones have not yet been institutionalised, it makes more sense to put stronger emphasis on the opposite perspective, on the practice → structure relationship – i.e. to see how collective actors, given greater structural indeterminacy (greater 'room for manoeuvre'), have more opportunities to shape institutions according to their conflicting interests and ideologies. In this case, actors are not so much the puppets of the system as rather its creators. Therefore concepts like choice, strategy, and class struggle are more relevant than those of 'laws', overdetermination, structural causality etc.[95] This is not to deny, of course, that in all cases a social formation should be seen from the point of view of both structures and practices, i.e. it should be seen how its institutional structures impose constraints on specific actors, and how these actors either accept or try to overcome such constraints.

D   Conclusion

The above criticism of Althusserian Marxism would not be adequate without a brief discussion of possible alternative paradigms more useful for the study of development. I already mentioned Marx's 'genealogical' method, to be found not only in his discussion of primitive accumulation but also in his study of pre-capitalist economic formations.[96] However, this is by no means the only method for dealing with problems of transition and development. I think it is possible to move towards a more holistic approach — without having to adopt Balibar's or Althusser's holism — via those who see wholes in terms of configurations of actors rather than of systems and sub-systems; those (including Marx himself in his earlier work) who study the development of class struggles in a thoroughly comprehensive and global manner.

For instance, if one looks at the work of such sociologically-minded historians as Hobsbawm, Braudel, P. Anderson, Lublinskaya,[97] or of historically-minded sociologists like Bendix, Moore or Wallerstein,[98] one finds theories which try to account for development and transition as a very intricate game of collective actors (peasants, landlords, or merchants): here development or underdevelopment is the more or less unintentional result of a variety of strategies and counter-strategies of groups which, within the limits imposed by various structural constraints, try to promote their interests through changing or defending the *status quo*. In these works, systemic structures are not dispensed with but made to recede into the background as collective actors occupy the centre of the stage. Here, although we are dealing with collective actors as more or less autonomous actors, the approach is neither idealistic-psychologistic nor empiricist. Althusser, having got stuck in a nineteenth-century debate, cannot see for instance that, when dealing with actors, writers like B. Moore or Hobsbawm do not talk about 'man' in general or about man's spirit, neither do they deal with historical events in the conventional historio-graphic manner as a series of conjunctural happenings and of great men's deeds.

Which is to say that it is possible to be holistic and provide non-empiricist, non-descriptive explanations of development without resorting to an obsessive, single-minded structuralism. This is what Althusser, fixated in a sterile philosophical debate on the role of the 'subject' in history, does not realise. Thus the pseudo-choice he offers us — systemic holism versus psychologism — must be dismissed. The crucial problem in sociology today is not a crude choice between systems (structures) and actors (practices), but rather the problem of finding out when and under what conditions the emphasis should be on the system → actor relationship and when on the actor → system one; and also on how to change over from a system to an action approach and vice versa. Given the particular problematic of the sociology of development, there is no doubt in my mind that, as in all cases of transition, class analysis should constitute not the exclusive but the major research strategy.

This is particularly so for the case of Greece. As I shall have the opportunity to emphasise in various parts of this volume, what more than anything gives the Greek social formation its specific character is the position of the Greek diaspora merchants. This diaspora bourgeoisie which, in financial terms, was and is more powerful than its indigenous counterpart, played a decisive role in the formation of the Greek State and in the development of the country's major institutions. For instance, only the considerable financial contributions of the nineteenth-century Greek merchant communities abroad can explain the overinflated character of the Greek educational system, the development of which was out of proportion to available indigenous resources.[99] It was also their enormous financial power which can partly explain why, even before Western imperialism took the direct form of economic penetration, Greece had the most commercialised economy[100] in the Balkans without, at the same time, having a strong autochthonous bourgeoisie. Such peculiarities which lie at the core of modern Greek society cannot, I believe, be accounted for in terms of tendencies of the CMP or the 'laws' resulting from a combination of modes of production. In Chapter 4 it is exactly this which will be my argument against an Althusserian-oriented theory which attempts to explain the overall development of Greek agriculture in terms of some 'inherent' tendency of the CMP.

Finally, I do believe that the most convincing argument against both Parsonian functionalism and Althusserian structuralism is a comparison of writings on development based on the above paradigms with writings which make serious use of class analysis (like the above-mentioned works by B. Moore, Wallerstein, etc.). As I will argue in the next chapter, there is no doubt in my mind at any rate, that the latter are much more fruitful and enlightening than the empiricist social stratification studies of functionalist sociology,[101] or the highly abstract, system-oriented economic models that both non-Marxists and certain Marxist economists delight in constructing.[102]

Of course, it is true that at the present moment there is no serious metatheoretical work which strikes a proper balance between a system and an action approach. The existing dominant paradigms in the social sciences either one-sidedly emphasise one system approach or another (Parsonian functionalism, Althusserian Marxism), or they go to the other extreme and overemphasise individual actors and their orientations to such an extent that systemic structures are considered as illegitimate reifications and banned from the analysis (social phenomenology). From this point of view the metatheoretical elaboration of the complex and dialectical relationship between systems and actors, between structural constraints and class practices, seems to me one of the most urgent tasks in sociology today.

3 The Relevance of the Concept of Class to the Study of Modern Greek Society

INTRODUCTION

In the light of the general theoretical debate on the nature of capitalist underdevelopment discussed in the previous chapter, here I will try to narrow the focus of analysis and examine the sociological literature on modern Greece — more specifically, the way in which the concept of class is used in the study of Greek development/underdevelopment. Within this limited perspective, there will be no attempt to provide an exhaustive or even systematic account of all sociological writings on modern Greece; neither shall I try to give an overall view of various Marxist and non-Marxist theories of class and the complicated problems they engender.[1] Rather, the emphasis will be on the underlying conceptual frameworks, paradigms or metatheories[2] that are discernible in representative studies of the Greek social structure and its development. In identifying and comparing such conceptual frameworks, their sociological adequacy and utility for the future development of Greek sociology will be assessed. Finally, although a study of the sociology of Greek sociology could be extremely useful, this paper does not attempt to do this — i.e. to find out how and why a certain sociological paradigm has been widely accepted by most Greek sociologists; the only goal it has set itself is to

An earlier version of this chapter was given as a paper to a conference organised by the New York Academy of Sciences on Modern Greece in 1975; for the Proceedings, cf. M. Dimen and E. Friedl (eds), *Regional variation in Modern Greece and Cyprus: towards a perspective in the ethnology of Greece*, New York 1976, pp. 395–409.

point out the limitations of the dominant paradigm and the need for an alternative or rather a complementary one.

1   FUNCTIONALISM AND THE SOCIAL STRATIFICATION APPROACH

A. I think that the most fundamental split in the social sciences today lies between those who place individual or collective actors at the centre of their analysis, and those who relegate actors to the periphery and view society primarily from a functionalist point of view, i.e. as a system of 'depersonalised' processes or institutional structures that contribute negatively or positively to its basic needs or functional requirements. From this perspective, various conflict theories and certain brands of Marxism[3] could be seen as following the former tradition, whereas Parsonian functionalism, which is dominant in Anglo-Saxon academic sociology, represents the latter.[4]

As is well known, the starting-point of Parsonian analysis are the core values of a societal system, and their institutionalisation into more specific norms and roles. Such norms form sub-systems that are conceptualised in functionalist terms: i.e., norms are viewed not from the point of view of actors, but so to speak from the 'outside', from the point of view of the system and its needs for maintenance and survival. It is these needs or functional requirements which indicate how the system is differentiated into sub-systems[5] — such sub-systems referring, if one views a society as a whole, to its major institutions (economic, political, etc.). In other words, the 'parts' of the social whole are not actors (groups, classes, etc.) but institutions.[6] This being the case, social development is seen as a process of functional-structural differentiation of roles and institutions as one moves from simple to complex social systems. This neo-evolutionist view of change underlies many functionalist studies of third-world countries which conceptualise the development of these countries as a gradual move from 'tradition' to 'modernity', from a state where one social role 'differentiates between two or more roles which function more effectively in the new historical circumstances'.[7]

Taking this highly elliptical summary of Parsonian functionalism, let us see in greater detail how it deals with actors. In so far as they appear at all, they are portrayed very passively. This is the case even on the level of individual actors; they are viewed as role players whose actions are controlled, puppet-fashion, by an all-embracing social system. Parsonian functionalism emphasises the manner in which values, institutionalised in the form of norms and roles, shape an individual's activities through the mechanisms of socialisation and social control. The direction of influence is from the system to the individual. Roles, status and norms are seen 'as things out there', existing in their own right.[8] As recent critics of conventional role-theory have pointed out, the other side of the coin, i.e. the actor-system relationship, is hardly touched upon. Parsonian functionalism never shows how actors *construct* that reality which the roles and norms refer to.[9]

Functionalism's passive portrayal of actors is further accentuated if one moves from the role player to the level of collective actors: here actors disappear altogether. What takes their place is a set of statistical categories (social strata) that group together under a single label all members of a population who have one or more social characteristics in common, e.g. income, education, mobility chances, etc. Social stratification studies are, of course, useful for identifying the *distributional* aspects of a social system, the manner in which various social traits, especially rewards, are allocated among members of a society or of smaller social entities (organisations, communities, etc.). To a limited extent, they can also show how such distributions are correlated with each other. They cannot, however, *explain*[10] such distributions; they can never tell us how and why they came about. Neither do they tell us to what extent the characteristics which all members in a social stratum have in common are or could be the basis of what Giddens calls *class structuration* or *boundedness*: the development of various degrees of class-consciousness and of organisational links between them.[11]

Take for instance Dimaki's study in the sociology of Greek education.[12] In a professionally very competent manner it measures the inequalities of the Greek higher educational system as far as student recruitment is concerned; it shows how educational chances are unequally distributed among the various social strata of Greek society. Furthermore, it shows how such inequalities are related to such things as the student's family environment, his geographical origin, the social origin of the father, etc.[13] Dimaki even tries to explain such correlations in socio-psychological terms. For instance, the finding that peasants' sons participate in university education to a greater degree than do the sons of blue-collar workers is explained in terms of the villager's urge to leave the village, his relatively greater ignorance of the meagre job chances that poor university graduates have, and his greater appreciation of jobs that require university degrees.[14]

At this point we reach the limits of the social stratification approach. What it cannot do without changing problematic and methodology is to explain sociologically how such inequalities ever emerged in the first place, and what made them take their specific form. For instance, in a very interesting chapter, Dimaki points out that despite the obvious injustices of the Greek educational system it is surprisingly open, even when compared with those of highly industrialised countries such as France.[15] But how is this openness and the relatively high social mobility that results from it to be explained? How did it come about?

B. By its very nature the social stratification approach cannot be of any great help in answering such questions. The way to answer them is to move from *stratum* to *class*, to ask *who*-questions on a historical and collective level. Who were the main actors involved in shaping Greek educational institutions, and under what type of constraints were they operating? As C. Tsoukalas has attempted to show in a yet unpublished dissertation,[16] one cannot understand the overinflated character of the Greek educational system without reference to the diaspora Greek bourgeoisie which, through its formidable financial power and its specific relationship to the Greek State, contributed to the shaping and development of most institutional structures in nineteenth-century Greece. As far as nineteenth-century education is concerned, not only did the Greek merchants living abroad create a considerable demand for educated young men (who could staff their offices), they also gave vast amounts of money for the development of various educational establishments. For instance, up to 1870, the funds available for education from the State budget were much lower than the donations for schools provided by rich diaspora Greeks.[17] Whatever the validity of such a thesis, what is important from our point of view is that here the bourgeoisie is not seen as a mere category whose properties can be ascertained by measuring the attributes or attitudes of its individual members. The diaspora bourgeoisie is here portrayed as a collective actor, whose impact on the Greek institutional order can be grasped by looking at it in relation to other actors (State officials, indigenous merchants, politicians, rentiers, peasants etc.). Here relationships do not refer to logical or statistical comparisons (e.g. 'category A has more income than category B'), but to actual organisational links between concrete groups which, in trying to promote their own interest, enter into historically specific relationships with each other. In other words, actors here are not portrayed in a Durkheimian fashion as mere *products* of society, they are its *producers* as well.

I am not, of course, arguing that Dimaki's and Tsoukalas' approaches are contradictory. They are *complementary*, both being necessary for a well-rounded study of Greek education. If I am emphasising the limitations of the social stratification approach, it is because large amounts of energy and financial resources, both in Greece and elsewhere, have been spent in that direction and relatively little has been achieved, in academic sociology at least, in so far as class analysis is concerned.

In Greek sociology this discrepancy is quite obvious. Most sociological studies of modern Greece are inspired by the social stratification paradigm: whether one looks at studies of emigrants,[18] Greek women,[19] the military,[20] political elites,[21] etc., the mode of analysis always comes down to the measurement of respondents' attitudes or other traits and the establishment of correlations between crucial variables.[22]

Given this state of affairs, very few Greek sociological studies deal seriously with problems of development and underdevelopment. The reason is not simply ideological; there are epistemological obstacles too, for Parsonian functionalism simply does not have adequate conceptual tools for handling problems of change.[23] Given the disappearance of collective actors, functionalists deal with development by *either* (1) emphasising the importance of certain institutions or 'values' as obstacles or catalysts of growth, in which case, in the usual social stratification manner, research focuses on entrepreneurial norms, attitudes and other social characteristics; *or* (2) by describing developments in terms of the structural—functional differentiation of roles and institutions as a society moves from 'tradition' to 'modernity'.[24]

For instance, Alexander's work on Greek industrialists very clearly represents the first variety. In the tradition of Hagen's and Mclleland's individualistic theories of development, Alexander tries to assess the economic-occupational origins of Greek industrialists, their social mobility, etc.[25] In similar fashion Pepelasis links Greece's economic backwardness to the persistence of traditional values and of various institutional structures.[26] On the other hand, Kourvertaris' work on the Greek military, although not directly involved with problems of economic development, is clearly based on a 'tradition-modernity' typology that simply describes role differentiation and specificity as the Greek military move away from traditional roles (the *leventis-philotimo* syndrome) to more modern quasi-managerial roles and attitudes.[27] Or there is Legg's work on the Greek political system, which is a combination of (1) a social stratificational study of Greek political elites, (2) straightforward conventional political history, and (3) an analysis of political roles and institutions in terms of functionalist, political modernisation theories. From this last perspective, the Greek political system, characterised mainly by personalistic parties and clientelism, is assessed in the light of more modern political systems where universalistic values and greater differentiation between kinship and political institutions has been achieved.[28]

All the above studies provide measurements and descriptions, but do not go far as explanations of social development and underdevelopment. As long as the Greek economic, military and political 'elites' are portrayed as static aggregates of individuals, there can be no move from description to explanation. Moreover, whether change and development are seen in terms of structural functional differentiation or in any other way, there can be no effective accounting for it without serious reference to collective actors (classes or other interest groups) — i.e. to people as constructors of their social world.

2   CLASS AND THE MARXIST ALTERNATIVE

A. As has been argued in the previous chapter, Althusserian Marxism, by portraying agents as the passive products of structures, has drawbacks similar to functionalism. But despite the considerable influence of the Althusserian paradigm among present-day Marxists, it is mainly, though not exclusively, through Marxist theory that the emphasis on class, or more generally on collective actors, has returned to the forefront of sociological analysis. If one looks, for instance, at the literature on the sociology of development, it is quite clear that Marxist-orientated writers regard development and underdevelopment as the outcome of choices, policies, and strategies of concrete interest groups competing with each other over scarce resources on the national and international level. More specifically, the obstacles to economic growth are not viewed in purely cultural or institutional terms, but in terms of dominant groups, both foreign and indigenous, whose interests are opposed to the type of resources-allocation that could bring about balanced and autonomous growth.[29]

As far as Greece is concerned, such Marxist historians or social scientists as Kordatos, Skliros and Psiroukis show modern Greek development and underdevelopment as a drama played out by collective actors (peasants, industrial workers, entrepreneurs, State bureaucrats, foreign financiers, military chieftains) who try to maintain or change a system of dominance and exploitation. They do not consider the major institutions of Greek society from the point of view of structural-functional differentiation, but rather as the direct outcome of historically specific struggles among antagonistic interest groups.[30] For instance, both Skliros and Kordatos emphasise the role that the bourgeoisie (especially the island shipowners, and Greek merchants and professionals resident abroad) played during the War of Independence against the Turks, in contrast to the ambiguous role of the more traditional oligarchy (*Kotsabassides*, higher clergy). The latter, seeing in the Greek uprising a serious threat to their interests, were quite hostile to it; they only joined the revolution when they realised its irreversibility.[31] On the other hand, V. Filias in a recently published work questions theories that view the Greek War of Independence as a bourgeois revolution. He acknowledges that the middle and small bourgeoisie of the diaspora, together with the Western-trained intelligentisia, played an important role in mobilising the peasant masses during the initial stages of the nationalist uprising: but he argues that ultimately, given the backwardness of the Greek infrastructure, it was the more traditional landowning local notables who took control of the revolt and managed to suffocate all attempts for an autonomous bourgeois transformation.[32] This victory of the traditional elites, combined with the fact that the revolution was ultimately salvaged by the intervention of the foreign powers, had far-reaching consequences on the shaping and development of the institutional structure of modern Greece. More than anything else, it explains the underdeveloped and dependent character of the Greek economy and polity.[33] However, in an intensive analysis of social conflict during the first seven years of the Greek uprising, N. Diamandouros argues that the 'modernisers' (the Western-orientated bourgeois and intelligentsia elements) managed to impose their views on the organisation of political institutions (i.e. a centralised State) *against* the will of the autochthonous elites,[34] despite their inferiority in terms of resources.

It is beyond the scope of this paper to assess the empirical validity of these positions.[35] What is important, from our point of view, is to stress that such theories take us closer to an explanation of the Greek social structure than any neo-evolutionist analysis of the structural-functional differentiation.[36]

Needless to say, there are limitations to class analysis, and often Greek Marxists are not very careful or successful in avoiding the pitfalls.

B. If social-stratification writers tend to reduce real group structures to an aggregation of isolated individuals, Marxists often go to the other extreme and overemphasise the 'conscious action' aspects of classes and large collectivities, especially when referring to dominant classes; they sometimes present them as anthropomorphic deities controlling everybody and manipulating everything on the social scene.

For instance, after reading Kordatos' voluminous writings on the history of modern Greece, one is left with an image of the bourgeoisie and its foreign masters as omniscient and omnipotent entities exercising total control behind the backs of military and political leaders; moreover, one gets the strong impression that, in a rather mechanistic manner, Greek development is fitted into the procrustean bed of Marx's highly misunderstood[37] stage theory of Western European history.[38] Even a more sophisticated Marxist like Psiroukis links, for instance, major political events (the Metaxas dictatorship) to infrastructural developments (the concentration of Greek capital) without any *serious* attempt to explain the mediating structures or mechanisms linking economic to political power. Any autonomy of the political sphere is therefore denied, and the tacit assumption made that an economically powerful bourgeoisie will, quite automatically, resort to a dictatorial political solution.[39]

If one goes to less well-known Greek Marxists, analysis disappears altogether and Greek history is reduced to a manichean battle between the forces of evil (the 'establishment' and its foreign masters — dealt with in an undifferentiated sweep) and those of good (the 'people').[40] Inevitably, this type of analysis (or rather non-analysis) not only leads to the reification of the concept of class, but disregards conscientious research in favour of ready-made formulas and prefabricated answers to all problems of development.

Such shortcomings are not innate to class analysis. For instance, concerning the relations between economy and politics, Marx and many serious-minded Marxists[41] have repeatedly pointed out that there is relative autonomy between infrastructure and superstructure — the degree of autonomy depending both on the type of mode of production dominant in a social formation, and on the specific conditions of each concrete case.

Take for instance the case of the 1909 military coup.[42] Non-Marxist historians usually explain it in purely contingent terms: in terms of the economic crisis, the defeat of Greece in the 1897 war with Turkey, the unsuccessful management of army affairs by the King's sons, etc. If one wants to go beyond this superficial listing of factors and analyse what happened in class terms, one does not have to establish a direct relation between, let us say, the officers who led the coup and their class origins and ideology. In fact, the 1909 coup, as Kordatos points out, may be seen as representing a conflict between the rising bourgeoisie and the *tzakia*. This conflict should not be conceptualised as a direct clash between a group of notables and a group of merchants, with the latter 'pulling the strings' behind the officers' backs. The 1909 military intervention in politics was a 'bourgeois' coup in a more indirect way: in the sense that it was clearly related to the rise of the 'new' middle and lower urban classes generated by the Trikoupis reforms and, more generally, by the intrusion of Western capitalism into the Balkans during the second half of the nineteenth century.[43] These new middle classes (professionals, *nouveau riches* merchants, State bureaucrats etc.) did not 'fabricate' the coup; it is simply that their economic and social activities provided a fertile soil for its realisation. There is no doubt that no satisfactory explanation of the 1909 coup can be given without serious consideration of the changing socio-economic background that made the intervention of the army not only possible but relatively successful.

Thus the emergence of a new, politically articulate bureaucratic, professional and commercial middle class was obviously linked with the widespread popular dissatisfaction with parliamentary politics at the beginning of the century — a type of politics in which power was still the exclusive preserve of a handful of oligarchic families. For instance these rising social strata were certainly behind the systematic newspaper campaigns which, in the years before the coup, were violently criticising the malfunctioning and 'corruption' of the political system.[44] Moreover, the clear emergence for the first time in Greek history of organised pressure groups which, through a variety of means, were agitating and trying to influence 'public opinion',[45] was another obvious way in which economic developments since 1880 are relevant for understanding the creation of a climate of general dissatisfaction with the political establishment (including the throne) and the enthusiasm with which the urban population accepted the coup. In other terms all the above developments were clear signs of a limited type of political mobilisation generated, in a more or less conscious manner, by a rising middle class which was determined not to be left for long outside the power game.

If one sees the 1909 coup within the context of this mobilisation, and if one realises that a similar coup would have been inconceivable in the early Othonian period, giving the coup of 1909 the epithet of bourgeois is justified. It should also be added here that the 1909 military intervention was even more 'bourgeois' in its later effects:[46] it opened the doors for

Venizelos' extensive bourgeois reforms, and for the accelerated development of the capitalist mode of production after 1922 (cf. above,
Chapter 1).

A similar point (i.e. about the often indirect relationship between class
and politics) can be made by referring to such widely used terms in
Marxist literature as class dominance, dependence etc. Frequently such
relationships, although very real and constraining, do not take an overtly
'anthropomorphic' form — in the sense that it is difficult to identify a
specific class fraction or group of people who *directly and actively* control
all political levers in society. Thus, to speak of the dominance of the
bourgeoisie in modern Greek society does not necessarily imply specific
'bourgeois' pressure groups influencing day-to-day political decision-
making (although, of course, this is possible too). Rather, the importance of
such dominance can be grasped when it is understood that most decision-
making groups, especially in the political sphere, operate within an
institutional framework that guarantees the 'hegemony' of the commercially oriented Greek bourgeoisie — in the sense that it legitimises and
sustains a capitalist solution to the economic organisation of the country.[47]

A parallel argument can be advanced concerning the dependence/
dominance relations between Greece and more advanced capitalist countries. As Furtado has pointed out, exploitation and dominance of metropolitan over peripheral countries does not only or not necessarily imply
greedy foreign corporations taking out of the country more than they put
into it, or a local comprador bourgeoisie receiving orders direct from
London or New York. That Greece, for instance, has adopted types of
technology and consumption more appropriate to the developmental
requirements of advanced industrial societies implies a dependence and
'disarticulation' of the Greek economy that cannot be overcome by just
being 'tough' with corporations and other specific interest groups.[48]

C. Another type of abuse in class analysis is to be found in Marxist
writings which systematically underplay or dismiss altogether the possibility that in certain types of society political cleavages do not *directly*
reflect class divisions, but are more closely linked with developments in
the religious, ethnic, caste or patronage spheres. To take the case of
patronage as especially relevant in the Mediterranean context, Luciano Li
Causi has criticised anthropologists who study Mediterranean politics
purely in terms of patronage and who thus tend to neglect the class
structures underlying the clientelistic practices.[49] Although he is right in
insisting that clientelistic practices should be linked with the class
structure, I think he goes too far when he argues that clientelism is an
'epiphenomenon', a mere ideology useful for concealing the underlying
structures of exploitation. According to the author, in the rural areas of
Italy, for instance, one always finds exploiting landlords behind the
patrons, and exploited peasants behind the clients. Thus, from a theoretical point of view, patronage is a non-existent problem!

By dismissing patronage in this facile manner, Li Causi eliminates a crucial problem in Mediterranean politics: i.e. the examination of the conditions where political cleavages reflect and are directly linked with the dominant structures of class exploitation, and those where they are not (at least not directly). In other words, Li Causi's contention totally misses the fundamental point that political conflict along clientelistic, 'vertical' lines often cuts across and inhibits the political organisation of the dominated classes (e.g. the peasantry) along 'horizontal', class lines; as well as the fact that in many cases a variety of 'vertical' and 'horizontal' political organisations co-exist and alternate in importance according to the political conjuncture.

At the risk of overgeneralisation, it would be possible to say that political conflict tends to take a directly class character in social formations where capitalism is both dominant and has expanded widely in the economy (as in western Europe). In such cases there is: (*a*) a widespread process of social and political mobilisation, as the rural periphery loses its self-containment (through the development of national markets, communication networks, education etc.) and the working masses are drawn into the political process;[50] (*b*) within the context of parliamentary regimes, conditions are favourable for the gradual decline of clientelistic/personalistic politics and the development of political organisations which try more or less successfully and autonomously to articulate and promote the collective interests of the dominated classes.

On the other hand, in social formations where the capitalist mode of production is peripheral, or where its dominance takes an enclave form (as in most Mediterranean societies), conditions are less favourable for a shift from patronage to class politics. In such cases the dominated classes either fail to organise themselves politically, in which case their vote is manipulated through clientelistic networks controlled by parties of the dominant class; or if they do manage to establish autonomous political organisations, these organisations present such a threat to the *status quo* that they are forcibly suppressed. (As I will argue in Chapter 5, Greece during the inter-war period was a good example of the former case, and Bulgaria of the latter.[51]) In other words, in underdeveloped capitalist social formations, given the difficulties of political organisation of the masses, clientelism persists in varying forms, and therefore the linkages between class 'places' and political practices are not as direct as in developed capitalist formations.

The above argument must not be read as a defence of the way in which functionalist political scientists and conventional anthropologists analyse clientelism — i.e. by making simplistic connections between 'modernity' and mass politics, and 'tradition' and patronage politics. For instance, Legg's already mentioned study,[52] by using such ideal typical dichotomies, not only gives us an oversimplified picture of Greek politics, but also fails to account for the fact that the Greek political system has changed *in fundamental ways* since the emergence of the modern Greek State at the beginning of the nineteenth century.

Granted that clientelism is very important in Greek political life, still one has to account for and analyse the various forms that clientelism has taken through the different phases of Greek historical development, as well as to relate such forms to the changing infrastructure. For instance, I believe that patronage under Otho or Trikoupis (i.e. before the dominance of the capitalist mode of production) was quite a different system of exchange from clientelism under Karamanlis. In the latter case, although clientelism did not disappear, given the development of capitalism and the entrance of the masses into politics, political conflict ceased to be the exclusive affair of a handful of privileged families – as broader class issues started, in a more direct manner, to break through clientelistic networks.[53] Similarly, to argue that most Greek political parties have always been parties of personalities, rather than 'modern' parties of issues, is partly true but hardly illuminating. Such an argument could become an easy way of avoiding the laborious and serious task of studying how political party organisations have changed through time. Surely, the parties admirably analysed by J. Petropoulos[54] for the period of the early years of Greek independence were quite different animals from the parties of the inter- or post-war periods. It is such differences that one should try to examine, rather than persist in elaborating generalisations on the personalistic character of Greek politics – generalisations that can be derived automatically from any textbook on the politics of modernisation.

In conclusion I would like to stress that a successful analysis of Greek clientelism presupposes the rejection of both the ahistorical, classless type of analysis of functionalist sociology and anthropology, and that of a certain 'economistic' version of Marxism which insists on ignoring the fact that often there is no one-to-one correspondence between class 'places' and political practices.

D. It might be objected that with the above qualifications, which help to avoid the presentation of classes as omnipotent anthropomorphic entities, we are back to a mere reductionist static concept of class – a concept not far removed from the way in which functionalists deal with social strata. I think that this is not so; even if class is not seen in a simple-minded anthropomorphic manner, class analysis is far removed from the measurement of isolated individual traits, as in social stratification studies. Its focus of analysis is on 'emergent' configurations, which are identifiable as one moves from the individual to group levels of analysis.

These emergent configurations (for instance power relationships between specific groups) should be grasped in their totality, rather than reduced to the attitudes or traits of the specific individuals which are at their base.

To be more specific, in order to understand the power position of the Greek peasantry, for instance, and its role in the development of modern Greece, it is not enough to study individual peasants through the use of questionnaires in order to measure, *à la* Lerner, their attitudes on a variety of dimensions.[55] One has to shift the focus of analysis from individual respondents to the actual ways in which the peasantry relates to merchants, usurers, bankers, State officials, etc.[56] In both cases, of course, one ultimately studies actual human beings, but by looking at them from different vantage points. In social stratification studies the focus is on the individual peasant seen as an isolated part of an aggregate. In class studies the focus shifts from aggregates to structures or configurations that are only 'visible' if one adopts a broad focus of analysis.

This is not to deny, of course, that a risk of portraying classes in static, passive ways does exist within Marxism. As already pointed out in the previous chapter, such a tendency is quite obvious in Althusserian Marxism, where in some respects analysis of class comes near the analysis of social strata. Here I would simply like to say that it is perfectly well possible to avoid the ultra-voluntaristic, 'anthropomorphic' conception of class without going to the other extreme, without portraying classes as static status groups (as is done in social stratification studies), or as mere 'effects' of structures (as Althusser does). I think that an effective class analysis implies a balance between structures (systems) and practices (actors), and such an analysis is indissolubly linked with a view of collective actors as producers as well as products of structural constraints.[57]

This being the case, one can examine social phenomena from an action point of view, even if one accepts the obvious fact that such broad formations as whole classes (e.g. the peasantry) cannot *act* in the strict sense of the term. Even in the case in which class-consciousness and organisation is completely non-existent, one can still ask 'action' questions: i.e. what is the relationship between the peasantry as a relatively amorphous whole, and smaller more self-conscious and cohesive interest groups and organisations within and outside the peasant class? Why do peasants find it difficult to become class-conscious and to establish 'horizontal'[58] coalitions and organisational links? As far as Greece is concerned, why did Greek peasants, for instance, fail to organise themselves politically during the inter-war period — at a time when powerful agrarian parties played dominant roles in the politics of all other Balkan countries?[59] Or why did the nineteenth-century bourgeoisie fail to play the same autonomous role as their Western European counterparts?[60] All the above are 'action' questions. They derive from a point of view of the peasantry and the bourgeoisie as real or potential historical agents of change.

In a nutshell, the argument in this section has been that class analysis sensitises the student to the *configurational* and *voluntaristic* aspects of social life. And these aspects must be taken into account if one wants to understand development and underdevelopment.

3 CONCLUSIONS

I think that the concept of class, provided it is used in a non-reified and non-deterministic way, can be very useful to the sociological study of modern Greece. It will not only fill a gap in the existing sociological literature, but will also bring closer together disciplines which, although concerned with similar problems, seem to develop in isolated compartments without any cross-fertilisation of ideas and methods.

If at the present moment one takes a rapid panoramic view of studies on modern Greek society, one sees very little communication between historical and social science disciplines. As far as history is concerned, with some significant exceptions, one is confronted with:

(a) the conventional historical approach which portrays the development of modern Greece in terms of personalities and *ad hoc* political events;

(b) a Marxist historiography that, while going beyond mere description, often lapses into schematic formulas and mechanistic explanations of social life.

The sociological and anthropological approaches attempt, respectively, to do the following (with very little historical perspective):

(a) measure, as already mentioned, certain distributional aspects of the Greek system or sub-systems within it;

(b) study, in the conventional anthropological manner, the social structure of village communities, without paying serious attention to the changing national and international context within which such communities are embedded.[61]

Class analysis, more than any other concept, can bridge the gap between history and sociology. More than any other concept, it can give to the historian the sense of *structure*: Marx's fundamental idea that, although men make history, they do not make it any way they like.

It can also inject new life and dynamism into an academic sociology that often hides the atheoretical, empiricist character of its activities under the use of unnecessary jargon and sophisticated statistical techniques. For adequate class analysis is inextricably linked with a serious consideration of historical developments: it is impossible to get an idea of how social groups act (or do not act) if the analysis is limited to the present. It is only from the perspective of relatively long time spans that one can become aware of the fact that human groups are both creatures and creators of their social world.

Moreover, the concept of class not only leads the sociologist to realise the importance of *context* in so far as time (i.e. history) is concerned, but also in terms of *space*. It necessarily leads him away from the timeless and spaceless generalisations that positivistically-minded sociologists are so fond of: the establishment of universal 'law'-like generalisations which often take the form of correlations between variables, conceptualised in such a way that the historical and socio-cultural context in which such variables are embedded is ignored.[62] Class analysis is, by its very nature, *context-bound*. A class, and smaller configurations within a class, make sense only if viewed in relationship to other classes and groups, as they form alliances or enter into conflicts with each other over specific issues through time.

Naturally enough, anthropologists studying small communities are more suspicious of too abstract generalisations and more aware of the importance of context. But, as mentioned before, as far as Greece is concerned, they usually limit their analysis to the village level.[63] When they attempt to move from the local to the national level, they adopt what Richard Fox calls the 'village outwards' perspective[64] where the links between periphery and centre are examined through local brokers, clientelist networks etc.[65] According to Fox, a second solution for moving from the village to larger social wholes in complex societies is the 'cellular' approach, which focuses on the way in which such relatively self-contained wholes as regional marketing areas and extensive lineage groups are related to each other and to the central State institutions.[66] I would argue that there is a third solution: that, as present-day complex societies (both the economically developed and the underdeveloped) are moving away from cellular or, to use Durkheimian terminology, segmental principles of organisation, *class* rather than *segment* is the concept that can help anthropology to broaden its focus of analysis and to become more sensitive to the importance of larger configurations.[67] This is *particularly* so for cases like Greece which, though underdeveloped, are ethnically homogeneous and highly 'modernised' (in terms of the early commercialisation and monetisation of agriculture, urbanisation, State expansion etc.). In such countries, in contrast to some contemporary African societies, class rather than region, tribe, or ethnicity is becoming a major vantage point for understanding social change.[68] This being the case, class analysis becomes an indispensable tool, especially if one wants to examine the social structure and its development in a total manner. For, as Gurvitch has pointed out, social classes are 'suprafunctional', i.e. they are macrostructures combining within themselves a variety of unifunctional or multifunctional groups and organisations, and as such they are the most appropriate categories for analysing the total structure and development of industrial societies.[69]

The breadth of this outlook does not necessarily imply a flight into all-inclusive grand theories, nor does it imply a less empirical and less rigorous approach to the study of society. It merely signifies a reorientation of empirical research and the setting of different standards of rigour and precision. Class analysis is not hostile to 'middle-range' or limited generalisations, but it advocates a *different type of limitation* from that of sociological positivism. The latter limits its scope by studying parts (i.e. variables) in relative isolation from the whole. By doing so it can afford to extend its analysis to a larger number of cases and therefore presents the

type of mathematical rigour that highly developed statistical tools make
possible today. Serious class analysis advocates a different type of
limitation. By its emphasis on the importance of seeing parts within a
whole, it suggests the opposite strategy: the study of a few cases *in
depth* – i.e. by taking *seriously* into account, while social phenomena are
being studied, the past and present socio-cultural context in which they
are embedded.

Finally, the above criticisms of sociological studies on Greece should be
put into a more balanced perspective: my argument is not that the
quantitative study of how various social traits are distributed among a
certain population is wrong or useless.[70] I think that they are and will
remain indispensable tools of social analysis. But these tools will become
more effective, and Greek sociology the richer, if class studies complement
social stratification studies.

Through the criticism of Althusserian Marxism in the previous chapter
and of Parsonian functionalism in this one – two influential paradigms
which, given their passive portrayal of classes, lead to different types of
ahistorical sociology[71] – my intention was to make the case for a class
analysis which would lead to rapprochement between history and sociology. This rapprochement, which was a distinctive mark of classical
sociology, broke down with the spectacular development of the functionalist and positivist sociologies during the 1930s, but it is emerging
again in sociology with the excellent work of such historically-minded
sociologists as Barrington Moore, Reinhard Bendix, and Emmanuel Wallerstein.[72] This chapter is a plea that this new awareness be infused into the
study of modern Greek society.

POSTSCRIPT: EMPIRICIST FALLACIES IN THE GREEK SOCIAL
SCIENCES

The most frequent criticism made by Greek academic sociology and
history against recent books[73] which, with varying degrees of success, use
the sort of Marxist class analysis discussed above, is that their global
examination of social phenomena and, therefore, their abolishing of the
conventional frontiers between the social sciences (those separating economics from political science, sociology, history etc.), results in their doing
everything and nothing. Not basing themselves on serious quantitative data
and trying to provide very broadly synthesized theories of Greek develop-
ment/underdevelopment, they merely produce a set of general ideas and
tentative explanations which might be interesting as literary essays but
have no value whatsoever as scientific theories. This criticism is of
fundamental importance. It raises questions on the definitions of 'data'
and on the role they play or should play in the construction of a scientific
theory. The problem is highly complex because it involves very basic and

complex issues on the nature of science, on the differences between social and natural sciences, etc. It is impossible to deal with all of these problems here. This postscript will merely give a brief outline of some basic misconceptions on which the above criticism is based, misconceptions which were pointed out long ago by philosophers of science, in both the Marxist and neo-Marxist camp,[74] in their fight against the narrow-minded empiricism which confuses scientific research with mere statistical measurement or descriptive classification.

A. The most frequent reason given by empiricist Greek historians and sociologists for refuting the kind of theoretical generalisations implied by class analysis is that empirical research on modern Greek society is at so low a level that any attempt to use such a thin empirical basis as the foundation for broad theories on the structures and overall development of such a society is 'dangerous' and 'anti-scientific'. According to this view it is necessary to wait until enough empirical data on narrow specific topics have been accumulated before it is possible to risk the formulation of any broad theory. The researcher who spends years measuring a single variable over a short period of time, and who is keenly aware of the huge gaps that exist even in his narrow field, quite naturally looks with great suspicion at works which set out not only to describe, but even to explain developments ranging over decades if not centuries. From his point of view it would require hundreds or thousands of monographs before attempting a more general interpretation of Greek development.

This type of argument is based on the idea that a scientific theory is nothing more than an inductive generalisation which emerges more or less automatically once enough data have been gathered. But such *statistical* generalisations (which abound in functionalist sociology and whose logic of construction C. W. Mills has rightly called *abstracted empiricism*) is radically different from the truly *theoretical* generalisation which characterises scientific work both in the natural and the social sciences. The statistical generalisation, when it is based on mere quantitative measurement or simple description, is as far removed from scientific theory as are, at the other extreme, the purely metaphysical theories which have no empirical basis whatsoever.[75] In fact, in true scientific research there are no data outside the context of a specific theoretical problematic. Data as such do not exist 'out there', ready to be picked up by anyone with enough patience and good statistical tools. What constitutes an empirical datum and what does not can only be determined by the theory itself. Just as the discovery of new data, when guided by a theoretical orientation, can have serious repercussions on the theory, so has the theoretical elaboration of a problem repercussions on the identification and search for empirical data.

This means that the logic of scientific research implies a constant dialectical relationship between theory and data, which makes completely absurd and unacceptable the empiricist position: first enough data and then a theory — first the empirical floor and walls, and later the theoretical roof. This attitude results in a situation where building of the floor and walls never ends, it goes on and on, producing an interminable series of data, a mosaic of disconnected observations and measurements — which lead nowhere. From this perspective, theory remains a distant vision, a goal which may be desirable but is not for the here and now, something only 'future generations of scholars' can afford to cope with.

B. A second basic weakness of empiricism in the social sciences is its reductionist tendency; its refusal to acknowledge the existence of different levels of analysis as one moves from the study of micro- to that of macro-systems — i.e. from the study of small groups to that of whole societies, or intersocietal systems like the world capitalist market. The passage from a 'lower' to a 'higher' level of analysis is not, as empiricism usually holds, a mere additive linear progression. For instance, studying *ad infinitum* the village economies of all rural communities will not provide data sufficient for the construction of one general theory about the overall structure and basic dynamic of Greek agriculture. For such a more general problematic, the data needed are not necessarily those gathered by the conventional anthropologist of the Greek village who studies its structure in isolation from the wider social context; rather, the required data should refer to the position of Greek agriculture in the whole economy, its relations to industry and commerce, its mode of integration with the world capitalist market, etc.[76] In other words, passing from a lower to a higher level of abstraction and analysis, new problems and phenomena emerge which cannot be reduced to a mere aggregate of their constituent parts. Moreover, theories on a lower level of abstraction have no logical priority or scientific superiority over more abstract or synthetic ones. It is possible to construct good and bad theories on every level of analysis.

C. This brings us to another common empiricist misconception, concerned with the manner of proving or disproving a theory. There is the view that in order to disprove a theory it is only necessary to show that any detail or part of it is based on false data or forecasts. Example: Marx predicted that the development of capitalism would tend to produce the pauperisation of the Western European working classes. This, from a certain point of view, has not happened, therefore Marxist theory is wrong. This well-known example demonstrates clearly the naïveté of the assumption that proving or disproving a theory lies simply in breaking it up into a mosaic of statements, from which one can be selected at random and 'checked against the facts', without serious reference to the overall structure and problematic of that theory.

Now a theory is not an aggregate of statements; it is a system of interconnected propositions, criticism of which on both the logical and the empirical level can only be valid when this system is seen in its entirety. Just as one cannot identify an empirical datum outside a theory, so one cannot define what is valid proof of a theory outside the theory itself. As

Braithwaite has rightly pointed out, it is the internal organisation of a theory which dictates the style of its empirical validation.[77] It is for this reason that all successful criticisms (negative or positive) of a scientific theory is done from 'within', i.e. takes seriously into account the terms of reference, conceptual tools and level of analysis on which the theory is based.

From this point of view it is quite obvious that to judge whether the empirical data used in a theory are adequate or not, one must see them in relation to its basic problematic. Thus a series of data can be crude and totally inadequate if the relevant theory moves on a low level of abstraction and is concerned with the detailed analysis of a very narrowly defined area; yet these same data can be perfectly adequate for a different theory dealing with a much broader problem. A mistake in the empirical measurement or description will, of course, have very different repercussions on the validity of the above two theories. A wrong date or name can completely distort and invalidate the conclusions of the first, without at all affecting those of the second. It should be obvious, then, that the mode of criticism in these two cases cannot be the same.

D. The above arguments on the importance of theory do not, of course, support or defend the theoretical verbalism and formalism of all those who, influenced by German idealism and legalism, have for decades been disorientating whole generations of Greek students;[78] neither does it advocate a flight from the difficult and time-consuming task of data-gathering in favour of armchair theorising which, for instance, characterises a large part of contemporary French Marxist thought. I also readily admit that some of the Marxist-orientated writings on Greece that I have referred to above could have been much improved if supported by more systematic empirical research. If, however, it is granted that science is something more than precise measurement or the mere correlation of variables, then it is high time to stop making a fetish of empirical data and viewing theory as a secondary, decorative element in the process of scientific research. It is time for the collection of data, the empirical work, to be done not in an *ad hoc* manner or by following what is called 'common sense'. The construction of theory, as of class-oriented theory for instance, does not mean neglect of empirical research; it simply means the adoption of a new type of empirical research where the collection of data is constantly guided and interlinked with the elaboration of theory.[79]

4   Capitalism and the Development of Agriculture

In this chapter I shall try to complement as well as to make more concrete some of the theoretical points of the two previous chapters by a detailed analysis of two books on development:

  (a) S. Amin and K. Vergopoulos, *La question paysanne et le capitalisme*;[1] and

  (b) K. Vergopoulos, *The agrarian problem in Greece: The issue of the social incorporation of agriculture.*[2]

These two works reflect, in varying degrees, two recent interconnected trends in Marxism which have stimulated important theoretical debates and fruitful empirical research in a number of different areas. The first refers to Althusser's work which, by advocating a return to the type of rigorous analysis found in Marx's mature writings, constitutes the basis for a critique of theories which were alleged to have been only superficially or eclectically Marxist.[3] The second trend is the development of a new type of Marxist anthropology which, influenced to some extent by Althusser's work, has tried to assess how far certain Marxist concepts (especially that of modes of production and their varied articulation in social formations) could help in their study of the so-called primitive societies — in particular, how these societies are incorporated into the world capitalist system.[4] In fact, these two books constitute an interesting attempt to use some of these new insights in order (a) to build up a general theory on the development of agriculture under capitalism, and (b) to apply this theory to a specific social formation, namely that of Greece.

An earlier version of this chapter appeared in the *Journal of Peasant Studies*, July 1976.

1 PEASANTS AND CAPITALISM

In *La question paysanne et le capitalisme*, Amin provides a general introduction in which the major themes of the theory are formulated in broad terms; the bulk of the book is written by Vergopoulos who, in a more rigorous and systematic fashion, sets about to elaborate and build them into a coherent theoretical framework. I shall leave aside the differences between the two authors, and concentrate mainly on Vergopoulos' contribution.[5]

Vergopoulos starts with a critique of the classical Marxist position on the development of agriculture as found, in a more or less emphatic way, in the works of Marx, Lenin and Kautsky: the well-known thesis that, with the growth of the capitalist mode of production (CMP), agriculture will tend to follow the same path of development as industry, i.e. that there will be land concentration, the emergence of large-scale enterprises, the elimination or proletarianisation of small landowners etc. — these processes leading eventually to the narrowing of the gap between town and countryside, between industrial workers and peasants.

Amin and Vergopoulos argue that these developments have in fact taken place only in exceptional circumstances, and that the main trend in twentieth-century capitalism has been the persistence of small peasant ownership and the functioning of the rural economy on the basis of the small family exploitation, in accordance with the principles elaborated long ago by Chaianov.[6] But if the CMP (characterised mainly by the use of wage labour) has not succeeded in establishing itself in the countryside, it has incorporated the rural economy in such a way that its own development takes place at the expense of those involved in agricultural production. In fact, the major focus of Vergopoulos' work is the study of the way in which the CMP dominant in the urban centres articulates with the mode of simple commodity production prevailing in the countryside. This perspective sees the articulation of these two modes as such that resources are systematically transferred from the rural to the urban centres — to the extent that the small agricultural producer, despite his formal land ownership, is reduced to the status of a proletarian who 'works at home'. In fact, he and his family work for long hours, not for profit but for survival — for the simple reproduction of their mode of existence.

Vergopoulos sees the profound reasons for this state of affairs as connected with the fact that

'land in the capitalist social system is regarded as a 'perverse' element in direct conflict with all other goods and factors of production. Despite the fact that productive land is increasingly the result of labour, its participation in the social process of production is subject to two exceptional constraints: (*a*) the social availability of cultivable land is relatively limited compared to the *a priori* unlimited availability of other goods and economic factors. From the social point of view land is the only commodity neither freely extensible nor reproducible at will. (*b*) Investment in the primary sector meets with a constraint specific to land, that of *decreasing returns*. For whereas in all other branches of production additional investments succeed in bringing down total cost per unit, it is only in primary production that capital investment comes up against the barrier of constant or increasing costs in relation to the invested capital' [my translation] .[7]

Therefore, these two constraints — the rigidity of land supply and the decreasing returns of agricultural capital — ascribe a social scarcity value to land as a factor of production which can lead to monopolistic situations and to the imposition of rent by those who control it. Feudal rents (or land rents in general) are the direct result of such monopolistic control. In such cases, the big landlord's power over cultivable land results, by means of the rent collected, in vast transfers of resources from the non-agricultural to the agricultural sector; transfers which reduce profits and slow down the development of industrial capitalism.

With the gradual decline of the landowning classes in the twentieth century, land rent tends to disappear and no longer constitutes a serious obstacle to the development of capitalism. But if the feudal landlords, through the development of a capitalist agriculture, were to be replaced by a big agrarian bourgeoisie, a new obstacle would emerge: the latter would exercise a similar quasi-monopolistic control over the land so as to realise, in addition to the normal capitalist profits, super-profits resulting from the 'perverse' character of land as a factor of production. In other words, big landed property, because it takes advantage of the rigidity of land supply, whether in capitalist or feudal form, constitutes an obstacle to the growth of industrial capitalism. Small producers, on the other hand, given their usual lack of organisation and weak power position, not only do not profit from the peculiarities of the land factor, but can easily be forced to work — not for profit, but for mere survival.

In this way a set of conditions is created (e.g. low prices of agricultural products, high prices for industrial products used in agricultural production) which are inimical to attracting private capital into agriculture. In fact, private capital tends to shun the countryside, preferring to squeeze the direct producer in the sphere of circulation through the impersonal market mechanism — the State becoming the main provider of capital in the rural economy. Thus we have a situation where the agricultural producer, under the strict control of merchant/industrial capital and the State, is constantly forced to modernise his exploitation and to increase his productivity, not in order to maximise his profits but in order to cover his expenses and to meet his debts.

In conclusion, according to the Amin-Vergopoulos thesis, the development of agriculture in the CMP cannot be understood by looking only at the internal dynamic of the rural economy; the key to its development lies in the way in which urban-industrial capitalism articulates with the simple commodity agricultural production — an articulation which contributes to the continuous growth of industrial capital and the corresponding marginalisation of the agricultural producers.

2   CAPITALISM AND GREEK AGRICULTURE

In *The agrarian problem in Greece*, Vergopoulos attempts to assess the development of Greek agriculture in the light of his general theory. After a brief survey of agrarian conditions in the Byzantine and Ottoman empires, he examines in greater detail developments since the establishment of the modern Greek State in 1821. Concerning the nineteenth century, he emphasises the following points:

(*a*) Contrary to a widespread myth, the land which had belonged to the Turkish landlords was not taken over on their leaving by their Greek counterparts, but by the State. The State managed quite successfully to keep under its direct control most of the Turkish lands (called *national lands*), and in this way prevented the emergence and consolidation of a strong, autochthonous landowning class. In the Peloponnese, therefore, from the very beginning — apart from the State-controlled national lands — the smallholding was dominant. The situation was different in Attica where — because it was not incorporated into the Greek State until 1833 and due to a special agreement with Turkey — big landed property persisted after liberation.

(*b*) Half a century later, in 1871, when the Greek State decided to distribute the national lands among the peasants, its main concern was again to ensure that the land reform would not result in the concentration of land in private hands. The policies of Koumoundouros, the statesman responsible for the distribution of national lands, ran counter to the interests of Attica's big wheat-growers (he adopted a liberal, non-protectionist policy on wheat imports) and profited the Peloponnesian small raisin growers and industry (by a protectionist policy as far as industrial products were concerned).

(*c*) This situation changed with the annexation of Thessaly in 1881. Here the agrarian property pattern which emerged was similar to Attica's rather than that of the Peloponnese. The Turkish landlords of Thessaly managed easily enough to sell their big estates to Greeks, especially to the financially strong Greek diaspora bourgeoisie. The latter succeeded in not only maintaining the considerable land concentration that had existed before the national liberation; they also, through the introduction of Roman law with its strong emphasis on private property rights, abolished the few remaining rights over the land which the actual producers had been enjoying under Ottoman law. In this way the Thessalian peasant was subject to expulsion from the land at the landlord's will. The developments in Thessaly were coupled with a change in State policy on big landed property. Prime Minister Trikoupis, contrary to his predecessors, began supporting big landowners and adopted a tariff policy for the protection of cereal production — a policy which resulted in an increase in the cost of living and a rise in industrial wages.

In other words, the end of the nineteenth century witnessed an attempt to forge an alliance between big landed property and industrial capital in the Greek social formation. According to Vergopoulos, as big landed property is inimical to the development of industrial capitalism, such an alliance could not but be precarious, since protection of the big land-owners was slowing down the industrialisation of Greece and acted, therefore, against the long-term interests of the ascending bourgeoisie.

(*d*) It is not surprising, therefore, that during the first quarter of the twentieth century, as the rising middle classes were gaining more power (especially after the 1909 coup) — and after a series of dramatical historical events (the First World War, the influx of the one-and-a-half million Asia Minor refugees in 1922) which made land reform imperative — this alliance between landoweners and urban bourgeoisie broke down. The land reform in 1917, which began to be implemented rigorously only after 1922, irreversibly abolished big landed property in Greece, thus contributing considerably to the development of Greek industry. It also established the permanent pattern for the articulation of simple com-modity production dominant in agriculture and the CMP dominant in the urban centres: the pattern of incorporation-marginalisation by which industrial capital heavily exploits the small cultivator by incorporating rather than destroying simple commodity agricultural production.

(*e*) Finally, in examining the post-war period (1950–70), the author shows in concrete terms how the mechanisms of incorporation-marginalisation contribute to the over-exploitation of the small producer-owner to the benefit of urban-industrial capital. In this context he examines the various State policies (on taxation, credits, price controls) which create a situation where the small owner and his family have either to work extremely hard with very little compensation, or must abandon the land altogether. Vergopoulos sees the mass desertion of the Greek countryside in the fifties and sixties as the only defence left to the Greek peasants against the pattern of incorporation-marginalisation which the development of urban capital had imposed on them. For him, the most crucial problem facing Greek agriculture today (from the point of view of the further development of the CMP) is not — as generally accepted — the problem of land fragmentation and low productivity, but the problem of stopping the massive rural exodus: the problem of persuading the remain-ing cultivators to stay at their posts and continue to work hard for the benefit of industrial and merchant capital.

Therefore, looking at the overall development of Greek agriculture, the Amin-Vergopoulos thesis seems to fit the facts pretty well — at least as far as big landed property is concerned which made its relatively late appearance towards the end of the nineteenth century, only to disappear again four decades later and leave the smallholding as the dominant form of ownership in the Greek countryside. These developments, according to Vergopoulos, were due mainly to the fundamental incongruity between capitalism and big landed property, an incongruity deriving from the 'perverse' character of land as a factor of capitalistic production.

3 CRITIQUE

A. I think that Vergopoulos' work is a very important contribution to recent attempts at analysing in a more historical and at the same time theoretical manner the social structure of modern Greece. In that sense, and together with a few other recent writings on Greece,[8] it stands out as a serious effort to get away from both the so-called bourgeois sociology — characterised by a blind and narrow-minded empiricism — and the dogmatic, mechanistic type of Marxist analysis which underlies many Marxist writings on Greece.[9] It is definitely the most significant study of the Greek peasantry since the publication of Karavidas' book in 1931.[10] In fact, it is the first serious attempt to go beyond the totally atheoretical conventional studies of Greek agriculture which either (a) give a straightforward historical account of agricultural developments (mainly in terms of the history of agrarian State policies),[11] or (b) set out to measure certain aspects of the past or present agrarian structure of Greece.[12]

Vergopoulos' attempt to look at the overall development of Greek agriculture from the point of view of a specific *problematic*, derived from a long and stimulating theoretical debate on the relationship between capitalism and agriculture, not only helps us to see some basic features of the Greek agrarian structure in a new light; it also shows clearly the limitations of thoughtless statistical calculations or pedantic historiographic studies of trivia. It seems to me that, in a more general way, the books under review reflect very clearly the growing reaction among social scientists in western Europe (Marxists as well as non-Marxists) against the crude pseudo-scientific empiricism which dominated the social sciences in the fifties and early sixties.[13]

Moreover, despite Vergopoulos' emphasis on Marxist theory, he has not succumbed to the temptation of indulging in the usual casuistic exegesis of Marx's 'sacred texts'. Although he does concern himself in some detail with Marxist writings on the development of agriculture, he is fortunately less worried about what Marx 'really meant' by this or that, and interested rather in the application of some fundamental Marxist tools in order to build up his theory of agricultural development in capitalism.

B. Having said this much, I shall now try to show some of the weaker points in Vergopoulos' work. If Vergopoulos has managed to avoid theoretical dogmatism, he has been less successful in avoiding another serious risk of theory-making: over-generalisation, the attempt to give quasi-universal character to a theory which, in fact, is only relevant in a restricted number of cases. More specifically, Vergopoulos' theory claims to deal with some fundamental trends to be found *in all social formations dominated by the CMP*. My contention is that, firstly, his thesis is valid only under certain conditions (which are not specified in his book); secondly, and more seriously, that certain fundamental aspects of his theory seem, with a few reservations, to have greater validity for *some* metropolitan societies of western Europe and less for peripheral capitalist formations such as that of Greece.

A case in point is the way the CMP is articulated to the simple commodity production dominant in agriculture. Vergopoulos' theory posits that the articulation of the two modes takes such a form that the transfer of resources from the countryside to the urban centres does not affect agricultural productivity. The impoverished and chronically in-debted peasants, in their endeavour to pay their debts and feed their families, embark on a process of 'wild' investments and intensive mechan-isation, resulting in continuous productivity improvements — which bene-fit not the direct producers themselves but big industrial and finance capitalism. In other words, Vergopoulos argues that over-exploitation not only does not lower the small owner's productivity, but actually increases it. In order to make the Greek case fit his theory, Vergopoulos tries, on the basis of very thin evidence, to persuade us that Greek agricultural productivity is high — something which is patently not so, especially if one compares it with that of Western European agriculture.[14] Vergopoulos attempts to prove his point by merely providing figures showing the increase in the use of tractors in the Greek countryside.[15] But such figures mean very little outside a comparative perspective. Within such a perspec-tive, however, one realises immediately that Greece, in terms of most indices of agricultural improvement (i.e. mechanisation, use of fertilisers, crop yield per hectare etc.) lags far behind Western Europe.[16] Moreover, whereas in all Western European countries per-capita productivity has risen faster in agriculture than in other sectors, the opposite is true of Greece.[17]

Thus, the aspect of Vergopoulos' theory which refers to the high productivity of the small agricultural unit is more relevant to the small French or Belgian cultivator than to the Greek, Portuguese or Spanish one, not to mention other, even more obvious, examples outside Europe. There is, in fact, a fundamental difference in the way in which the CMP incorporates simple commodity agricultural production in metropolitan and peripheral capitalist formations; a difference which is never mentioned in Vergopoulos' 'universal' theory, and which can be expressed in the following way. In Western Europe, industrialisation has meant either the destruction of simple commodity production in agriculture and artisanal industry (as was the case in some parts of England, for instance), or its incorporation into the CMP in such a manner that the small producers, whether in agriculture or industry, managed through rationalisation and specialisation to increase their productivity and to establish a *positive complementarity* with big industry. This meant that technological progress, originating chiefly in the CMP, was quickly passed on to the simple commodity production sectors, with consequent beneficial effects on the size of incomes, the expansion of internal markets etc.[18]

In the Greek social formation, as in many third-world countries, the CMP is 'negatively' linked with the non-capitalist sectors. The fact, for instance, that in contrast to the West, there are no serious Greek industries making agricultural implements, is an obvious indication of the lack of positive complementarity between agriculture and the industrial capitalist sector. For despite the rapid spread of the CMP — with the help of foreign capital in the sixties — into key manufacturing sectors (metallurgy, chemicals), it has not succeeded in expanding or transferring its dynamism and its high productivity to the technologically backward, small-commodity production sectors of the economy. These sectors were neither destroyed nor have they benefited from the industrial growth, they remain stagnant and technologically backward.[19] In consequence, not only is productivity in the agricultural and small industry sectors very low, but the productivity gap between these sectors and the capitalist-industrial one is widening fast; this gap is in any case much higher in Greece than in Western European countries.[20] It is precisely this coexistence within the Greek economy of sectors with very different rates of productivity which explains why income distribution in Greece is much more unequal than in Western Europe. For in addition to the usual inequalities between labour and capital in the sectors where the CMP is dominant, Greece has inequalities resulting from the persistence of vast productivity differentials between the capitalist and the simple commodity sectors of the economy. Therefore, to build a theory which does not distinguish between the standard of living and productivity of the Greek or Portuguese producer on the one hand, and the French and Dutch on the other, is, to put it mildly, misleading.

My argument is that the mode of articulation between the CMP and simple commodity production in the West is radically different from that of most third-world countries including Greece. And it is exactly this difference, i.e. the more negative type of articulation found in peripheral social formations, that many neo-Marxist writers, including S. Amin, call *underdevelopment*.[21]

No wonder that Vergopoulos, brushing aside this fundamental point at the beginning of his book, argues that the Greek economy, as far as its internal development is concerned, resembles the developed economies of western Europe; and that it is mainly in the international capitalist market that it should be compared with the underdeveloped countries of the third world.[22] I think that this is simply not true. The dependent and peripheral character of the Greek social formation can only be explained by the persistence of the underdeveloped character of its internal economy — an underdevelopment which not only persists, but has been accentuated since the relatively rapid industrialisation of the country with the help of foreign capital in the sixties.[23]

So despite Vergopoulos' healthy aversion for linear evolutionist explanations of development (he is against the idea that agriculture will follow the same path of development as industry), he has not managed to avoid the evolutionist trap altogether — for he does not seem to realise that agricultural development in Greece is following a course very different from that of France, for instance.[24]

C. Concerning Vergopoulos' more theoretical work, one can cite a number of other cases which do not fit his general theory at all well, even within merely the confines of Europe. Agricultural development in Spain, for instance, seems to defy the author's thesis in a different way. In Spain, despite the rapid industrialisation of the last decade (which, in many ways, is more spectacular than that of Greece), big private landed property has not only survived but seems much more efficient than the small family exploitations of northern Spain.[25]

Of course, this example is not meant to refute Vergopoulos' over-generalisation by producing an equally unacceptable counter-over-generalisation on the efficiency of large-scale agriculture. It is impossible to argue about the efficiency or inefficiency of large-scale capitalist agriculture in a general way. This clearly depends on a variety of factors which cannot be discussed here. What can be said with greater certainty, however, is that industrial capitalism in the twentieth century can very easily prosper *with or without* the existence of big landed agricultural property. Because, with the gradual shrinking of the agricultural sector in most European countries (both in terms of the labour force employed and in terms of agriculture's contribution to the GNP), the eventual rents or superprofits coming to the holders of big landed estates can hardly be considered a serious obstacle to the development of industrial capitalism, especially if big landed property is rationalised and its returns productively invested. As a matter of fact, what is apparent in countries like England today is that the 'agrarian problem', in terms of land distribution, is often not solved but by-passed — in the sense that, given the increasingly subordinate role of agriculture, it makes very little difference, from the point of view of the overall development of the CMP, whether big landed property is maintained or destroyed.

D. The limited application of Vergopoulos' general theory becomes even more obvious if one tries to apply it to the overall historical development of European agriculture. From such a broad perspective, it becomes all too apparent that the pattern of agricultural development which Vergopoulos elevates to a universal trend in the CMP, is simply one among many in the fascinating and complicated rural history of the continent.

It is well known that the modernisation of agriculture and the development of capitalism followed a radically different course in Eastern Europe (e.g. Hungary, Poland) before the establishment of the people's democratic regimes at the end of the Second World War. There, contrary to what happened in most Western European countries, big landed property had not only survived but was politically dominant, imposing its own logic of development on the weak bourgeoisie of the cities. This does not mean, of course, that there was no agricultural modernisation. Although agricultural reforms (i.e. the abolition of the 'second serfdom' and the various other feudal rights of the nobility, the reinforcement of the Roman-law type of private property etc.) and technological improvements came much later than in the Western part of the continent, nevertheless Eastern European capitalism was in every respect more advanced than that of the Balkans.[26]

The Balkan pattern of agricultural development has been strikingly different from both the Western and the Eastern European models. Although over roughly the same period (nineteenth century), agricultural rationalisation followed the same process as in Eastern Europe — i.e. the establishment of Roman-law notions of private property etc. — here its modernisation took place in a context where the small owner-cultivator was dominant (except in Rumania). This, of course, was not at all due to any inherent trends or laws of the CMP, but to the simple fact that with the gradual decline of the Ottoman empire, as Turkish landlords were forced more or less suddenly to leave, the peasants managed to possess themselves of the lands before the weak autochthonous landlords had a chance to get hold of them.[27] And the more sudden the Turkish withdrawal, the easier it was for the Balkan peasants to take over the land they were cultivating. This explains, for instance, why from the very start Bulgaria had a much more egalitarian agrarian structure than Greece or Serbia.[28]

My argument here is, in other words, that if one looks seriously at the development of capitalism and its relation to agricultural 'modernisation' in Europe, one cannot fail to see at least four strikingly different patterns of growth: the Iberian, the Eastern European, the Balkan, the Western European. I think that Vergopoulos' thesis is properly relevant to the last, and partially relevant to the Balkan pattern. I also maintain that if one wishes to account for the different ways in which agriculture is articulated to industry, one must pay less attention to any inherent trends of the CMP and more to the *class structure* of the societies under consideration. Or, to put it another way, trends and laws only make sense when they take a less universal form and are seen *in context*. In this specific case, Vergopoulos' ideas about capitalism and agriculture would have been much more effective and illuminating if he could have *built into his theory* the conditions under which his generalisations hold true and those under which they do not, i.e. if he could have delineated, among other things, the class configuration within which the articulation he emphasises between urban capitalism and simple commodity agricultural production are to be found.

E. To be perfectly fair, it must be emphasised that Vergopoulos, in his more theoretical book, makes it quite clear that his theory does not postulate 'iron laws' of agricultural development. In fact, he does not believe that such laws exist. He simply tries to point out some general *trends* discernible in the development of the CMP and its relation to the countryside — trends which can be explained by considering the 'perverse' character of land in capitalism.[29]

But whether they are called laws or trends does not change the fact that some of Vergopoulos' generalisations, given the universal, contextless way in which they are presented, are quite unacceptable. Take for instance his basic assumption that the most favourable land solution for the development of industrial capitalism is the small owner-cultivator who can be exploited and pushed to overwork with no chance of realising an adequate income or profit. Can one really say that, *in the long run*, this is the most profitable solution for the development of industrial capitalism? How about the argument that a fundamental precondition for the development of industry is the widening of internal markets such as can partly result from a rise in agricultural incomes? Contrary to Vergopoulos' argument, this is exactly what did happen in Western Europe and what *is not* happening in Greece and other underdeveloped societies.

In the last analysis, the answers to such questions vary from case to case and can be solved only by empirical investigation rather than by the formulation of general principles. As far as Greece is concerned, an answer must again refer to the class structure and its development during the last two centuries.

F. The concept of classes is not absent from Vergopoulos' exposition. Even in his theoretical book he emphasises that the relations of production (which directly refer to the class structure) are crucial for an understanding of the way in which the forces of production develop in capitalism. But he only pays lip-service to class analysis. In his theoretical book, despite his statements on the importance of relations of production, the class issue remains peripheral. Even in the case study, where class analysis plays a somewhat more prominent role, social classes are still portrayed in a typically Althusserian manner as the passive products of the capitalist *system*. The analysis moves always from the system to the collective actors (the 'bearers of structures', as Althusser would say), never the other way round. Collective actors, classes, interest groups are never shown as *both shaping and being shaped* by the CMP.[30]

In this respect Vergopoulos' analysis reminds one of Parsonian functionalism, where institutions seem to appear and disappear according to their positive or negative contribution to the social system: big property is bound to disappear because it is 'dysfunctional' to the requirements of the CMP, whereas small landownership, being functional, is here to stay. I am not saying that this type of functionalist analysis (which, of course, one finds in Marx's work as well) is wrong. But it is definitely incomplete and becomes misleading unless it is linked with a class analysis — i.e. unless one tries to do what Marx achieved so admirably: to combine a 'system' with an 'action' approach, to portray human beings as both the products and the producers of their social world.[31]

If too much emphasis is put on the system and its structure, when actors and classes become the 'mere bearers' of systemic-structural determinations, then the analysis is bound to be limited to the level of description. For in so far as collective actors are portrayed as passive puppets of a mysterious system with its laws or trends, it is impossible to explain why and how social structures either change or persist.

In brief, to find out why small property-holdings prevailed in Greek agriculture, why agricultural productivity is low, why industrialisation took an enclave form, one should look less at the general trends or laws of the CMP and more at the historical development of the class struggle: at the complex way in which various collective actors — landowners, peasants, merchants, foreign investors, bureaucrats — in their attempts to defend and promote their own interests, were 'making history'. For instance, the fact that land reforms in Greece were imposed basically from 'above'; the fact that the Greek peasants, for a variety of structural and conjunctural reasons, failed to organise themselves into a strong agrarian party (in contrast to developments in all other Balkan countries during the inter-war period); and the fact that peasant demands were always represented, through the major bourgeois parties[32] are more relevant for understanding the present pitiable state of Greek cultivators than any general trends of the CMP.

The conflict between system and action explanations, between structuralism and voluntarism, is as old as the social sciences themselves. It is a debate which runs through the whole of Marxist literature. If a decade ago the fashion was greater stress on and appreciation of the more historical-voluntaristic elements in Marx's work, today Althusser's important impact has shifted the pendulum considerably to the structuralist side. This influence is clearly reflected in Vergopoulos' work. My own position is that going too far into system explanations, where laws and trends replace class struggles and strategies, means moving away from the possibility of satisfactory explanations of social change. Of course, it would be equally inadequate to emphasise actors to such an extent that any system analysis disappears. Indeed, the most difficult task in social analysis is how to strike a balance, how to combine those two types of explanation — to show how actors create structures and, at the same time, how these structures impose limits on collective action.

It must be obvious from what has been said above that my criticism of

Vergopoulos' work does not imply a rejection of his theory. It simply suggests that it could become more effective if he specified more clearly the conditions under which it does and those under which it does not hold true; and that, if this is to be done seriously, classes (as collective actors) should play a more important role in the theoretical analysis of the relationship between capitalism and agriculture.

Part III
Class Structure and Politics

5 Greek and Bulgarian Peasants: Aspects of their Socio-Political Situation During the Inter-War Period

INTRODUCTION

Part I of this book provided an overall view of the historical development of Greek capitalism, whereas in Part II an attempt was made to examine, critically and in the light of the Greek case, some crucial debates in the sociology of development literature. These two frameworks (the historial and the theoretical) laid the ground for a closer examination of the relationship between class structure and politics in certain crucial phases of Greek underdevelopment. The aim in Part III is not to give a systematic account of the development of Greek society and polity from the nineteenth century onwards; but rather to focus selectively on certain 'turning-points' in this trajectory.

One such turning-point was undoubtedly the way in which the peasantry, mobilised during the inter-war period by the disruptive effects of capitalist development, were brought into the political process. For once mobilisation occurs, the mode of 'bringing-in' the peasants into active politics is extremely crucial for understanding the structure and further development of a social formation. Concerning this 'bringing-in' process, one sees a striking difference between Greece and its Balkan neighbours. In fact one of the most interesting features of Balkan politics during the inter-war period has been the spectacular rise of peasant movements and parties which have had a profound influence on the social structure of these societies. The only Balkan country which did not experience a strong peasant movement was Greece — where peasants were brought into the

An earlier version of this chapter was published in *Comparative Studies in Society and History*, January 1975.

political game through their dependent integration into the major bourgeois parties. As I shall try to argue below, the development of Balkan
peasantism can be seen to a large extent as a political reaction to the
strains and disruptions created by the increasing penetration of Western
capitalism into this underdeveloped part of the world. Since this penetration was as strong in Greece as in the other Balkan countries during the
inter-war period, the failure of Greek peasants to organise themselves
politically poses an interesting problem for anyone concerned with the
past and present development of modern Greek society.

The problem becomes even more interesting if one tries to compare
Greece with its northern neighbour, Bulgaria — a country with which
Greece shared many historical experiences and whose institutions, at least
up to the Second World War, were quite similar to those of Greece.[1]
Bulgaria, during the inter-war period, had the most powerful peasant
movement in the Balkans. This paper attempts, through a comparison of
certain features of the Greek and Bulgarian social structure, to provide
some tentative explanations of the striking difference between the political
organisation of the peasantry in these two countries.

1   CAPITALIST PENETRATION

Any study of Balkan peasant conditions during the inter-war period must
necessarily start with an examination of the changing relationship between
south-eastern and Western European countries at the end of the nineteenth
century. Whereas previous to this time Western powers were trying to
control developments in the Balkans through traditional diplomatic and
military means, by the end of the century European imperialism assumed a
more economic character. As is well known, increasing competition among
industrial countries for new markets was not confined to the outright
acquisition of colonies. It was also extended into other economically
backward countries which, although not directly annexed, provided
considerable opportunities for the rapidly accumulating European capital.
It was, in fact, during this time that Western capitalism penetrated in a
very intensive and systematic manner into the Balkan peninsula.

This economic penetration initially took the form of private and public
loans advanced to the chronically impoverished Balkan governments and
of investments in railways, roads, bridges, ports, etc.[2] Of course, the
pattern of these investments, as in other colonial or semi-colonial situations, was not always dictated autonomously by the internal requirements of the economies involved; it was much more a function of the
strategic, political and economic needs of the Great Powers. For instance,
the first two railway lines in the Balkans (from Varna to Ruschuk, and
from Constantsa to Cernavoda) were constructed according to British
interests after the Crimean War in order to tap the commerce of the

Danube area; and proposals for trans-Balkan railway lines were promoted or boycotted according to the strategic interests of the powers most concerned.[3]

In addition to the need for social overhead capital, Balkan governments had to depend on Western capital for the build-up and maintenance of their comparatively huge military establishments as well as for their over-inflated and 'corrupt' public bureaucracies. As these types of investment were not very productive and as even infrastructural investments could only pay off in the very long term, Balkan governments became increasingly indebted to their foreign creditors.[4] As their financial condition became more and more precarious, creditors would only advance new loans under the condition of having direct control of the resources guaranteeing loan repayments. For instance, in 1902 Bulgaria had to accept the foreign control of its revenues from a special tobacco tax as a precondition for obtaining a consolidation loan.[5] Not so many years earlier, Greece had been forced to grant even more humbling concesssions when, chiefly as the result of the shrinking world market for its main export crop of currants, the country had to be declared bankrupt. An international financial commission was appointed on Greek territory which controlled the main Greek revenue sources and had a major say in currency issues, new loans, and in fact the entire range of State finances. For many years Greece had to submit to having its vital executive and legislative functions exercised by a foreign group of bondholders directly appointed to the Financial Control Commission by the creditor States.[6]

As in all similar cases, the class which suffered most from the disruptive impact of foreign penetration was the peasantry. The inundation of the country districts with cheap Western industrial goods (facilitated by improvements in transport), as well as the increasing need to find cash for the payment of taxes, were pushing the peasants to abandon their subsistence style of life and to start producing for the national and international market. The unavoidable risks of transition from a subsistence to a market economy were accentuated in the Balkans by weak and corrupt governments which not only did very little for the protection of the peasant, but also were actively undermining his precarious position by the imposition of highly unjust and exorbitant taxes.[7]

A more positive measure of Balkan governments during the inter-war period was the important agrarian reforms which broke up the big landed estates (the chifliks) and, in an irreversible manner, established the small peasant holding as the dominant form of land ownership.[8] As far as Bulgaria and Greece were concerned, the inter-war land reforms were more extensive in the latter, Bulgaria having had an egalitarian agrarian structure even before the First World War.[9] But in both countries these reforms, although giving a final blow to the already declining landlord classes, did not contribute very much to the welfare of the peasantry. As indicated above, the assistance of the State (in terms of the provision of credit, technical assistance, education etc.), a fundamental precondition of successful land reform, was minimal if not lacking totally.[10]

The situation of the peasants was further aggravated by a spectacular population growth in the peninsula, a trend which started at the beginning of the 19th century and which accelerated during the inter-war period.[11] This resulted in the extreme fragmentation of peasant holdings and the lowering of agricultural productivity. It is not necessary to give detailed information on productivity levels or on the low standard of living of the peasantry; suffice it to point out that in most Balkan countries approximately half the rural population was redundant.[12]

One way of dealing with surplus labour in agriculture is, of course, industrialisation. As a matter of fact, during the inter-war period all Balkan governments made serious efforts to develop their industrial sectors, hoping in this way to solve both their chronic balance of payments difficulties and their problem of rural overpopulation. Although some industrial growth was achieved, and although, through the creation of relatively large wage-labour employing units the capitalist mode of production started playing a more dominant role in the social formation, the attempt at industrialisation was on the whole unsuccessful.

The reasons for this are not very different from the reasons why present-day underdeveloped countries fail to industrialise with the help of foreign capital: excessive profits going abroad, unsystematic development of natural resources, preference for the processing of raw materials and semi-finished products, avoidance of risky investments, etc.[13] Naturally enough, the peasants, given the type of 'negative' articulation between the capitalist mode of production prevailing in some industrial branches and simple commodity agricultural production,[14] had very little to benefit from the above developments. The State attempts at industrialisation not only failed to absorb the surplus labour of the countryside, but the high tariffs, which the protection of inefficient local industrial monopolies necessitated, radically increased the prices of industrial goods, thus further deteriorating the conditions of the peasantry.

Thus, whether one looks at the earlier phase of Western capitalist penetration (in the late nineteenth century), characterised by railway construction and the provision of loans, or at its later stage (inter-war period), characterised by attempts at industrialisation, one sees that it promoted an economy which was much more integrated with the developmental requirements of Western Europe than with the needs and resources of the Balkan regions. It set the basic pattern of growth, or rather of misgrowth or underdevelopment, which prevailed in all Balkan societies up to the Second World War: a pattern characterised by severe sectoral imbalances, by a lack of positive links between capitalist and non-capitalist modes of production and, more generally, by a fundamental incapacity of the economic system to use effectively all the natural and human resources available.[15]

Although the above distortions had an equally strong effect on both Bulgarian and Greek peasants, they each reacted in very different ways. In Bulgaria there emerged a very strong peasant populist movement with an anti-bourgeois, anti-establishment ideology.[16] The Agrarian Union had been, in fact, a considerable political force even before the Balkan Wars and the First World War. Its rise to power in 1919 and its subsequent electoral victories indicate the extent to which peasant voters in Bulgaria succeeded in breaking out of the older bourgeois political formations. Moreover, the anti-agrarian coup of 1923 and the savage assassination of Stamboliiski, the charismatic agrarian leader, show the extent to which the Bulgarian elite felt threatened by the political rise of the peasant class. Finally, despite this setback and the subsequent harassment and persecution of Agrarian Union members, there was a remarkably rapid recovery of the movement after 1923; in the elections of 1931, the moderate wing of the agrarian party, in coalition with a group of liberal bourgeois politicians, succeeded once more in forming a government which lasted until the coup of 1934.[17]

In Greece, on the other hand, the dominant classes managed to contain peasant discontent and to keep the peasantry within the 'safe' boundaries of bourgeois political debates. In fact, the Greek bourgeois parties, profoundly split during the inter-war period over the issue of the monarchy, succeeded in drawing into this essentially intra-bourgeois conflict the peasant masses – thus diverting their attention from their desperate economic situation. The Greek Agrarian Party which was established as late as 1922 was, both in terms of membership and in terms of political impact, an insignificant force in Greek political life.[18]

The basic argument to be developed in the rest of this paper is that these radically different political reactions to the intrusion of Western capitalism can be understood in terms of the different ways in which the peasantry was integrated into the State and other dominant bourgeois institutions of the two countries.

2   THE HISTORICAL DEVELOPMENT OF THE GREEK AND BULGARIAN BOURGEOISIE

A good starting-point for trying to understand the considerable differences in rural-urban relationships between Greece and Bulgaria is to go back to the time when both societies were under Ottoman rule. A striking phenomenon in the economic history of the Ottoman empire is the early rise (in the fifteenth and sixteenth centuries) of the Greek Orthodox merchant, not only in the Balkans but in most territories of the empire. In the eighteenth century, Greeks (and to a lesser extent Jews and Armenians) managed to control a considerable portion of the empire's internal and external trade.[19]

Other Balkan merchants appeared on the scene much later and never managed to rival the Greeks in terms of power or wealth. This is especially true of the Bulgarian merchant class, whose beginnings are traceable only to the eighteenth century. An important obstruction to the development of Bulgarian commerce was the fact that Bulgaria constituted the hinterland and was the main agricultural provider for four major Ottoman cities: Constantinople, Adrianople, Philipopolis and Sofia. As a result, it was not allowed to engage in export trade. Even inside the empire the Bulgarians had few possibilities of developing trade activities. At the time of their emergence, the commerce between Constantinople and Bulgaria was already controlled by Greeks and Armenians who had a virtual monopoly of trade between the Ottoman capital and the eastern Balkans.[20] Trade opportunities were no better westwards, as most of Bulgaria's western neighbours (Serbia, Bosnia, Wallachia) were producing similar products. Finally, the fact that Bulgarians did not settle near coastal areas[21] was another important reason for the weak development of its merchant class.

A clear indication of the supremacy of the Greek bourgeoisie in the Balkans during the eighteenth and early nineteenth centuries is the fact that before the rise of separate Balkan nationalisms, Greek was the language of commerce and 'culture' all over the peninsula. For non-Greek merchants it was a sign of upward mobility and prestige to speak Greek and even to be considered Greek. As Stoianovich puts it, 'Men of wealth took pride in being called Greek, and Orthodox Albanian, Vlach, Macedo-Slav and Bulgarian merchants of the 18th century normally identified themselves as such. Class-conscious Slavic peasants also applied the term "Greek" to most merchants, particularly if they considered them rogues . . .'[22]

This hellenising process of the Balkan upper classes lasted up to the beginning of the nineteenth century when the development of Slav nationalism curtly interrupted it.[23] Good examples of this interesting process of acculturation were the two major trading groups which appeared in the eighteenth century and which played a crucial role in the commercialisation of the Greek economy: the famous maritime merchants of the Aegean (especially of Hydra, Spetsai and Psara) who were originally Albanians, and the land traders of Macedonia, Epirus and Thessaly who had predominantly Vlach and Macedonian origin. By 1800 the wealthy members of both groups were completely hellenised.

Moreover, the Greek bourgeoisie played a very important part in the early awakening of Greek nationalism and in the struggle for independence against the Turks.[24] The Greek merchants, especially those established in the Danubian principalities and in the major European capitals, transmitted French revolutionary ideas and provided leadership and considerable material resources to the insurrectionary movement. Through their commercial activities, their numerous contacts with the West and their financing of schools in which students were initiated into the rationalism and anti-clericalism of western enlightenment, they contributed significantly to the early 'modernisation' (i.e. Westernisation)[25] of Greek culture and society. The impact of Greek merchants becomes even more considerable if one takes into account that the more traditional elites of Greek society (i.e. the high clergy and the big landowners), having a greater stake in the *status quo*, had a much more lukewarm and ambivalent attitude towards the revolution; the majority of them joined the struggle only after they realised the irreversibility of the nationalist movement. This explains to some extent why the bourgeoisie became the value-originators and the standard-setters of Greek society, quite early shaping its major institutions along liberal bourgeois lines.[26]

The Bulgarians, on the other hand, remained under Turkish domination longer than any other Balkan people (except the Albanians). They achieved their independence half a century after the Greeks (in 1878). An important reason for this late emancipation was that Bulgaria was much more densely inhabited by Turks and other Muslims and, as it was near the empire's administrative centre, it was much easier for the Ottoman authorities to suppress any revolutionary attempts. More generally, due to its geographical position in the eastern part of the peninsula, both culturally and economically Bulgaria was much more oriented eastwards — towards Constantinople and Asia Minor rather than to the regions of central and Western Europe. In contrast to the Greeks and the Serbians, the Bulgarians did not directly experience the impact of Western ideas; 'progressive' Western ideas reached Bulgaria indirectly through the Greeks. Indeed, up to the middle of the nineteenth century, upper-class Bulgarians received their education in Greek schools either in independent Greece (Athens, the Aegean islands) or in Greek centres of the empire (Salonica, Yiannina, Smyrna). Moreover, on the Bulgarian mainland, until the establishment of the first Bulgarian school at Gabrovo in 1835, the only existing schools were either Church establishments with a traditionally ecclesiastical curriculum, or Greek schools with a secular, Western orientation.[27] Of course, this Greek influence did not prevent the Bulgarians from eventually becoming aware of their separate national identity and from using Western nationalist ideas against the cultural and religious hegemony of their Greek teachers,[28] but it indicates quite clearly the vast difference in the degree of 'Westernisation' of the two countries.[29] Finally, although wealthy Bulgarian merchants did contribute to the national awakening of the Bulgarian people, their role was by no means comparable to the role that the Greek bourgeoisie played in the Greek revolution. If for no other reason, the independence of Bulgaria was not so much due to an internal uprising (although there were numerous revolts before 1878), but was the direct result of the Turkish defeat in the Russo-Turkish War of 1877–8.

3   RURAL-URBAN LINKS

A   *The Commercialisation of Agriculture*

Taking the above facts into account, it is easy to understand why at the beginning of the twentieth century Greece had a much more complex and differentiated social structure than Bulgaria. For instance, the commercialisation of agriculture and the subsequent shifting of the labour force from the primary to the secondary and tertiary sectors started much earlier in Greece. Around 1930 the percentage of the labour force employed in agriculture was below 60 per cent in Greece and above 80 per cent in Bulgaria,[30] and although other Balkan countries at that period resembled Bulgaria more than Greece in the structure of their labour force, nowhere else in the Balkans did peasants resist market influences and attempt to maintain their old traditional life style more than in Bulgaria.[31]

Thus, at a time when the Greek peasant was fully exposed to the influence of the money economy, his Bulgarian counterpart was still immersed in the Zadruga family system[32] which, to some extent, protected him from the uncertainties of market forces. The contrast in degree of commercialisation can be seen on a more socio-psychological level in the differences in life styles between Greeks and peasants of Slav origin living in the north of Greece during the inter-war period. According to Daniilides, the Peloponnesian peasants, who were involved very early in the market economy, showed much more individualistic, 'modern' characteristics: i.e. less attachment to the soil, greater attraction to the city and willingness to adopt urban styles of life, development of a consumer mentality, chronic indebtedness to the grocer, merchant and the State bank. On the other hand, those Slav peasants who were still cultivating the land within the Zadruga kinship system were less dependent on the market for their food and clothing, more attached to the land, more hostile to urban values.[33] This difference in degree of commercialisation between Bulgaria and Greece was accentuated even further after the agrarian reforms in the two countries. Indeed, according to Mitrany, after the reforms many Slav smallholders reverted to subsistence farming in order to avoid the hazards of the market economy. This did not happen in Greece because the commercialisation of agriculture had advanced to such a degree that the return to subsistence was not possible.[34] This difference is of course very relevant to our problem. As has been pointed out in the literature on peasants, in a situation of relative autarchy the links tying the peasant to the dominant institutions of a capitalist society are weaker; and this lesser dependence of the peasant on the merchant and on State credit organisations gives him more room to manoeuvre and greater freedom to shift his political allegiances radically in times of stress.[35]

B   The Village community

If one now looks more closely at the social structure of the village community in its relationship to the urban centre, one can again discern systematic and significant differences between Bulgaria and Greece. The general point that can be made is that the Greek village was much more differentiated both in terms of occupations and in terms of wealth, prestige and power.

In the Bulgarian village of the inter-war period, those who were not directly engaged in agricultural activities were not only relatively fewer, but did not have the same power and influence as their counterparts in the Greek village. In fact, the Bulgarians remained agriculturalists to the extent that during the first quarter of the twentieth century, even in the large villages where a minimum of occupational differentiation did occur, the local merchant, the baker, the shoemaker, the blacksmith etc. were of foreign origin — Greek, Vlach, Epirote.[36] Moreover, so great and striking was the difference between peasants and non-peasants in the village community that the few Slavs who did engage in non-agricultural activities were considered foreigners.[37] In other words, as the Rumanian historian N. Iorga puts it, at the beginning of the century 'Serb always meant peasant'.[38]

In consequence, not only was there great hostility between the village community and the urban merchants, but even within the village community itself there was a serious split between those who were directly cultivating the land and those who were not. Because of this hostility it is plausible to hypothethise that the latter were unable to exercise effective leadership and to become effective intermediaries between the village and the town.

Another related and significant difference between the social structure of the Greek and Bulgarian village is the more egalitarian character of the latter. It is true that owing to the land reforms after the First World War in both countries big ownership was on the decline. But Bulgaria had an egalitarian structure much earlier than Greece. Even before the First World War Bulgaria had very few big estates.[39]

It has been argued that Bulgaria's agrarian structure before and after the First World War was not as egalitarian as the absence of big landed estates might suggest. This was so because at the end of the nineteenth century and the beginning of the twentieth there was considerable economic differentiation and concentration of landed property due to large-scale usury.[40] This meant that a great number of small peasants lost the ownership of their land and had to work it as renters or sharecroppers. From this perspective the emergence and rapid development of the Agrarian Union can be seen as a reaction to this type of exploitative situation.[41]

Although the above considerations are relevant for understanding when and how the agrarian movement started in Bulgaria, it does not provide a sufficient explanation for our problem. For undoubtedly similar processes of economic concentration, due to extensive usurious practices, were taking place in Greece during the same period.[42] Although there are no comparative statistics on this, there is no reason to believe that in Bulgaria usury was more developed than in Greece. If anything, the opposite must have been the case since both the co-operative movement and State-sponsored agricultural credit were developed earlier in Bulgaria than in Greece.[43] I would therefore agree with Gerschenkron, who argues that although usury was quite extensive in Bulgaria at the beginning of the twentieth century, it was drastically reduced even before the First World War through the development of the co-operative movement and through government intervention. With the galloping inflation during the war and the post-war years, peasant debts diminished even further.[44]

Moreover, those who emphasise usury and money-lending as a means of property concentration often neglect to take into account processes which work in the opposite direction. For instance, because wealthy peasant families tend to have numerous children, through equal partition at death (primogeniture does not exist in Bulgaria or Greece) there is a tendency towards economic levelling and what Shanin calls 'centripetal' mobility (i.e. the sort of intergenerational mobility which discourages the accumulation of economic advantages and disadvantages).[45] It is only if one takes into account such processes that it can be understood why even at the beginning of the twentieth century, when usury was still rampant, there was a tendency towards the relative growth of small property in the Bulgarian countryside.[46] In fact, Bulgaria, especially after the land reform of 1917 and the egalitarian measures implemented by the first agrarian government in 1921, moved further towards an equal distribution of land than any other Balkan country.[47] In Greece, although legislation against the big chifliks (which were dominant only in Thessaly and the north of Greece) started in 1917, its implementation was slow — land distribution was accelerated only after 1922 with the massive influx of Greek refugees from Asia Minor.[48]

As far as our problem is concerned, it is quite obvious that 'egalitarianism' is very relevant to the explanation of Bulgaria's agrarian populism. That absence of great social inequalities favours solidarity and the propensity for collective action is a point which has often been stressed in studies of peasant politics.[49]

In conclusion, the general picture which emerges if one looks at the structure of Bulgarian rural society at the beginning of the twentieth century is that of a quasi-subsistence, homogeneous mass of peasants in opposition to a handful of non-agriculturalists who, because of their small number and of the peasant hostility towards them, could not operate as effective mediators between the village and the national centre. In the Greek, relatively 'commercialised', village on the other hand, not only was differentiation in terms of occupation and wealth more extensive, but local notables and villagers not directly engaged in agriculture also constituted an effective bridge between the village 'periphery' and the 'centre'. Their leadership and strategic position as intermediaries being accepted, they could much more effectively channel peasant demands and incorporate the peasantry in the bourgeois political and economic institutions of the country.

C   Urbanisation and emigration

Another point which needs emphasis is the striking difference between the two countries as far as migration patterns (both internal and external) are concerned. As can be surmised from the figures for the labour force already given, the shifting of the population from the countryside to the towns started relatively early in Greece. Urban growth was significant towards the end of the nineteenth century and this trend accelerated dramatically during the inter-war period and after the Second World War. Greek villagers, pushed by the lack of economic opportunities in their village and pulled by the attractions of city life, started leaving their communities for the rapidly growing urban centres, particularly Athens. The spectacular population increase of the Greater Athens area during the inter-war period is a direct indication of the dimensions of this population shift. Whereas at the end of the nineteenth century Athens had fewer than 200,000 inhabitants, in the early 1920s its population reached the half-million mark, and had exceeded one million before the Second World War.[50]

This significant migratory movement was another powerful mechanism even further diminishing the gap between village and town, not only because those who moved to the cities usually maintained strong links with their villages, but also because their efforts and aspirations were, and are even today, constantly oriented to the city. There is hardly a village family that does not aspire to a good education for its children, helping them to find a 'place' in Athens.[51] Such a place, whether in private enterprise or in the public bureaucracy, is not simply a sign of prestige for the whole kinship group, it is also a means of facilitating the numerous dealings that villagers unavoidably have with the centre. To have the right contact, to establish connections in 'high places', whether these connections are relatives, friends or politicians, is not simply a matter of ambition or convenience, it is imperative in a village world widely permeated by external forces − both economic and political. In fact, as Lineton points out,

'. . . wealth. power and security in the village depended not so much on source of income, but on being or having connections with political and economic intermediaries. *Families did not seek to improve the position of peasant generally . . . but sought to push their members or climb themselves into a more powerful class.* Whether locally or nationally, this always involved some members moving to the city or establishing connections with members of a class based in the city' [italics mine].[52]

Undoubtedly, similar processes of urbanisation occurred in Bulgaria, but such processes were weaker than in Greece. For instance, as the following statistics show, during the late nineteenth and early twentieth centuries the proportion between the urban and rural population in Bulgaria remained more or less constant.

Year	% of the urban population in Bulgaria
1880	19.3
1887	19.5
1892	20.0
1900	19.9
1905	19.6
1910	19.1

From Popoff, op. cit., p. 11.

This means that the population shift from the countryside to the towns did no more than compensate for the low natural growth rate of the cities (due to lower birth rates); and although the growth rate of the urban population was slightly higher during the inter-war period, up to 1946 the urban/rural population ratio was 1 to 4.[53]

Another clear indication of the difference in geographical mobility between Bulgarians and Greeks is the pattern of external migration. During this period Greece experienced an exceptionally strong migratory movement to the United States. It started at the end of the nineteenth century and, due to various economic crises, gained momentum during the first two decades of the twentieth century; it slowed down after 1922 with the initiation of restrictive immigration policies by the American government. For instance, in 1907 alone, 36,580 Greek citizens emigrated to the United States. By the end of 1932, the total number of Greek immigrants in the States amounted to 445,122.[54] This contrasts sharply with the low level of Bulgarian immigration to the United States. For example, it was calculated that in the middle thirties, Bulgarian immigrants to the States (including those originating from Thrace, Macedonia and Dobroudja) did not exceed 35,000.[55]

This contrast is significant for two reasons. First of all it strengthens the point already made that Greek peasants were 'outward'-looking, less bound by kinship and other ascriptive local groupings than the Bulgarians. It is also significant because emigration, to a great extent, reduced surplus labour in agriculture without creating further unemployment in the city; in that respect it operated as a safety valve in Greek society. Because this solution was less operative in Bulgaria, where the strains created by rural overpopulation were relieved neither by internal nor by external migration, one can understand why its peasants were more susceptible to political programmes aiming at a radical improvement of their desperate state.[56]

D   Political links

A final relevant consideration is the extent to which the State administration *permeates* the rural periphery in the two countries. Since Greece emerged as an independent national State approximately half a century before Bulgaria, it is plausible to assume that during the inter-war period State institutions (administrative agencies, police organisations, schools, churches etc.) had more pervasive, stronger roots in the Greek than in the Bulgarian countryside. One way of assessing the relative strength of the State and its degree of penetration into the 'civil society' is to assess its tax-raising capacity — i.e. its ability to extract resources for self-maintenance and expansion as well as for the realisation of other public goals. In this respect Greece was far ahead of Bulgaria: whereas around the 1930s the Greek State managed to extract 83.40 French francs per head (calculated on the basis of pre-First World War purchasing power), it extracted only 28.08 francs in Bulgaria.[57]

A similar point can be made where political parties are concerned. Even where Greece was under an absolute monarchy (1827—43), there were already distinct political organisations, based on all-powerful local oligarchies.[58] Such oligarchies (especially during the early years of Greek independence) exercised quasi-total control over their territories. When eventually, with the strengthening of a national army, they were no longer able to prevent the centralising tendencies of the State, they succeeded in compensating for their loss of autonomy by controlling the State from within. In this way political factions with strong and extensive links in the countryside appeared very early in Greek political life.[59] Of course, they continued to thrive with the introduction of parliamentary politics in 1864. Operating as pressure groups and as patronage agencies, they managed to control and integrate the peasantry into the central institutions of the State. In fact Greek peasants were and are notorious for their political sophistication, their passion for political arguments and discussions. This strong involvement in party politics has often been portrayed as a distinctive trait of the Greek 'national character'. I think it can be explained in a much more direct way if it is related to the early dependence of the village community on the State, which makes involvement with patronage politics and the securing of a political protector a vital necessity for survival and advancement.

In the case of Bulgaria, as has been mentioned already, differentiation in terms of wealth and power was less accentuated than in Greece. The Bulgarian ruling classes, whether in the town or the countryside, never managed to accumulate the wealth or to achieve the power of their Greek counterparts. Moreover, the fact that Bulgarians got their independence from 'above', so to speak, means that from the very start there was no serious oligarchic challenge to the establishment of a centralised monarchical State. Thus there was a sort of political vacuum between the monarchical State and the peasantry — i.e. the political organisations in Bulgaria had less autonomy *vis-à-vis* the throne, and their roots in the countryside were quite weak. E. Dicey, visiting Bulgaria a decade after its independence, comments:

> 'Except in the large towns very little interest is taken in politics. To the great mass of the electorate it is a matter of utter indifference who their representatives might be. The difficulty is to get the electors to vote at all; and in the majority of instances the representatives [in parliament] are virtually nominated by the government of the day'.[60]

4 CONCLUSION

In conclusion, whether one looks at the processes which draw peasants into the market, the occupational structure of the village and the link between the local and the urban bourgeoisie, the migratory movements, or the degree of State penetration in the countryside — in all these areas one encounters a difference in organisation between Greece and Bulgaria during the inter-war period: the various mechanisms which incorporated the peasant into the urban centre were much stronger in Greece.

It is not surprising, therefore, that with the intrusion of Western capitalism the reaction of the peasant to the ensuing disruption was quite different in the two countries. Under the stress of the capitalist impact, the Bulgarian peasant, being more autonomous *vis-à-vis* the market, more hostile to a bourgeoisie which he identified with foreign oppression, less 'modernised' and less involved in the bourgeois State, was more available for mobilisation by leaders with a populist, anti-bourgeois, anti-town platform. The initial success of this movement had a profound impact on the structure of Bulgarian politics, in the sense that the major political cleavage took a 'peasant masses versus bourgeoisie' form.[61] Such a political split clearly reflects, on the level of the political institutions, the weak rural-urban links which, as indicated, constituted a major characteristic of Bulgarian society during the inter-war period. In Greece, on the other hand, where these links were stronger, the political cleavage continued to have an intra-bourgeois character, the peasants being firmly kept within the boundaries of the bourgeois political parties. Such differences however, should not lead one to neglect the obvious fact that, given the underdeveloped, 'enclave' type of capitalism that prevailed in both Greece and Bulgaria during the inter-war period, in neither country could the imported parliamentary institutions work in a way similar to the West. Neither Greece nor Bulgaria provided a fertile ground for the institutionalisation and long-term persistence of relatively autonomous political organisations able to articulate the collective interests of the working classes within a reasonably stable parliamentary system. As far as peasants are concerned, in Greece such an organisation did not appear at all; in Bulgaria it did, but was eventually suppressed by force.[62] From this point of view, Greek and Bulgarian inter-war politics present two different versions of the 'malfunctioning' of Western parliamentary institutions when transplanted into pre-capitalist or in underdeveloped/capitalist social formations.

If one tries to place these considerations in the more general debate on the nature and causes of populism, I think that the Bulgarian case does vindicate those theories which link populist movements in the third world with the disruptions produced by unbalanced and dependent growth within the context of capitalist relations between advanced industrial and underdeveloped countries.[63] But the Greek case indicates that unbalanced and dependent growth can occur without any serious challenge or radical political reaction from those who suffer most from it.

The Greek case makes sense theoretically if one refers to those theories which, in a more specific way, link peasant populism to the fact that peasants during industrialisation are in a very ambivalent and marginal position: they are sitting on the fence between 'tradition' and 'modernity'; they are partly drawn into the process of 'modernisation' and partly left outside it.[64] From this point of view, Greek peasants experienced this marginality much less; during the inter-war period they were resolutely placed on the 'modernity' side of the fence. In other words, compared with their northern neighbours they were more drawn in and less left out.[65]

A major reason for the mobilisation of Bulgarian peasants must, therefore, be sought in their relative isolation, in combination with the homogeneity of their economic interests which made them feel the strains of capitalist disruption in a uniform manner. We have already mentioned empirical studies in the sociological literature which emphasise the importance of homogeneity as a favourable condition for mobilisation. A similar support from the literature can be found as far as social isolation is concerned.[66]

In considering 'factors' or 'variables' favourable to mobilisation, it would be tempting to establish more abstract, law-like generalisations,[67] such as a positive correlation between social isolation and peasant mobilisation, or a negative one between the degree of 'modernisation' (urbanisation, occupational differentiation) and potential for peasant mobilisation during periods of intensive capitalist penetration, the argument being that the more differentiated the society is, the greater its capacity to absorb capitalist disruption without a radical political realignment of its peasantry. However, it seems to me that such generalisations are highly misleading, in that they draw the attention of the student away from the actual socio-cultural context in which such variables are embedded; this context is indispensable for understanding the significance and importance of the variables and the way in which they are inter-related. In other words, in order to make sense of the way in which peasants are politically organised in any specific country, one must take very seriously into account a variety of factors both synchronic and diachronic, whose specific configuration might invalidate 'universal' correlations between any two variables.

One cannot claim universal applicability for the relationship between rural-urban links and propensity for mobilisation. This type of relationship obviously does not hold true in cases where the peasants are related to powerful local landlords in a quasi-feudal manner.[68] In this case, isolation from the centre does not imply availability for mobilisation; peasants can be kept under strict control without the direct intervention of the State. Such considerations suggest that the limited generalisations formulated with respect to the political organisation of the Bulgarian and Greek peasantry, although relevant, cannot automatically be applied in the case of other peasant movements, not even within the Balkan peninsula.

A final note of caution is necessary here. This examination of the reasons for the lack of a peasant movement in Greece and for its strong development in Bulgaria is by no means exhaustive. It is hardly necessary to point out that the weak links between the peasantry and the State in themselves cannot generate a peasant movement; they simply constitute favourable soil for its eventual development. From this point of view the explanation developed in this paper does not imply contradiction of other explanations which refer, for example, to the extraordinary charisma of Stamboliiski and the lack of a personality of similar impact in the Greek Agrarian Party, or to the fact that the Bulgarian ruling class was discredited by defeats during the Balkan Wars and the First World War.

The present analysis claims to be complementary to such explanations. It points to more long-term developments and to those less rapidly changing aspects of the social structure which constitute a kind of framework limiting the choices that collective actors have at any specific historical moment.[69]

6 Class Structure and the Role of the Military in Greece: An Interpretation

INTRODUCTION

If the issue of the political organisation of the peasantry is crucial for understanding Greek society, so is the problem of the military and the role they played in the development/underdevelopment of modern Greece.

In this chapter there will be no attempt to give a full explanation or even a systematic historical account of the role played by the military in Greek politics; rather, the aim will be to locate the 1967 military dictatorship in a broader historical context by considering it in the light of (a) previous military interventions during the inter-war period, and (b) Greece's changing class structure. Since earlier chapters (especially Chapter 1) have already outlined some basic features of the Greek economy's development, here the focus will be on the political superstructure: on its basic transformation as Greece, with the general dominance of the capitalist mode of production, moved from oligarchical to mass politics. In a way this essay, by providing an overall sketch of long-term politico-military developments, prepares the ground for the next chapter which tries to explain the rise and fall of the Greek junta in terms of the post-war capitalist underdevelopment of Greece.

1 HISTORICAL BACKGROUND

A major feature of Greek politics during the early years of national independence in the nineteenth century was the attempt of the newly-born State to reduce the autonomy of the all-powerful local oligarchies (notables or military chieftains) and to expand its dominance to the periphery.[1]

Not unlike the earlier struggles of western European nobilities against the absolutist tendencies of monarchic States, Greek State expansionism was resisted by Greek local notables for as long as they could.[2] Thus Capodistria's and later King Otho's efforts to establish an absolutist system of government were eventually thwarted by an oligarchy which found in the recently imported Western libertarian ideas of 'freedom' and 'democracy' a convenient ideological vehicle for the maintenance and promotion of its interests.[3]

The tension between the centripetal tendencies of the throne and the centrifugal tendencies of the various oligarchies reached equilibrium with the 1864 Constitution which considerably restricted the powers of the throne and allowed the Greek notables to maintain a great deal of their local influence and power. Despite the existence of universal suffrage, the broad mass of the people, through patronage and other forms of vote manipulation were safely kept under the control of their traditional masters. From this perspective the period between 1864 and 1909, which could be called the period of *oligarchic parliamentarianism*, was both stable and unstable.

Indeed, on the level of parliamentary politics, the system was character-ised by extreme instability as the continuous succession of short-lived governments[4] was a reflection of the weak institutionalisation of an imported system of government which did not correspond to Greek infrastructural realities. But this type of political instability (which in this paper I shall call *parliamentary instability*) operated within a more general socio-political framework which proved surprisingly stable. In fact, during the whole of this period (1864–1909) despite the chaos and other obvious 'dysfunctions' of parliamentary politics, there was no serious attempt by the military, the throne or any other political force to disrupt the basic parameters of the system: the balance of power between the throne, the oligarchy, and the people.

The reasons for this remarkable 'macro-stability' are not very difficult to find. In a pre-capitalist, predominantly agrarian social formation, the slow rate of economic growth ruled out the possibility of any serious threat from below. The throne, despite constitutional limitations, was in actual control of military and foreign affairs,[5] and the oligarchy had no interest in changing a system which ensured it both a relative autonomy *vis-à-vis* the throne and the continuation of its dominance *vis-à-vis* the rest of the people.

This combination of parliamentary instability and constitutional macro-stability was not very favourable for the collective intervention of the military in politics. The army had not as yet emerged as a distinct interest group and the military elites were not clearly differentiated from their political counterparts. Since they had both descended from the same oligarchical families (the so-called *tzakia*), their interests virtually over-lapped.[6]

2   THE INTER-WAR PERIOD

A. Oligarchic parliamentarianism could not, of course, last for ever. Already during the last decades of the nineteenth century the penetration of Western capitalism in the Balkans[7] and the related Trikoupian reforms of the 1880s (i.e. social overhead investments, administrative rationalis-ation, etc.) ushered Greece into a transition period during which the capitalist mode of production, although not yet dominant, was gradually gaining ground[8] – generating thus new social forces (clerical workers, professionals, a new merchant and industrial bourgeoisie) which would eventually challenge the quasi-monopoly of power enjoyed by a handful of oligarchic families.[9]

From this point of view the military coup of 1909 is a crucial turning-point in Greek history. It marks the end of oligarchic parliamen-tarianism, the breaking of the nineteenth-century macro-stability based on the balance of power between monarchy, oligarchy, and the people. There are many conjunctural factors which might be used to explain the military intervention of 1909: the economic crisis, the defeat of Greece in the 1897 war with Turkey, the unsuccessful management of army affairs by the royal princes etc. But there is no doubt that there can be no satisfactory explanation of the 1909 coup without serious consideration of the development of capitalism and the ensuing changing of the whole socio-economic background which made the intervention of the army not only possible but relatively successful.[10]

Thus the widespread popular dissatisfaction with parliamentary politics at the beginning of the century (as reflected in the press for instance),[11] the clear emergence of organised pressure groups,[12] and the enthusiasm by which the population in the urban centres accepted the coup[13] are clear indications of a limited type of mobilisation in which middle-class elements played a leading role.

In consequence it is possible to call the 1909 military intervention a 'bourgeois' coup without implying that dissatisfied merchants, in a highly conspiratorial manner, were pulling the strings behind the military's back. Given that, at this stage the links between class and politics was still fairly indirect, the rise of the new middle classes and the socio-economic changes associated with them must be seen, not as the immediate cause of a coup but as a limiting framework which favoured certain political solutions and discouraged others.[14]

This framework is also relevant to an understanding of the major political events that followed the coup: the army's summoning of Venizelos (the great Cretan statesman) to act as its political adviser, his spectacular entry into Greek politics, his unprecedented electoral victory of 1910, etc. The election of December 1910, in which the *paleokom-matikai* (the old political leaders) were routed, opened the door to active politics for the rising middle classes. The old *tzakia* were not swept away altogether, but they were *increasingly forced* to share power with lawyers, doctors and new-rich businessmen.[15]

This change in the composition of political leadership was to affect the balance of power between throne and oligarchy. The decline of the *tzakia* automatically brought a relative decline in the power position of the throne, the newcomers being less loyal to the King,[16] or rather less prepared to see military and foreign affairs as the exclusive preserve of the monarchy.[17]

The inevitable clash did not take long to come. It took the form of a disagreement between the liberal Prime Minister Venizelos and King Constantine over the policy Greece should adopt during the First World War. The disagreement led in 1916 to the *dichasmos*, the schism between Venizelists and anti-Venizelists which profoundly marked the course of Greek politics during the inter-war period.[18] From our perspective, this split over the monarchy meant the end of half a century of macro-stability — a type of stability which will never again happen in Greek politics. From then on the endemic parliamentary instability was to continue within a broader framework which in itself was in permanent imbalance. For with the *dichasmos* the throne had utterly ceased to be 'above' politics. By becoming totally identified with one fraction of the dominant class, it generated a type of conflict which could no longer be contained from above. As the political pendulum swung from Venizelists to anti-Venizelists and back to Venizelists again, a political imbalance appeared which was quite different from the parliamentary instability of the nineteenth century. Given this type of disequilibrium, the door was wide open for the institutionalisation of military intervention in politics. From this point onwards the inter-war period was to be marked by a series of coups and counter-coups (some successful, some unsuccessful)[19] as antagonistic political groups with the help of army factions tried to defend their political interests and forcibly impose their conflicting views on the new constitutional order in Greece.

It lies outside the scope of this paper to analyse the intricate course of Greek politics during the inter-war period.[20] What should be emphasised here is that all political conflicts (at least up to the Metaxas coup of 1936) were essentially conflicts *within* the ruling class. For despite inter-war efforts at rapid industrialisation (a Balkan phenomenon), the Greek masses were safely kept outside active politics. Contrary to what was happening in Bulgaria, for instance (a country which developed at the same period a formidable peasant party with an aggressive anti-bourgeois, anti-establishment policy), Greek peasants failed to organise themselves politically. Their interests were misrepresented through the major bourgeois parties (especially the Venizelist party).[21] One could argue that it was precisely because the intra-bourgeois schism was so deep and violent that the peasants and the growing urban masses were so easily drawn into a conflict (over the fate of the monarchy) which had very little to do with their own vital interests. For if Greek irredentism in the form of the *Megali Idea*[22] was an ideological force hindering the development of class consciousness among the lower strata, the *dichasmos* was a greater one still.[23]

B. Given this general background, let us focus our attention on the role of the Greek army during the inter-war period (up to the Metaxas coup of 1936). The following points are of chief relevance:

(*a*) After the Balkan Wars and the First World War, the size of the army increased spectacularly.[24] At the same time, as more middle-class people were accepted in the Military Academy and as, due to the long war years, mobility up the ladder of the military hierarchy became easier, the officer corps lost its 'aristocratic' (*tzakia*-style) orientation. It acquired a more middle-class character,[25] and emerged for the first time as a pressure group, anxious to promote the economic and professional interests of its members.

(*b*) Its emergence as a distinct interest group at a time of political transition, when the usual parliamentary instability was coupled with constitutional instability, made the army's intervention a quasi-certainty — especially when one takes into account the fact that among 'politicised' interest groups the army, because of its control of the social means of coercion, is in a particularly advantageous position for seizing power.

(*c*) However, despite the strategic position of the Greek military, they never managed during the inter-war period to constitute an autonomous political force in the manner of Kemal Ataturk's army in Turkey, for instance.[26] They were either brought into the political arena through the initiative of politicians (e.g. Venizelos' 1935 unsuccessful coup) or, whenever they themselves took the initiative, the active support and collaboration of politicians was always sought (which was also true in the case of General Pangalos who tried to establish a long-term personal dictatorship).[27] In other words, there was a two-way penetration between the military and the political spheres. It was not simply the military who were interfering in politics — politicians were also interfering in military matters, in the sense that political factionalism and patronage politics permeated the army organisation from top to bottom.[28]

(*d*) Despite this interpenetration and the fact that the army was not pursuing autonomous goals, one could generalise that up to the Metaxas dictatorship the army as a whole had a mildly progressive-liberal orientation; if this did not apply to the motivation of individual officers, ideologically at least most military officers were more prone to favour anti-monarchical reforms. However, this reformism did not go beyond the bourgeois notions of formal equality and freedom. Having been drawn into politics through a strictly intra-bourgeois conflict, their ideological orientation was kept within the boundaries of this conflict.

(e) Given the lack of autonomy of the army and its ideological orientation, as well as the general class situation in Greece during the inter-war period, one can understand why, up to the Metaxas dictatorship (1937—41), the military could not realistically aim at and had never seriously tried to establish a long-term dictatorship in Greece. The attempt of General Pangalos to imitate Mussolini and set up a long-term personal dictatorship was the exception which confirmed the rule: the operetta-like character of the short-lived dictatorship and the ease with which it was overthrown were not simply a reflection of Pangalos' quasi-farcical character; they also indicated to what point a long-term dictatorial solution was incompatible with the overall configuration of forces in inter-war Greece.

(f) Finally, considering more specifically the relationship between the social classes and inter-war coups in Greece, one should point out that the connections between the two were indirect not only in 1909 but also in subsequent military interventions. Thus in order to understand the latter, more attention must be given to the Venizelist/anti-Venizelist pendulum mentioned above, and especially to the form that this conflict took within the army.[29] For instance, for an understanding of Leonardopoulos' unsuccessful attempt to seize power in 1923, class changes are not as relevant as developments within the army and within the political sphere.[30] Thus up to the 1930s the military-political dynamic had a relatively high degree of autonomy *vis-à-vis* the socio-economic infrastructure. It was only with the Metaxas coup of 1936 that the relationship between class developments and military intervention became more direct.

(g) With the Metaxas coup the pattern of military intervention and the role of the army started to change in a way that presaged the post-civil war developments. The change had a structural basis. Although the monarchy issue was still all-important and directly related to the coup, with the dominance of the capitalist mode of production in the decades after 1922, a new problem emerged: rapid industrialisation and urbanisation, the influx of the Asia Minor refugees and the depression of the thirties began for the first time to pose a real threat from below.[31] A small fraction of the urban working class and of the refugees was mobilised by the Greek Communist Party which, despite its relatively small electoral support (5.7 per cent of the vote) in the 1936 elections, managed to play a crucial balancing role in parliament between the two major bourgeois political parties. Therefore, if the consolidation of the monarchy was Metaxas' (and his patron's) major aim,[32] the growing unrest from below became the second important task of the dictatorship — a task demanding, of course, a different type of repression from that exercised for instance under Pangalos. Though the intra-bourgeois conflict was still strong, it was further compounded by a working class versus dominant class conflict.

Therefore, the dictator not only purged the army of all republican officers; he also inaugurated the type of large-scale repression and all the related 'techniques' which were to be developed fully by the 1967 regime.

Thus from now on the army became the guardian of the bourgeois system of power against threats from below. This new role became increasingly important not only because of the disruptions created by the development of industrial capitalism; but also because of the mass mobilisation of the peasantry and the urban working classes by the Left during the Greek resistance against the Germans and the subsequent civil war. From the civil war onwards, as Greece was entering the era of mass politics, the popular masses could no longer be kept outside active politics without large-scale repression. Given this situation, the army's major aim became the 'containment' of the masses, the task of keeping 'the lower strata in their place'.

3   ARMY AND MASS POLITICS: POST-CIVIL WAR DEVELOPMENTS

The Greek civil war ended with the victory of the right-wing forces which, with the help of the British and later the Americans, established a quasi-parliamentary regime in Greece – a regime in which the defeated Communist Party was outlawed and its followers and sympathisers systematically harassed and persecuted. Within this context the army, and more specifically an extremely powerful group of anti-communist officers (the IDEA group)[33] who were holding key positions in most control agencies of the State, had as one of their major tasks to make sure that this type of limited democracy functioned smoothly and that left-wing 'agitators' were kept firmly under control.

At the level of the political parties, the early post-civil war period was characterised by a strong polarisation between Left and Right. The Right, represented mainly by the ERE (the Radical Union) under the strong leadership of Papagos and then Karamanlis, managed to rule for eleven continuous years (1952–63). The Left, represented by the EDA (the Democratic Left), the only non-personalistic party in modern Greek politics, managed by ideological and organisational means to constitute a fairly important and cohesive force despite continuous harassment of its members.[34]

Between the two extremes, the forces in the middle of the political spectrum remained fragmented and weak. It was the achievement of George Papandreou to unite the small parties of the centre and to establish an opposition (the Centre Union) strong enough to successfully challenge the supremacy of the Right (it won the 1964 election with an unprecedented majority of 53 per cent). A second significant development during this time was the further differentiation of the Centre Union by the emergence of a strong and active left wing under the leadership of Papandreou's son Andreas. Andreas Panandreou propagated a pro-growth and egalitarian ideology which appealed to all rising social strata whose demands and growing expectations could be met neither by the empty anti-communism of the ERE nor by the dogmatics of those who at that time were controlling the EDA.

In fact, the impressive development of capitalism during the post-civil war period, the activation of the Cyprus problem which started stirring the masses in the fifties, the strengthening of the Centre Union and its persistent fight against electoral fraud and repression and its implementation of a limited programme of political liberalisation once it had taken power — all these factors lay behind the more active participation of the masses in politics during the sixties, a phenomenon noted by most political analysts.[35] Given this rising tide of mass mobilisation (by no means entirely communist in orientation), the mixture of liberalism and repression which characterised politics during the 1950s and 1960s could no longer be sustained. The balance had to tilt either on the side of liberalism (opening-up of the system to the masses), or on the side of repression. The colonels and those who were behind them decided on the latter solution; setting themselves against rising pressures for broader political participation (a concomitant of capitalist growth), they had to establish a repressive apparatus much more complex and far-reaching than anything experienced during the inter-war period.[36]

However, one must be careful not to go to the other extreme and identify the 1967 dictatorship with right-wing totalitarian regimes. If it is important to distinguish the 21 April coup from inter-war coups, it is equally important to see the differences between the Papadopoulos dictatorship and fascist or even quasi-fascist regimes of the Spanish and Portuguese type. In fact neither Papadopoulos nor his short-lived successors managed in any serious way to build up totalitarian organisations for mass mobilisation and support on the pattern of Nazi Germany or Fascist Italy. In the latter regimes the State managed to permeate the civil society and to mobilise and control the masses to a degree which until then was unknown in bourgeois societies. Such a vast mobilisation presupposes for its success not only that fractions of the ruling class give active support to the regime; it also presupposes large-scale popular support in the town and/or the countryside.

The Greek colonels did not manage to build any serious political organisation either in the countryside or among the urban masses. Due partly to their lower-middle-class origin, they did not even manage to win the *active* support of the Greek establishment.[37] In fact, during their seven-year rule, right-wing opposition was often more active and effective than opposition from the Left. And if the business world had to accept the 'realities of power', Athenian high society adopted an attitude of disdainful tolerance, looking down on the colonels as social upstarts totally lacking in skills and social graces.

The deeper reasons for such an attitude are not difficult to find. Although there was mass mobilisation during the Papandreou government, the threat from below was not serious enough to alarm the bourgeoisie to the extent of giving wholehearted support to a military dictatorship. In fact, just before the coup, the right-wing political leadership decided against a military solution and accepted the risk of an electoral confrontation with Left and centre-Left.[38] The political mobilisation and Papandreou's liberalisation measures were more threatening to those occupying key posts in the repressive State and army apparatus (mainly IDEA officers) than to the economic establishment of the country and to those politicians who represented their interests in parliament. The assessment of the situation by the latter was quite realistic. The *objective conditions* for the creation of a genuinely revolutionary situation (which could jeopardise the economic dominance of the bourgeoisie) were as lacking in the Greece of 1967 as they are today.

In fact, looking first at the countryside where the land reforms of the inter-war period had irreversibly abolished big landed property and established the smallholding as the dominant form of ownership in rural Greece,[39] contrary to the situation in Republican Spain or pre-fascist Italy, there is no Greek rural proletariat or land-hungry peasantry which could be mobilised against a class of powerful landlords (who in turn could resort to a fascist solution to maintain its privileges).

Conditions in the towns are equally non-conducive to revolutionary upheaval. Despite the rapid post-war economic growth, industrialisation in Greece is relatively weak and of a type which does not favour the development of a strong and class-conscious industrial proletariat (persistence of artisanal forms of production, of numerous familial, small-sized firms, etc.).[40] So it is not surprising that the Greek trade union movement during most of its history has been under government control.[41] Finally, despite the underdeveloped features of the major Greek towns (i.e. over-inflated service sector, a plethora of parasitic intermediaries etc.), for reasons which cannot be developed here[42] there exists no huge slum-dwelling *Lumpenproletariat* (another possible basis for mass mobilisation in third-world countries).

Given the above socio-economic conditions, and the fact that large-scale emigration in Greece operates as a huge safety valve further eliminating politically explosive situations, one understands why the Greek bourgeoisie intuitively felt that it could maintain its dominance without the establishment of permanent military rule. It is precisely for these reasons that the Greek junta did not succeed, despite its long survival, in sinking deep roots in Greek society — i.e. to transform itself into a fascist or quasi-fascist dictatorship. The same reasons, of course, explain the surprising suddenness and ease with which the dictatorial regime collapsed in July 1974.[43]

4   CONCLUSION

In conclusion, in this chapter I have argued that the role of the army
during the largest part of the inter-war period was quite different from
that of the post-war period and that this difference is linked with the
changing infrastructure of the Greek social formation. Inter-war military
interventions were connected, in a more or less direct manner, to the
monarchy issue, an intra-bourgeois type of conflict which, I think, has its
distant roots in the socio-economic transformation of the 1880s – transformations which generated a new middle class unwilling to accept the old
oligarchic establishment's power monopoly. In other terms, given that a
considerable time lag is often necessary for infrastructural developments to
be felt on the level of politics, I would argue that the monarchy issue and
the type of military interventions associated with it are typical of the
'transition' period.[44] Whereas with the dominance of the capitalist mode
of production and the gradual entrance of the masses into politics, the
issue which gradually became dominant (especially since the 1940s) was
the 'containment of the masses'. Given this situation, the role of the army
changed accordingly: from being partly participant and partly arbitrator to
intra-bourgeois squabbles, it acquired not only a more dominant position
in the power structure, but it also became the overjealous guardian of a
capitalist system which, because of its underdeveloped character, was and
is still generating profound popular unrest and discontent.

7 Capitalism and Dictatorship in Post-War Greece

The seven-year rule of the Greek junta, from 1967 to 1974, has received much attention but little satisfactory analysis. It has been used as the basis for case studies of imperialism, CIA conspiracy, and third-world development. But the specificity of the Greek social formation and its relevance for understanding the roots and nature of the dictatorship remain relatively unexplored. The aim of this chapter is to examine some of the structural causes for the rise and fall of the Greek military regime. It does not attempt an account of the complicated events surrounding the actual seizure of power, but will concentrate on the long-term effects of economic and class developments, for these, although they do not directly determine, set limits to what is possible on the level of the political superstructure at a given historical moment.

First, it is important to emphasise something which will be argued more fully later. By the 1960s, the major axis of strain within Greece was between the *form* of bourgeois rule which had emerged out of the civil war, and the *changes* which Greek capitalism needed to undergo in order to remain competitive. After 1949 the ruling class was no longer threatened. Neither the bourgeois State as such, nor the capitalist mode of production itself were at risk; their enemies had been effectively destroyed for generations. It is necessary to grasp this political fact before considering the development of the Greek economy. The path forward for Hellenic capitalism was never seriously disputed by any section of the ruling class. The latter's crisis, on the contrary, was a political one: how to control the

In an earlier form, this paper was published in *New Left Review*, April 1976.

masses who would have to suffer the 'inevitable' consequences of that path. The choice was straightforward enough: either to 'incorporate' the masses by means of parliamentary democracy, or to subordinate them to direct domination by the army.

1   THE POST-WAR STATE

Despite the fact that the Left constituted the major resistance force during the German occupation and was in actual control of most Greek territory when the occupying forces started withdrawing, for a variety of reasons which cannot be developed here it subsequently suffered a complete military defeat. After its victory, the Right imposed a quasi-parliamentary regime on the country: a regime with 'open' franchise, but systematic class exclusion. The Communist Party was outlawed and an intricate set of legal and illegal mechanisms of repression established in order to exclude left-wing forces from political activity. The job of guaranteeing this regime fell to the agency which had created it: the army. The State was nominally headed by the monarchy, and political power was supposedly vested in parliament. In reality, however, the army, and more specifically a powerful group of anti-communist officers within it, played the key role in maintaining the whole apparatus. We must start, therefore, with a few words about the political conflicts which divided the Greek army during its 1941–44 exile in the Middle East and in particular about the IDEA group (the Sacred Bond of Greek Officers), which was to play a key role in post-war politics.

When Nazi Germany invaded Greece in April 1941, the bulk of the Greek army, along with the royal family and a government-in-exile, embarked for Egypt. Immediately a political cleavage developed, with the Right on the defensive. Within the army, now under the British Middle East Command, as also among the population in the Greek peninsula, it was the Left which took the initiative. The first secret organisation to appear, ASO (Anti-Fascist Military Organisation) was anti-royalist as well as anti-fascist; it made three separate attempts to take control of the army and the government-in-exile.[1] ENA (Union of New Officers), the immediate ancestor of IDEA, emerged in order to counteract the 'subversive' activities of ASO. This conflict between republican and royalist elements in the army was finally resolved by the British authorities. After a 'mutiny' of left-wing soldiers in 1944, the British decided to disband the regiments. They imprisoned left-wing or republican officers and soldiers in various detention camps in Africa and the Middle East. From the remaining personnel a new, 'ideologically reliable' body was formed (the Third Mountain Brigade), which took part in the Italian campaign and later, in December 1944, fought with the British against the Greek communists in mainland Greece.

A group of these rightist Greek officers organised themselves into IDEA.[2] They played a decisive role on the side of the British during the battle of Athens in December 1944; then, after the end of the hostilities and the establishment of a precarious agreement between Left and Right — the Varkiza Agreement of February 1945 — their major effort was to sabotage any permanent compromise settlement. More specifically, they sought to ensure that articles of the Varkiza Agreement which provided for a purge of all those who had collaborated with the Nazis from the army, police and other State agencies would remain a dead letter. In the army, at least, they were very successful. Republican officers appointed immediately after the Varkiza Agreement were dismissed from the forces. Officers who had participated in the Security Battalions (right-wing organisations collaborating openly with the Germans), on the other hand, were readmitted to the service. By 1946 the aims of IDEA were fully achieved: the Greek army was totally purged of 'unhealthy' elements and IDEA officers were firmly established in key positions within it. Once this anti-communist army had been constructed and blooded in the civil war, it was only a matter of time before the same spirit and organisation permeated all other State agencies.

It lies outside the scope of this article to trace all the steps in the establishment of the anti-communist State.[3] Here, it need only be emphasised that after the Communists' final defeat in 1949, with the extermination or imprisonment of thousands of left-wing resistance fighters and their leaders, military reaction assumed full control over the whole of the Greek territory and consolidated a system of repressive parliamentarianism or 'guided democracy'. This was controlled by a triarchy of throne, army and bourgeois parliament. Within this power bloc it was the army, the victor of the civil war, which played the dominant role.

The fact that the officers who controlled the army were royalists did not, most emphatically, mean that the army was a mere instrument of the King. King Paul knew of the existence of IDEA, but both he and especially Queen Frederica were apprehensive of its growing power. The rise of Marshal Papagos whom King Paul did not trust, Papagos' enormous prestige among officers and his successful entrance into politics in 1952 through the creation of a popular right-wing movement (the Greek Rally), were indications of the army's autonomy from the crown.[4] Papagos' electoral successes in 1952 and 1953 confirmed the military's domination of the parliamentary forces. They also marked the beginning of more than a decade of uninterrupted right-wing rule (1952—63), during which the cleavages within the ruling bloc were kept at a minimum and the IDEA group went through a period of quiescence. Although it would be a gross error to see the throne, the army, and the right-wing parliamentary leadership as a monolithic alliance, it is quite true that in the early fifties, when the system of repressive parliamentarianism was working quite smoothly, these three power centres presented a united front to the outside world. Their differences would only emerge once the existing system of political controls could no longer cope with the massive social changes and popular dissatisfaction of the late fifties and early sixties.

As these conflicts were, and are still, more or less directly linked to developments in the infrastructure, it is necessary to make some reference to the model of capital accumulation in post-war Greece.

2   POST-WAR CAPITAL ACCUMULATION

A. The Second World War and the civil war had devastating effects on the Greek economy. For instance, at the end of the Second World War 9000 villages and 23 per cent of all buildings had been destroyed.[5] It was partially a sign of the vitality of Greek capitalism that by the middle of the fifties, pre-war levels of output had been reached again and the economy was growing at a fast rate (the average growth rate in the fifties was 6 per cent).[6]

On the level of relations of production, the post-war Greek model of capital accumulation bears some similarities to nineteenth-century German and French development, in that the banking system, in close collaboration with the State, played a major role in the growth and direction of the productive forces. In fact, the most striking economic characteristic of the post-war era was the spectacular growth and concentration of finance capital and its tight control over the whole of the economy. Whereas during the early inter-war period there was a plethora of small banking establishments, after the 1929 economic crisis amalgamations began. Then, after the civil war, a very complex process of mergers and takeovers resulted in the emergence and consolidation today of a duopolistic situation in which two giant commercial banks control virtually all economic transactions: the National Bank of Greece, which is mainly owned by a variety of public corporations through which the State has majority control, and the privately owned Commercial Bank of Greece. To give an idea of the degree of concentration in banking, it suffices to say that in 1962 the assets of these two concerns amounted to 96.3 per cent of the assets of all Greek commercial banks together.[7] If one also takes into account that Greek banking capital is growing much faster than industrial or merchant capital,[8] the enormous power of these two establishments becomes clear. Between them they handle not only 90 per cent of the country's considerable savings, but also participate directly in the ownership and management of an important part of the insurance and industrial sector. As far as industry is concerned, quite apart from enterprises under direct bank ownership. the banking system has very tight control by means of its credit policies. This control is particularly strict in

Greece because, due to the exceptional weakness of the stock market, not many alternatives for financing are available to Greek entrepreneurs.[9] At least up to the late fifties, Greek industrial and commercial capital was highly dependent on the commercial banks, not only for short-term but also for long-term financing.[10]

The degree of concentration of the banking system is at the same time a clear indication of the extent to which the Greek State controls the economy. For not only does the State control the National Bank (the stronger of the two banking giants), but through its powerful Monetary Commission it regulates in great detail the credit policy of all banks, setting limits on the manner and extent of their operations. It is not, of course, only through the banking system that the State exercises control over the country's economic life. In 1957 its direct investments in the economy amounted to approximately $113 million, i.e. 4.7 per cent of the GNP. This rose to $538 million, or 9.2 per cent of the GNP in 1970. Furthermore, if one considers that the State budget, which constituted 16—17 per cent of the GNP before the war, now amounts to more than one-third of it, one can understand why a Greek Marxist economist in a recent book talks about State-monopoly capitalism in Greece.[11]

But despite the impressive rate of growth, the concentration of finance capital and, through this, the tight State control over the whole social formation, the Greek economy of the fifties did not manage to overcome a major feature of its underdevelopment: its weak manufacturing sector. Greek capital, whether in its mercantile, industrial or finance form, was unable to orient itself towards the manufacturing sector — especially in those key branches (chemicals, metallurgy) which can contribute most to a rapid growth of the industrial sector.

Thus, given the fact that profits were much higher in the commercial sector, it is not surprising to find that the two banking establishments often failed to dispose of the 15 per cent of their funds they were obliged to advance for the development of the industrial sector.[12] Moreover, it should also be taken into account that in the fifties the commercial banks were reluctant, despite pressure from the State, to provide industry, and especially small industry, with cheap credit. For not only was the structure of commercial banking totally unfit for long-term industrial finance, but banking capital could also be placed much more profitably elsewhere. Besides, the strong links of banking capital with the already existing highly inefficient traditional industrial monopolies made it reluctant to help in the creation of serious industrial competitors.[13]

Neither, of course, did Greek capital orient itself towards the agricultural sector. Given the low profitability of agricultural investments, big private capital shunned the countryside even more than it did the manufacturing sector.[14] As far as agriculture is concerned, capital operated in the sphere of circulation rather than production. In fact, whether catering for the domestic or the international market, merchant capital has managed quite effectively to squeeze the small and unorganised farmers and has contributed to a great extent to the *relative* pauperisation of the Greek peasantry and the systematic transfer of resources from the countryside to the urban centres.[15]

As far as shipping is concerned, this was a sector which assumed colossal proportions in the post-war period.[16] In certain respects the impact of post-war Greek shipping on the economy was similar to that of Greek migration to the West. For, as in the case of Greek migrants to Western Europe (mainly Germany), Greek seamen helped the economy by reducing unemployment and by providing valuable foreign currency through their remittances home. On the other hand, since shipping capital lies outside the effective control of the Greek State (it can always be moved elsewhere if the State bothers it with heavy taxes or other restrictions), it becomes increasingly an avenue of escape for Greek merchant capital. In this way, if migration robs Greece of its most valuable human resources, shipping plays a similar role with respect to the country's financial resources.

To sum up, then: until the late fifties Greek capital, ever searching for higher profits and lower risks, preferred to orientate itself mostly on borrowed money[17] towards the non-manufacturing sectors, and then to transfer a substantial share of its revenue either to banks abroad or to shipping. This, not unexpectedly, resulted in Greece exhibiting the usual features of an underdeveloped economy: the tertiary sector expanded rapidly, the feeble manufacturing sector came almost to a standstill, and agriculture remained badly organised. Even as late as the end of the decade, more than half of the working population was employed on the land, and industry managed to contribute no more than 25 per cent to the GNP. Not only is this a low figure as such, but manufacturing was in fact the most laggard in growth of all industrial sectors, with concomitantly an actually decreasing contribution to total output.[18]

The seriousness of this structural weakness of the manufacturing sector becomes more obvious if it is seen against the fact that during the fifties Greece's now communist Balkan neighbours, who had limped so far behind during the inter-war period, were starting to industrialise at a very

Index of Manufacturing Production (1958 = 100)

	1938	1948	1959	1965
Greece	52	34	101	155
Yugoslavia	28	44	114	226
Bulgaria	10	21	121	272
Rumania	24	20	110	248

Source: *United Nations Statistical Yearbook 1966* (from Table 50)

fast rate. The figures in the Table above illustrate strikingly the growing crisis of Greek merchant capitalism in the late fifties and early sixties. Given this type of impasse, and the State's long-term commitment to a free-enterprise economy, there was no solution for Greece other than to resort to the help of foreign capital.

B. It was at the beginning of the sixties that foreign capital (in the form of direct investments) came into the country on a large scale and had a serious impact on the structure of the economy.[19]

By the end of 1973, foreign capital invested in Greece had risen to a total of approximately $725 million,[20] an amount which is not very impressive if one takes into account that in a single year (1969) $2,504 million went to the gross formation of fixed capital in the Greek economy.[21] Nevertheless, as foreign capital was mainly directed to the key manufacturing sectors, its impact on the economy was much greater than its relatively small size would suggest. In fact, especially during and after the years 1962–3, when the metallurgical, chemical and metal construction industries experienced a great boost due to foreign investments, one can speak of a qualitative break in the growth of Greek industry. Not only did the industrial sector start expanding at a much faster rate, but there was an important shift in investment from light consumer goods to capital goods and durables. Whereas in the period 1948–50 light industry represented 77.5 per cent of total manufacturing output, its share went down to 60.9 per cent in 1963–70.[22] This important shift is clearly reflected in the changing structure of the Greek export trade. In 1960 agricultural products constituted 80 per cent of the country's exports, but this figure went down to 54 per cent in 1966 and 42 per cent in 1971, as Greece started to export industrial goods. Thus the sixties saw a qualitative advance in the industrialisation of modern Greece.

There can be little doubt that the ability of the Greek economy to reap the benefits from concentrated foreign investment in manufacturing was due to its own pre-existing capitalist development.[23] This was not able to generate a significant industrial sector autonomously, but it could adapt itself to and consolidate one with exceptional rapidity. Yet this type of capitalist growth not only failed to eliminate some fundamental aspects of Greek underdevelopment, but on the contrary accentuated them, creating disruptions and dislocations which are directly relevant to an understanding of developments in the political superstructure. To assess the scope of such disruption, we shall have to examine how the spectacular growth of the productive forces was linked to the relations of production during the sixties.

The intrusion of foreign capital, in close collaboration with Greek capital and the Greek State, reinforced the already impressive degree of capital concentration in the economy. A first rough intimation of this is conveyed by the enormous size (in terms of assets) of such giants as ESSO-Pappas or Pechiney,[24] or the fact that out of the 200 largest companies in terms of fixed capital, seventeen were fully foreign-owned and in another thirty-nine foreign capital had a degree of participation varying from 10 to 90 per cent.[25] As the share of foreign capital in the GNP steadily increased (from 2.15 per cent in 1962 to 8.15 per cent in 1972), the monopolistic tendencies of the Greek economy were markedly accentuated. In the fifties, monopoly or oligopoly were due mainly to indiscriminate and nepotistic State protectionism; in the sixties they were due rather to the capital-intensive nature of the new industries and the small size of the Greek market.

This impressive concentration of industrial capital did not eliminate the plethora of small industrial units which for the most part are of family-oriented, artisanal character. Indeed, one of the most striking characteristics of Greek industry is the persistence, especially in the more traditional sectors of the economy (footwear, clothing, leather, wood products), of small low-productivity units side by side with large firms that exercise a quasi-monopolistic control of the market.[26] For a variety of reasons, including indiscriminate State protectionism and the inability of small firms to grow,[27] any increase in demand for indigenous industrial products creates a proliferation of additional tiny units instead of consolidating existing ones.[28] These small units remain, on the whole, unspecialised and highly inefficient, and survive only either because their elimination is politically undesirable, or because big industrial capital realises super-profits by tolerating them.

As far as agriculture is concerned, here again one sees the persistence of small, family-based, low-productivity units; very few rural holdings employ wage labour. Despite the dramatic decrease of the agricultural population of the fifties and sixties, there is no marked tendency towards the emergence of large-scale capitalist enterprises in agriculture.[29]

C. By attracting concentrated doses of foreign direct investment, the Greek capitalist class has managed to even out somewhat the imbalance between itself and its northern neighbours. But it has achieved this at the cost of greatly amplifying inequalities at home. The general standard of living, it is true, has undoubtedly risen. Gross per-capita income, approximately $550 at the beginning of the sixties, had reached the $1000 level by the end of the decade.[30] But the few rough calculations which have been made in the absence of complete data leave us in no doubt as to the inequalities which disfigure this spectacular gain. For instance, according to a relatively recent estimate, 40 per cent of the lowest income groups receive 9.5 per cent of the national income (after deduction of taxes and social benefits), whereas the 17 per cent in the top income brackets receive 58 per cent.[31] From 1954 to 1966, when the national income approximately doubled, profits tripled (banking profits between 1966 and 1971 quadrupled).[32] Obviously, as the relative share of big capital increases, the relative share of all other income decreases.

Those engaged in agriculture are, as usual, the worst off. Thus in 1951 agricultural per-capita income amounted to 83.3 per cent of the average national income; the proportion dropped to 60.3 per cent in 1962, and 51.1 per cent in 1971.[33] Given this situation, the mass exodus of the rural population and its migration into the industrial centres of Western Europe is at least partly understandable. Moreover, given the insignificant development of the capitalist mode of production in agriculture, farmers' income differentials are not very important. It is the quasi-totality of the agricultural labour force which is being squeezed by the more or less impersonal mechanisms through which simple agricultural commodity production is incorporated into the capitalist mode of production dominant in the urban centres.

If one now considers the situation in the cities, income differentials here can be seen to have been not only enormous, but continuously increasing. Comparison of industrial wages (at constant prices) with increases in labour productivity show clearly that, in terms of industrial income, the relative share of labour has been decreasing, whereas that of capital has been on the increase.[34] What is also interesting is that, given the coexistence within industry of sectors with very different rates of productivity, there have been increasing inequalities *within* the industrial labour force and *within* the lower middle classes. For instance, with the relative scarcity of skilled labour in the Greek economy, wages have increased at a much faster pace in industries employing a highly skilled workforce — especially those of the new dynamic manufacturing sectors.[35] Similar if not greater income differentials have become discernible among the middle and lower middle classes. Certain white-collar categories (executives, professionals, employees working on advertising, communications or other fast-growing sectors) have seen their incomes rise rapidly beyond those of the rest of the white-collar sector and the 'old' petty bourgeoisie (small shop-owners and craftsmen).[36] These intra-working class and intra-middle class inequalities, which provoke each individual to draw obvious comparisons with the situation of others in the same social milieu, create acute dissatisfaction and frustration among all social groups — from cleaners to colonels.

As far as the State is concerned, it has not done much to change the inequalities generated by the Greek model of capital accumulation. Indirect taxation, which particularly hits low income groups, has not only provided more than half of the enormous State revenue, but also tended to increase in relation to direct taxes. Moreover, even direct taxation seems to hit small and medium incomes harder than big ones.[37]

Finally, the leniency of the State *vis-à-vis* big capital reaches its zenith in the enormous privileges accorded to foreign capital. Taking into account the variety of the privileges which foreign and mixed capital enjoy in Greece (in terms of taxation, credit facilities, cheap energy, etc.), it would not be an exaggeration to say that in many cases industrial expenses and risks are socialised, whereas the fruits of any such industrial success go solely to private capital. In other words, the State revenue derived from the taxation of low incomes is mainly used to consolidate and develop big capital. Of course, given the model of capital accumulation that Greece is following, this taxation policy is congruent and necessary. If the dynamism of the economy is based on the willingness of indigenous and foreign capital to go on investing in Greece, any serious attempt to change the fundamental structure of income distribution would result in a deterioration of the 'favourable climate' for private investment in the Greek economy.

D. To use a more rigorous terminology, the major points may be summed up by saying that the capitalist mode of production, dominant in the Greek social formation, is linked to the mode of simple commodity production (agriculture, 'small' industry) in such a way as to keep growing continuously at the expense of the latter – neither destroying it completely, nor helping it to develop.[38] And it is precisely here that the most crucial difference lies between the Western European and the Greek models of industrialisation. The former involved either the destruction of simple commodity production in agriculture and industry, or its articulated incorporation into the capitalist mode of production through a specialisation which established a positive complementarity with big industry. As a result, the effects of technical progress, which originated in the dynamic sectors, spread fairly quickly to the rest of the economy, with beneficial consequences for income distribution, the expansion of internal markets, and so on. In the Greek social formation, by contrast, capital-intensive industrial production has taken an 'enclave' form. Despite its rapid growth in the sixties, it has not succeeded in expanding or even transferring its dynamism and high productivity to the backward sectors of the economy. Thus simple commodity production looms large within the Greek economy. It gives a lot (directly and indirectly) to the capitalist mode of production, but takes very little in return – just enough to reproduce itself. As a consequence, inequalities in Greece are much greater than those found in the West. For in addition to the usual inequalities between labour and capital in the sectors where the capitalist mode is dominant, Greece has inequalities resulting from the persistence of vast productivity differentials between 'modern' and 'backward' sectors of the economy.

The sharply uneven development of the forces and relations of production in post-war Greece is directly connected to the rising social unrest and political mobilisation of the late fifties and sixties. The inequalities generated by the Greek model of industrialisation – whether seen in terms of income and wealth differentials, of geographical imbalances, or of the way in which different modes of production are articulated in the Greek social formation – have unavoidably created severe disruptions and social unrest.

To illustrate this point one has only to mention the huge rural exodus during the last two decades: out of a population of nine million, a million-and-a-half people have had to leave the countryside. Given the low labour absorption of Greek industry, the majority of these have had to vegetate in parasitic jobs in the tertiary or artisanal sectors, or to emigrate to the industrial centres of western Europe. To a certain extent, massive foreign migration has operated as a political safety valve. It has reduced unemployment in the towns and, through the migrants' remittances, improved the Greek balance of payments and strengthened the meagre incomes of village households. On the other hand, this migration, by dislocating thousands of families, has created resentment and discontent, not only among those who have had to leave their country, but also among those who have been left behind. Moreover, the increased geographical mobility of the population, partially a result of both internal and external migration, has weakened traditional loyalties and orientations, widened the social horizon of villagers and made increasing social inequalities both more visible and less acceptable. These rapid changes have taken place in a country in which a large-scale civil war had already made the rural population politically aware. As a result, the system of patronage through which the Right used to maintain political control of the countryside has been steadily and threateningly eroded.[39]

At the same time the spectacular development of communications — the media, tourism — and, through them, the encouragement of a consumptionist mentality, has created needs and raised expectations far beyond the rise in the standard of living. The capitalist course which Greece embarked upon held out the promise of integration into the capitalist world at large and the European Common Market in particular. But, as a corollary, it involved widespread social disintegration, specifically threatening the political controls established in the aftermath of the civil war.

3   POLITICAL DENOUEMENT

A. What has been described above constituted the basic socio-economic context for the political mobilisation of the late fifties, as right-wing forces gradually lost their hold in the countryside and the towns. A clear sign was the spectacular 1958 election gains of the left-wing party EDA; with the continuing fragmentation of the centre parties, the latter, for a time, became the main opposition in parliament. This development immediately put the whole repressive apparatus on the alert. IDEA was fully reactivated and participated in the elaboration of the notorious 'Pericles' contingency plan; devised for the purpose of neutralising the communists in case of war, this was used instead by the Right to achieve victory in the 1961 elections.[40]

However, this blatant intervention of the para-State in the electoral process was also the starting point of *Anendotos* — the fight against the repressive policies of the Right launched by George Papandreou, who managed to reunite the centre parties. In the 1963 elections, Papandreou's Centre Union successfully challenged the electoral dominance of the Right. In the elections of the following year, it further consolidated its position by gaining an unprecedented 53 per cent majority. Meanwhile, a strong left wing emerged within the Centre Union under the leadership of Papandreou's son Andreas.

When George Papandreou became Premier he made a half-hearted attempt to purge IDEA. A number of rightist officers, including Papadopoulos and some of his close associates, were removed from their key positions and sent to frontier posts. But Papandreou was not willing to attack the structure of the power bloc. He never attempted to deliver an effective blow to the para-State, or to challenge the power of the army except in the most lukewarm manner. Under the pressure of social unrest and mounting political mobilisation, he did seek to liberalise slightly the system of repressive parliamentarianism imposed after the civil war by ending open political intimidation in the countryside. He also placed minor checks on the growing economic inequalities, by slackening controls on wages and increasing State expenditure on education and welfare. But these reforms, together with Papandreou's feeble attempt at gaining control of the military, alarmed and aroused the army officers without seriously limiting their powers.

Nevertheless, Papandreou's moves, however inadequate, combined with the growing political unrest which sustained them, threatened the balance of power between throne, army and parliament. To put it more generally, the Greek model of capital accumulation had created conditions which by the middle sixties were incongruent with the existing political super-structure. By favouring big capital (indigenous, foreign and mixed) at the expense of the rural population, workers and also important sections of the old and new middle classes, it had created a level of discontent which could no longer be contained within the prevailing system of repressive parliamentarianism. This system had to be either abolished, or reinforced by the total removal of parliamentary rule.

To see why this was so we must examine more closely the triarchy of army/parliament/throne, within which the army was dominant. The crucial issue was this 'structure of dominance' itself. An important part of the bourgeoisie, despite its apprehensions at the growing number of strikes and Papandreou's liberalisation policies, did not feel threatened enough to opt for a dictatorial solution. Why should it have? There was no chance of a communist takeover, no revolutionary situation, no serious challenge to the bourgeoisie as a class.[41] The parliamentary Right decided against a dictatorial solution; Kanellopoulos, its leader, finally accepted the risk of an electoral confrontation set for April 1967 and came to a secret agreement with Papandreou.

In 1967, therefore, a solution was possible in which the parliamentary forces, through pressure from the mobilised masses, could have established a less subordinate role in the triarchy. Such a development, however, would have weakened the army's dominance within the State. Obviously, no bourgeois parliamentary State exists without an army to ensure the ultimate rule of the class — *in extremis*. This 'determinate' role of the armed force must be clearly distinguished, however, from control over policy and personnel. It was this aspect of the Greek army's activities which would inevitably have been dissolved by clear-cut election results and the establishment of parliamentary dominance within the State. The formation of a strong parliamentary regime posed no substantial risk to the bourgeoisie as a whole, give or take a few reforms, and certainly did not threaten the existence as such of a Greek bourgeois army. But it would undoubtedly have undercut the position of the actual army within the State, and thus would have had a particularly acute impact on those exercising crucial repressive functions within it. Given the degree of popular support for the left and centre parliamentary forces, it could not hope to retain its hold over parliament by intervention on the hustings, as General Papagos had done so successfully in the fifties. In order to safeguard its rule, it was obliged to make it unilateral and direct.

The third force in the hierarchy — the throne — stood to lose either way. In the previous chapter reference was made to the long-term changes in the structural position of the throne and to the fact that with the advent of mass politics the 'monarchy' issue was increasingly becoming secondary to the 'threat from below' issue. Given the long-term gradual decline in the power position of the throne, the apparent high degree of political power still wielded by this latter-day monarchy stemmed from the degree of manoeuvre allowed it by the conflict between army and parliament. At the apex of both — Commander-in-Chief of the one, appointer of premier to the other — the high tide of royal interference was naturally reached when a hostile stalemate existed. When the politicians hesitated to mobilise support for a real purge of their military counterparts, and the latter held back from direct rule, then the King could 'make history'. This explains the King's ambivalent behaviour during the crisis. He exacerbated political relations when active, prevaricated when faced with a real choice (elections or dictatorship), and was simply impotent when this choice was made by the army without his assent.

B. Although the army was agreed on the need to defend its position by striking pre-emptively to stop the elections, it was also divided. There were two conspiratorial groups: the 'big' junta, on the one hand, and the 'little' junta of IDEA officers under the leadership of Papadopoulos on the other. The latter decided to stage its coup a few days before the date set for the 'big' junta's coup (24 April), and thus to present it and the King with a *fait accompli*.[42]

Less clear, however, are the reasons underlying the split between the 'big' and the 'little' juntas, two groups of officers with fundamentally the same aims. The usual explanation in terms of CIA decision to support lower-ranking officers who were under its direct control is unconvincing and superficial. Unconvincing, because no one has yet shown why the CIA, or any other foreign agency, should have had any interest in taking the enormous risk of withdrawing support from the right-wing establishment in favour of obscure, lower-ranking officers. Superficial, because such an easy explanation draws attention away from the underlying structural reasons within the army itself, which can throw light on this fundamental split, and from the more general conditions in the army conducive to the mobilisation of junior officers for a coup. For while it is clear why the personnel of the two juntas wanted to stage a coup, it is less clear how and why they managed to mobilise and gain the support of those below them.

For an explanation of this, one has to look at the promotion structure of the post-war army. During the civil war, the newly established Greek army had to expand hurriedly. Standards were lowered and the training period shortened so that new officers could be created in large numbers.[43] After the civil war, with the number of top posts limited, there was a serious constriction in the career possibilities of junior officers. According to a reliable report,[44] there were 2000 captains in the Greek armed forces before the 1967 coup. The average rate of promotion was between 100 and 150 annually. Therefore, those who were bottom in seniority would have to wait fifteen years for promotion. A similar problem, although not so acute, existed among officers in higher ranks. In this climate of general dissatisfaction and frustration, it is not surprising to find that prior to the 1967 coup, 200 captains had formed an association for the advancement of their professional interests. Aside from this bottleneck, there was also a distinct class difference between high- and low-ranking officers which accentuated the gulf between them.[45] It is in these terms that one can better understand the split between the two juntas and the reasons why the Papadopoulos group found such fertile ground for its conspiratorial activities among the junior officers.

C. The events of April 1967 in Athens were primarily a struggle between groups within the State. Given the chronic weakness of the Greek bourgeois parties and the dominant position of the army within the enormous State apparatus, this struggle was settled by a straightforward dictatorial solution imposed by the military. In contrast to what happened in Chile, for instance, where the generals managed to organise a massive social campaign and were supported by sizeable sections of the populace in their decision to overthrow Allende, the Greek colonels intervened strictly 'from above', not to defend their country from Marxism but to defend their own role within the State. They not only lacked any popular base in 1967, they were not even able to win one after their seizure of power. As mentioned in the previous chapter, the colonels failed to build the totalitarian structures for mobilising the masses which would have given a fascist character to their rule. Because of this failure, the junta had to operate more or less in a social vacuum. Having no mass base and no strong roots either in the towns or the countryside, in an atmosphere of increasing social discontent its position became more and more precarious. Despite the absence of serious armed resistance, when pressures from below increased, the junta had no means of dealing with them. It could not resort to more repression, since it lacked the means — mass organisation — for embarking on a process of wholesale totalitarian mobilisation. Neither was it able to deal with social discontent through a genuine opening up of the system. The colonels' fierce anti-communism and their belief in a 'disciplined' and 'healthy' political order supervised by the army allowed them to offer only the merest gesture of representation.

Why, then, was there not more widespread opposition to the junta? In the first place, given the overwhelming power of the State and the fact that the working-class movement had been catastrophically defeated and physically decimated in the civil war, armed resistance could find no popular base. Secondly, the working class was not prepared either for organised civil opposition to the junta's seizure of power. The mobilisation around the Centre Union had been party-political in the strictest sense; the CU had never prepared its supporters to defend parliamentary rule as such, for to have done so would have encouraged the masses to impinge directly upon the character of the State. Finally, although the parliamentary and journalistic fragments of the bourgeoisie's political leadership were dismayed by the Papadopoulos coup, they could not oppose its economic policies, for these did not in any way differ from their own.

In fact, the colonels accepted the pre-existing model of capital accumulation and simply sought to remove all obstacles to its full development. Using a dictatorial system of controls, they created a political superstructure designed to deal more effectively with the rising social discontent and to create a more 'favourable' climate for the growth of both indigenous and foreign capital. The liberal mythology now rampant in Greece which portrays the colonels' economic policies as radically different from those of their predecessors is a facile ideological mechanism by which the bourgeoisie is trying to shift the attention of the masses away from the fundamental and persistent contradictions of the post-war Greek social formation.[46]

The colonels, by following the logic of the economic model they had inherited, gave their unlimited support to big capital, foreign and indigenous. They made sure through repression that the ensuing growing inequalities would be accepted unconditionally, without protests or strikes to frighten capital away. After a short period of hesitation, and once the colonels' credentials were fully established, private investment rose again and foreign capital continued its penetration of the Greek economy. The rate of growth soon surpassed pre-dictatorial levels and sustained an impressive acceleration. This achievement was a clear indication of the 'fit' between rapid capital accumulation and the dictatorship. Moreover, as already pointed out, despite growing inequalities, the standard of living grew steadily during the period of the dictatorship. The colonels brought to fruition a process of dependent industrialisation that had started before them. They did not initiate it, but given their capacity to eliminate by force any attempt to disturb this process, they pursued it with ruthless consistency.

On the other hand, though this successful expansion of the productive forces may have contributed to the longevity of the regime, it could not lead to its permanent consolidation. For at the same time, on the level of relations of production, all the trends already mentioned not only continued but were accentuated: increasing concentration of capital, growing inequalities, scandalous concessions to foreign capital, mass migration of labour, sectoral stagnation and the rest. Discontent continued to rise, as social injustice was coupled with large-scale repression. If this discontent did not take a very acute form when the economic going was good, it became more visible and stronger with the economic crisis of 1972–3. In a way, the junta was the first victim of the world recession which brought the expansion of the Greek economy to an end and deprived the dictatorship of its momentum. Politically, the junta's foundations were too shallow for it to survive this down-turn. For even during the pre-recession years of the dictatorship, despite the rising standard of living, the masses refused to legitimise the regime by giving it any significant measure of support.

Passive rejection by the masses was the main reason, of course, for the failure of Papadopoulos' attempt at liberalisation in 1973. On top of this failure and the growing economic crisis came the Athens Polytechnic massacre. Intra-junta fighting then resulted in the fall of Papadopoulos and the rise of Ioannides to the rickety pinnacle of power. All these developments accentuated the structural instability of the regime, cutting it off even further from any popular support. Its isolation meant that, increasingly, there was no correspondence whatsoever between developments in civilian society and the growing in-fighting between army cliques within the State; the base of the regime, already narrow, kept shrinking. From the point of view of this internal dynamic, the Cyprus adventure can be seen as a desperate last-ditch attempt by the Ioannides junta to consolidate its precarious position by gaining popular support through a nationalistic 'triumph'.[47] When the foolishness and miscalculation of this move brought the Greek army to the brink of a disastrous war with Turkey — a war which, both materially and politically, it was not prepared to fight — the immediate response of the general staff was to dissociate itself from the junta. For even if an eventual war had resulted in stalemate, the mass conscription of an already disenchanted populace might have led to a situation where not only army dominance, but even bourgeois rule itself might have been threatened. The leaders of the armed forces, therefore, swallowed their pride and turned to Karamanlis for exactly the same reason that both the 'big' and 'little' juntas had decided to put an end to the growing power of parliament in 1967: namely, in order to preserve the power position of the army intact.

4 THE DEBATE ON THE RISE AND FALL OF THE DICTATORSHIP

Taking into account what has been said above, I would like to comment briefly on the two types of analysis prevalent in the already voluminous literature on the Greek dictatorship. The first, in a highly simplistic manner, portrays the policies of the CIA and other American agencies as the main reason behind the rise and fall of the dictatorship.[48] The CIA is often represented as an omniscient and omnipotent deity regulating and controlling everything and everybody. Now there is no doubt that the CIA, both before and after 1967, had strong links with the IDEA officers and with the whole repressive apparatus of the State.[49] But there is equally no doubt that these links have often been exaggerated and a great number of myths created concerning the extent of CIA control over Greek affairs.[50] Given the scarcity of serious evidence, the extent and nature of foreign intervention in the 1967 coup and the events that followed it will long remain debatable. But what is certain is that it was limited, at least in the short term, by the socio-economic structure of the country.[51] It is this structure which is most relevant if one wants to go beyond *ad hoc* and superficial explanations of the Greek crisis.

On the other hand, those more serious Marxist analyses which shift attention away from the CIA towards the role of the class struggle, unfortunately often adopt an equally facile style of reasoning. By trying to establish *direct* links between the role of big capital (foreign or indigenous) and the emergence or fall of the dictatorship, they arrive at explanations which are hardly more convincing than the 'CIA' ones.

Developments in the class structure are, of course, crucial for understanding the dynamics of the Greek dictatorship. But the links between them and the politico-military events which led to the abolition of repressive parliamentarianism are much more complicated than simplistic ready-made formulas would suggest. For instance, there is no doubt that the coup was bourgeois in its general class character, in the sense that (1) big capital, merely by playing its normal role of making maximum profits in the context in which it had to operate, was at the source of the increasing inequalities and disruptions which generated the social unrest and mobilisation in the fifties and sixties; (2) important fractions of the bourgeoisie, by adopting an alarmist attitude towards the mildly liberal policies of Papandreou, created a climate highly favourable to the realisation of the military's aims; (3) the policy of the junta was to intensify the capitalist development of Greece. Yet these very obvious facts do not mean that 'the Greek bourgeoisie' or any of its fractions should be shown as the 'creators' of the coup, whose architects must be politically and institutionally defined — the IDEA colonels, highly specific interests within the previously existing State structure, etc.

Let us take a closer look at the type of theory which sees the rise and fall of the dictatorial regime as basically the result of in-fighting among different fractions of capital. For instance, according to Poulantzas,[52] the basic dimension for understanding both the rise and fall of the Greek dictatorship is the conflict between what he calls the 'interior' bourgeoisie (a more liberal fraction of indigenous capital which collaborates with European monopolies) and the more traditional, commercially oriented comprador bourgeoisie (which is much more dependent on American capital). However, despite the fact that this intra-bourgeois conflict is the foundation of Poulantzas' book, he provides no real evidence for any such conflict either before or after 1967 — indeed, he fails to provide any convincing empirical account of the existence of the two fractions at all. In fact, not only is there no serious evidence that these two fractions existed, considered their interests as opposed, and were fighting each other; but even from the point of view of *objective* class 'places' there is no reason to believe that such interests would have diverged significantly anyway. Given the close collaboration of autochthonous and foreign capital, and given the fact that foreign capital was mainly directed by the Greek banking and investment institutions into areas where Greek commercial capital was unwilling or unable to go, it seems obvious that such interests were more complementary than antagonistic.

Another and even more important reason for dismissing this type of explanation is the great dependence of the bourgeoisie on the State, and the overriding importance of the latter in the Greek social formation. There is nothing more misleading than to present the Greek State in such a passive manner — so that alleged conflicts between fractions of capital could more or less automatically lead to a change in political regime. I have already mentioned the extent to which the State, through direct investment and through its control of finance capital, influences the Greek economy. In order to give some historical perspective to this fundamental point, it should be recalled that at the beginning of the nineteenth century, when Greece emerged as an independent nation, a variety of causes brought about a spectacular development of State power and institutions, at a time when the autochthonous Greek bourgeoisie was insignificant and the forces of production were in a rudimentary state of development. Contrary to what happened in eighteenth-century England, for instance, the Greek indigenous bourgeoisie was highly dependent on the State for its consolidation and growth.[53] As Vergopoulos puts it:

'The functioning axis of the Greek social formation was not bourgeois civil society, as a certain liberal theory would imply, but the State. Ever since the middle of the nineteenth century, nothing could be done in

Greece without it necessarily passing through the machinery of the state. The State apparatus, as Gramsci would say, was the social machine *par excellence*.'⁵⁴

The State, as the general co-ordinator of the whole social formation, had to provide a favourable institutional framework for the enlarged reproduction of the capitalist mode of production — i.e. it had to use its enormous power to safeguard and promote bourgeois interests. In particular, after the civil war, the Greek State had to play its co-ordinating role in the absence of a Western-type, mass social-democratic party. In a political system characterised by 'modern' bourgeois mass parties, the autonomy of the State *vis-à-vis* the dominant classes is not so high as in cases where such parties do not exist. In the latter case, as the Greek experience shows clearly, it is easier for shifts of power to occur *within* the State; they then can present the bourgeoisie as a whole with an accomplished fact.

In conclusion, even if one admits a certain conflict of economic interests among fractions of the bourgeoisie before 1967, this conflict never assumed significant proportions. What the dominant classes had in common was infinitely more important than what divided them. The fundamental contradiction was between, on the one hand, an expanding model of capital accumulation which, by creating severe disruptions and inequalities, was mobilising and radicalising the masses; and, on the other hand, a political system of repressive controls, engineered to prevent the masses from taking an autonomous part in the political process. Confronted with the rising tide of political mobilisation, repressive parliamentarianism — characterised by the throne—army—parliament alliance in which the army was dominant — could no longer survive. Either parliament, through its opening up to the masses, had to become the dominant force in this triarchy, in which case the army would lose its leading position with inevitable internal consequences for those holding posts within it; or else the army had to prevent this by the overall abolition of parliamentary rule.

I have tried to show why, given the different reactions of various fractions within the power bloc and certain structural characteristics of the post-war army organisation, the latter solution ultimately prevailed. I have also tried to show how the persistence of the contradition between capital accumulation and political control after 1967 is relevant for understanding both the unpopularity and the collapse of the dictatorship. For the dictatorial regime proved as inadequate to cope, in a lasting way, with the disruptions created by the growth of the Greek economy as the repressive parliamentary order that had preceded it. It remains to be seen whether the new presidential regime of Karamanlis will be more successful in coping with the inequalities and social unrest which the further development of capitalism cannot but continue to generate in the Greek social formation.

8 On Greek Formalism: Political and Cultural Aspects of Underdevelopment

1 EXAMPLES OF GREEK FORMALISM

A striking characteristic of political and cultural practices in the Greek social formation is the extent to which conflicts and debates take a formalistic-legalistic character, shifting the attention of the masses away from 'substantive' issues (i.e. issues related to fundamental class antagonisms and to conflicting views of the world).

A. Concerning political practices, a typical political debate in Greece either takes the form of metaphysical discussions on such concepts as freedom, democracy, socialism, etc. – concepts which, used in a totally abstract manner, are far removed from the everyday problems and experience of the citizen; or it takes the opposite form: intense verbal competition on a purely personal level. Obviously, the two levels, the personal and the formalistic, are linked in a complementary manner. More often than not, behind the various abstractions and lofty ethical principles one finds particularistic interests and personal ambitions – not surprisingly so if one considers the still clientelistic orientation of most Greek politicians and parties.[1]

It is not difficult to see that this combination of verbalistic and personalistic orientations to political life is an effective mechanism for the maintenance of the *status quo*. It contributes, even more than any hegemonic ideology, to the systematic expulsion from the political arena of issues referring to class differences and to problems of basic reform. Of course, none of these 'displacement' mechanisms are specifically Greek phenomena. They exist in most political systems, and particularly in those of the underdeveloped countries. However, I think that in Greece political formalism, as a means for the maintenance of the *status quo*, has taken such proportions that it must be regarded as one of the distinguishing characteristics of modern Greek society.

Consider for instance the structure and development of Greek inter-war politics. Its main feature was the famous *dichasmos*, the split between Venizelists and anti-Venizelists[2] over the issue of the monarchy. Thus, at a time when all other Balkan countries had strong agrarian movements and parties which, more or less successfully, were trying to promote peasant interests, the throne issue managed to disorient the Greek peasants and draw them into a conflict which had very little relevance to their own interests. How far this conflict was removed from true peasant interests is seen by the fact that the miserable condition of the Greek peasantry changed very little after the monarchy had been abolished in 1923 and in the ten years of the subsequent Greek republic.[3]

The specific reasons for the Greek peasantry's failure to organise itself politically have been developed in Chapter 5. Here, I would like to focus on a discussion of the problem which is more general, i.e. applies to a type of political formalism which does not simply characterise peasant inter-war politics, but which runs through the whole of modern Greek history. For instance, a similar process of mystification and disorientation of the masses repeated itself a bit later after the disastrous end of the Greek campaign in Asia Minor in 1923. In this campaign the Greek bourgeoisie tried to make its dream of a Greater Greece come true by extending the frontiers of the Greek state across the Aegean Sea and establishing a Greek province in Asia Minor – in past centuries the home of prospering Greek minority communities. The total failure of this highly unrealistic military adventure brought more than a million Greek refugees to settle in mainland Greece. In the explosive situation which resulted from this massive influx of uprooted and totally dispossessed people, the *dichasmos* again worked miracles as a conservative mechanism. All these people, instead of turning their justified anger and frustration against both bourgeois parties as really co-responsible for this enormous fiasco, were drawn into operating politically within the *dichasmos* framework. They ended up by considering the royalists, who had been in power at the time of the defeat, as entirely responsible for the debacle and gave their massive support to Venizelos, who had actually been the architect of this imperialistic folly.[4] The Asia Minor catastrophe had another important impact on the ideological structure of the Greek social formation: it marked the end of the *Megali Idea* (the Great Idea), the grandiose vision of more or less resurrecting the lost Byzantine empire and reinstating Constantinople as the great spiritual centre of Hellenism. The sudden death of this dream left a great gap in the ideological armoury of the dominant Greek bourgeoisie. So the continuing *dichasmos* and, more generally, the personalistic-formalistic feuds continued to play an important role as mechanisms for the preservation of the *status quo*.[5]

These mechanisms did not stop with the inter-war period: despite the more direct links between class structure and politics in post-war Greece, the tendency of the political system to displace substantive issues by formalistic feuds is still quite strong. Such 'displacement' mechanism can be seen operating not only on the macro-political level but also in more restricted areas of social life. The student movement and the post-dictatorial educational reforms is a very good example. Immediately after the junta's fall the students, taking into account their role in bringing about the demise of the junta, possessed the prestige and the power to generate very radical changes in the antiquated Greek educational system. However, all this enormous potential was literally squandered in either struggling for the 'dejuntaisation' of the universities (i.e. removing from teaching posts all personnel who had collaborated with the junta), or in ultra-revolutionary rhetoric, very much removed from the immediate and pressing educational problems. The result was predictable: all that was achieved was a few changes in the teaching staff, while the basic institutional structure of the rigid and oppressive educational system remains intact.[6]

B. Formalism on the cultural level, being more obvious, needs less elaboration. A few striking examples will suffice to illustrate the phenomenon.

The split in the modern Greek language between *demotiki* (the popular, living language) and *katharevousa* (the 'pure', archaic language-construct) and the interminable battles fought over it, is surely unique even among countries with important ancient literatures. As a result of this split all Greek children up to the very recent present, were obliged to learn both *demotiki* and *katharevousa* at school — in addition, of course, to learning ancient Greek. The difference between the two versions of modern Greek is not the usual difference to be found in all literate societies between colloquial and literary speech, neither does it simply express class or regional variations. *Demotiki* and *katharevousa* have, to a great extent, different vocabularies and different grammatical rules, the *katharevousa* being an attempt to artificially re-create past linguistic forms and to impose them on both written and oral communication. The ultimate aim of the *katharevousa* movement is to replace to the maximum degree the 'vulgar' living language with one which would approximate more closely to that of the 'glorious ancient ancestors'. Needless to say, the school-children, being made to learn both, end up by learning neither properly. The conservative function of this linguistic split is quite easy to see. Not only does it create a great cultural chasm between the few who have mastered *katharevousa* (and who therefore have access to government publications, scientific textbooks, etc.) and the rest of the population; its artificial and archaic character has a deadening effect on all education and is the royal road to formalistic thinking — which is to say non-thinking.[7]

Another relevant example of cultural formalism is the manner in which ancient Greek is taught in the Greek secondary school (gymnasium). The emphasis on linguistic form is such that hardly any attention is paid to the content of the ancient texts which are being analysed. After six years' intensive lessons in ancient Greek, the typical Greek pupil knows by heart all the irregular verbs and the complicated rules of grammar and syntax, but has hardly any idea of the philosophy and teachings of the great classical writers. It is not surprising, therefore, that Greek gymnasium graduates, despite their longer schooling, seem so totally ignorant when compared with those of their counterparts who studied classics in Western Europe.

A final example: the fact that in Greek universities the mastery of a field of study, as far as examinations are concerned, usually still means the memorising of the professor's textbooks or notes, is another clear indication of the extreme formalism which characterises the entire Greek educational system.8

2   A TENTATIVE EXPLANATION

All the above examples are mere illustrations of the high degree of political and cultural formalism in Greece and the conservative role it plays — they do not give an explanation for it. As this all-pervasive style runs through the whole of modern Greek history, its systematic explanation is an extremely complex affair requiring analysis of the genesis and development of the major Greek institutions, in the context of the class struggles which can ultimately account for them. Such an enterprise is beyond the scope of this essay, however. All that can be attempted here is not a full answer to the problem, but a few suggestions indicating the areas where one should look for one. Hopefully these suggestions will also help to clarify further the concept of underdevelopment analysed in Chapter 2.

A. I would like to start with a brief dismissal of the usually psychologistic theories which attempt to account for Greek formalism in general and its various manifestations in the political and educational system in terms of the Greek 'national character' or the moral qualities of Greek politicians and teachers; or those socio-psychological theories which point to the faulty socialisation of Greek children at home and at school.[9] Such theories are inadequate, if only because they in turn would have to explain (and cannot do so within their frame of reference) why the Greek school and family socialise the children in the way they do, or why Greek politicians are so 'corrupt'. Actually, to take the second case as an example, if in Greece much more than in the West particularistic interests are hidden behind the formalistic political debates, this does not mean that Greek politicians are more hypocritical or egocentric as individuals than their Western European counterparts. It is merely that the latter operate within an institutional framework which allows them to realise their ambitions and use their talents by tackling issue of a more collective and substantive character. Whereas in Greece the political framework is such that unavoidably the fulfilment of any ambition (egocentric or not) is only possible by following the logic of patronage and the formalistic rules of the political game. It is for these reasons that, I believe, a more satisfactory explanation of the Greek tendency to transform substance into form must rather be of a historical and sociological character.

B. To start with, there could be a fairly general explanation of the phenomenon of political and cultural formalism. In all societies where institutions did not develop endogenously but, together with advanced technologies, were introduced or rather imposed by Western imperialism, the organic links between native and imported institutions are often lacking. The latter either play a purely decorative role (like parliaments in some African countries) or, when they take strong roots in the host country, do not merge effectively with the older institutional structures. Their co-existence is such that neither of the two works properly. *One* of the results of this disjunction is usually formalism on both the institutional and action levels.[10]

There is an interesting parallel here with developments in the infrastructure. I have already discussed the striking difference in the manner in which the capitalist mode of production works in metropolitan and peripheral countries as the essence of underdevelopment. Just as at the economic level, capitalism articulates negatively with the pre-existing forces and relations of production, so on the superstructural level, imported political and cultural institutions are 'negatively' linked with the indigenous ones. If capitalism takes an 'enclave' form on the level of the economy, imported political and ideological institutions occupy a similar position in the political superstructure. They neither destroy nor integrate positively pre-capitalist superstructural forms. The imported political and cultural ones function in a manner which is (*a*) totally different from the way they function in the metropolitan centres (*anti-evolutionist thesis*), and (*b*) less effective and satisfactory from the point of view of the interests of the majority of the people concerned (*misgrowth thesis*).[11] If on the level of the economy this lack of effectiveness, this disarticulation, results in a wasteful and anti-popular utilisation of economic resources (unemployment, non-productive use of surplus, transfer of wealth abroad), on the level of the superstructure it takes the form of political and cultural arrangements which ensure perpetuation of the infrastructural bottlenecks and contradictions. This precisely is the distinctive contribution of formalism to the maintenance of the *status quo*. To put it in another way, if economic underdevelopment is a process whereby the penetration of Western capitalism into third-world social formations mobilises and then misallocates indigenous economic resources (i.e. allocates them in a way which profits the metropolitan centres and a small local oligarchy to the detriment of the indigenous populations) — political and cultural underdevelopment is the process whereby the importation of Western political and cultural institutions results in the mobilisation of ideological resources (political support, legitimation) for the maintenance of the *status quo*, i.e. for the development of economic underdevelopment.

If one tries to see this process from the point of view of classes, one can argue that in an underdeveloped political system the ruling classes deal with the mobilisation of the rural and urban working classes (a concomitant of the dominance of the capitalist mode of production in a social formation) in a way which prevents their entrance into politics as *autonomous* political forces. For the autonomous political organisation of the peasantry or the proletariat is incongruent with the type of accumulation which characterises capitalist underdevelopment, in the sense that a politically autonomous working class would not accept the enormous inequalities and the one-sided sacrifices that are a precondition for the dynamic growth of the economy (cf. Chapter 7, section 2).[12] Given this situation, there are only two broad political alternatives which, in the long term, are congruent with the type of foreign-led capital accumulation characterising underdeveloped social formations today:

(*a*) The one is to use imported bourgeois parliamentary institutions in such a way that the masses are either kept outside active politics or are brought into the political process in a dependent, 'safe' manner. Before the dominance of the capitalist mode of production, as mass mobilisation is at a minimum, it is relatively easy for the traditional ruling oligarchy, even under conditions of universal suffrage, to control through clientelism the voting system in such a way that the working population is kept 'in its place' (cf. Chapter 6). But with the dominance of capitalism and the ensuing advent of mass politics, the problem of 'containing' the masses, i.e. the problem of politically integrating the working classes in a dependent manner, becomes much more difficult and problematic. One mode of 'dependent integration' is the way in which peasants and refugees were integrated into the dominant bourgeois, clientelistic parties in inter-war Greece (cf. above, Chapter 5); another is the way in which in some Latin American countries populist/charismatic leaders mobilise the masses while at the same time they monitor their trade union and political organisations from above, through paternalistic/quasi-corporatist state controls (e.g. Peron in Argentina). A third mode of dependent integration consists in restricting parliamentary 'freedom' to bourgeois parties only and using a variety of legal, quasi-legal or illegal techniques for excluding left-wing forces from the political process (this was the situation which prevailed in Greece during the two decades after the civil war – cf. Chapter 7).

(*b*) The other major political alternative, especially when the various modes of dependent integration fail, is of course to abolish parliamentary institutions altogether and to try, through dictatorial means, to reverse the process of mass mobilisation: i.e. to depoliticise the masses and exclude them from active politics. Given that this second alternative, as I have argued with the 1967 Greek dictatorship, is not necessarily more stable than the previous ones, one may witness an alternation of dictatorial and quasi-parliamentary solutions as the ruling classes try to cope with the problems of mass mobilisation and popular discontent generated by capitalist underdevelopment.

In conclusion, the basic difference between the political system of developed and underdeveloped capitalist social formations is that, in the former, capitalism is congruent with the relatively autonomous trade union political organisation of the working classes, whereas in the latter it is not.[13] Or to put it more cautiously, the forces and relations of production in developed capitalism provide a framework which makes possible (although, of course, not certain) the autonomous organisation of the working classes; whereas in underdeveloped capitalist countries the infrastructural setting does not leave much room for such an autonomous political solution. Therefore in the latter case the 'entrance of the masses' problem is dealt with either by dictatorial attempts at exclusion and depoliticisation or by quasi-parliamentary attempts at dependent integration. Given the above, it is easy to see why imported parliamentary institutions function both differently and in a less satisfactory manner (from the point of view of the majority of the population) in underdeveloped countries.

C. Greece, like many other 'late-comers' experienced a massive injection of Western culture, especially at the beginning of the nineteenth century, when she was established as an autonomous State. The previous four centuries of Ottoman rule gave Greek institutions a structure radically different from those of the West. Greece did not experience the great socio-political transformations which, following the feudal crisis of the fourteenth and fifteenth centuries, completely changed the face of Western Europe in the sixteenth century and led two centuries later to the development of industrial capitalism and its concomitant bourgeois political and cultural institutions (political liberalism, enlightenment, etc.). In the sixteenth century, when Western finance and commercial capitalism were inflicting severe blows on the disintegrating feudal system, Greece was an impoverished province of a patrimonial empire. Later on, the development of industrial capitalism and the creation of a world-wide capitalist market simply swallowed up the declining Ottoman empire and its Greek provinces as mere agrarian adjuncts to the dynamic Western centres.

Thus the large-scale adoption of Western institutions and civilisation during and after the revolution of 1821 unavoidably clashed with a pre-existing institutional setting characterised by a pre-capitalist, underdeveloped economy, a patrimonial structure of political controls, and the anti-enlightenment, anti-Western ideology of the Christian Orthodox Church.[14]

Of course, the clash between Western and indigenous institutions and the ensuing disjunctions (including formalism) are not unique to Greece; they are seen, for instance, in most ex-colonial countries of Africa and Asia.[15] However, in order to account for the specific form that this clash took in Greece, one must (a) place it within the context of the early class-struggles during the formation of the modern Greek State, and (b) find other distinguishing characteristics of the Greek social formation which can explain the extraordinary proportions attained by political and cultural formalism in the country.

3   THE AUTOCHTHONOUS OLIGARCHY AND THE IMPORTATION OF PARLIAMENTARY INSTITUTIONS

By the early nineteenth century Greece, as a province of the Ottoman empire, had gone a long way to becoming a peripheral, underdeveloped area of Europe. Its integration into the capitalist world market and its ensuing commercialisation of agriculture had brought profound changes in its class structure. In the countryside there was considerable concentration of land property at the expense of the small peasant owner, and a general deterioration in the living conditions of poor peasants. The latter had to endure a dual domination: that of the decaying and increasingly rapacious Ottoman State, and that of Western capitalism.[16] Elsewhere, similar developments took place: the artisanal industries which had flourished in Greece in the eighteenth century, unable to compete with Western industry, were completely destroyed at the beginning of the nineteenth century. Even the formidable shipping industry had to weather a very severe crisis which ruined the small shipowners and captains.[17]

Prior to the 1821 revolution, then, mainland Greece witnessed on the one hand the pauperisation of its peasantry and small artisans, and on the other the strengthening of the landowning classes, which, with the commercialisation of agriculture, were actively involved in import-export activities. Apart from the indigenous landowners/merchants and the big island shipowners, another group which profited greatly from the expansion of Western capitalism was the diaspora Greek bourgeoisie who played a crucial intermediary role in the trade between Western Europe and the Ottoman empire.[18]

This group, in contrast to the autochthonous landowner/merchants, played a leading role in the development of Greek nationalism and in the mobilisation of the peasantry against their Ottoman rulers. In fact, the Western-educated intelligentsia and part of the diaspora bourgeoisie not only provided the leadership and material resources of the revolutionary movement, but by disseminating French revolutionary ideas and Western culture generally on the mainland, they were the real catalysts for directing the peasant unrest towards nationalistic-revolutionary goals. Having the bulk of their fortunes outside Greece, the diaspora bourgeoisie were not running any great risks from the emergence of a modern Greek State, provided of course it remained within the capitalist division of labour imposed by the West — i.e., provided this new State rid itself of only the Ottoman, not the Western yoke. The autochthonous landowning/ merchant groups on the other hand, fearing that a war of liberation against the Turks might also jeopardise their own dominant position, were very lukewarm towards the revolution. They only joined it when they realised its inevitability, as well as the higher risks they were running by boycotting it.[19]

The only class whose objective interests were opposed to both the Ottoman and Western domination were, of course, the peasants and the urban poor.[20] And although it is from these classes that the bulk of the revolutionary forces later arose, ultimately they played a very small role in the shaping of the modern Greek State. After the 1824 civil war which defeated the popular forces, the 'masses' disappear from the scene of internal political strife.[21] From that date on and for several years to come, the basic conflict will be between the representatives of the two dominant classes: the autochthonous conservative landowning class, and the Western-oriented intelligentsia whose interests and views reflected those of the diaspora bourgeoisie. The former would ideally have liked to replace the departing Turks in their leading positions without effecting any funda-mental changes in the institutional structures bequeathed them by the Ottomans — whereas the latter wanted to 'modernise', i.e. Westernise Greek society along the liberal bourgeois lines of the European Enlighten-ment.

Thus, during the early revolutionary years, in most struggles and debates over the structure and role of the Greek State a basic split can be discerned between the 'modernisers' and the 'traditionalists'.[22] The latter were in favour of customary law, a weak army, and a decentralised ineffective executive which would leave intact their local power and prerogatives; the modernisers wanted the importation of Western legal codes and a strong, centralised State apparatus to unify the country by breaking up the military and political autonomy of the local potentates.

In this basic conflict the traditionalist, landowning classes were stronger in the sense that, being more deeply rooted in the Greek mainland, they were much more in control of local resources. However, the modernisers not only possessed administrative, diplomatic and legal skills which were indispensable for the running of the newly-born State, but also had greater support from the diaspora bourgeoisie and the foreign powers. With regard to the role played by the latter, it is well known that regional fragmen-tation during the revolutionary years was so strong that no internal force could emerge capable of imposing unity on the revolutionary forces, whether by force or persuasion. Thus the incessant fighting between regional fractions came very near to jeopardising the whole insurrectionist effort. It was only through the intervention of the three great powers

(France, England, Russia) that the Greek revolution was rescued from total collapse, and that the monarchical institution was imposed as a means of unifying the country. Of course this type of unity, maintained by pressure from outside, only reflected on the political level the dependency which already characterised Greece on the economic one. It is understandable therefore why the 'modernisers', despite their lack of material resources, managed to imprint their own views on the structure of the modern Greek State.[23]

However, in so far as foreign domination was leaving them any room to manoeuvre, the victory of the modernisers was very partial indeed. For if the traditional notables had to accept the new political and legal framework imported from abroad, they managed to distort it to such an extent that their basic privileges were left pretty well intact. More precisely, when it became obvious to them that regionalism was no longer viable and that it would be impossible to stem for long the expansionist tendencies of the State, they endeavoured to control it from within. Thus they tried to compensate for the loss of their local political autonomy by controlling the key posts of the expanding central bureaucracy.[24]

For such control the imported parliamentary institutions provided an excellent means, of course. It is not surprising, therefore, that the first constitutions drafted during the revolutionary years were the most democratic and liberal of Europe. And although these first constitutions were never seriously implemented, Western parliamentarianism – after a short period of absolutist rule (1828–43) – took strong roots in Greece. In fact, despite its obvious and continuous malfunctioning,[25] the representative system of government showed a remarkable resilience. It operated more or less uninterruptedly from 1843 to 1909. In a way it was its very malfunctioning which explains its astonishing longevity. For the dominant classes in the nineteenth-century Greece found in the parliamentary form a very effective way of maintaining or even furthering their interests. In fact, the famous *tzakia*, the oligarchic families dominating the various regions of nineteenth-century Greece, used the representative system of government as a means of protecting their privileges from *both above and below*. At the local level, using the traditional forms of patronage and clientelism, they could easily control the voting process and safeguard their representation in parliament. At the national level, their control of parliament was an effective brake on the absolutist tendencies of the Greek throne.[26]

I think that the above very sketchy analysis, although it provides no full explanation, does point out some of the mechanisms behind the specific form the disarticulation between imported and local political institutions took in Greece. It shows some of the reasons why parliamentarianism, although strongly rooted in the Greek mainland, was articulated with pre-existing political structures in such a way that the whole political system was made to function differently and less satisfactorily than in the West.

In the latter case, the development of bourgeois parliamentary institutions went hand in hand with the development of capitalism; Western political parties managing to organise and express effectively broad class interests. Greek parliamentarianism, implanted at a time when the capitalist mode of production was peripheral in the social formation, functioned in a very different manner.[27] The nineteenth-century Greek oligarchy used it as a means, not for overthrowing the inherited Ottoman structure, but for safeguarding as many of its features as possible. Of course, at a later stage, the development of capitalism broke down the political monopoly of this oligarchy and made possible the participation, first of the rising middle classes, and later of the working classes in the political process. But even after the dominance of the capitalist mode of production and the gradual advent of mass politics, as shown in the previous chapters, the underdeveloped type of capitalism that prevailed in Greece was incongruent with the autonomous political organisation of the rural and urban masses and therefore with the effective functioning of parliamentary institutions. Therefore a variety of methods were and are still used to bring the masses into the political process in a dependent, subservient manner. It is from such a perspective that, I think, one should look at the persistence of clientelism[28] and the resulting formalistic/personalistic overtones of the Greek parliamentary process. Its tendency to distort and conceal class differences through legalistic debates and personalistic feuds must be seen as one aspect of political underdevelopment — i.e. one aspect of the overall attempt to prevent the autonomous expression and articulation of working-class interests in the political process.

4   THE DIASPORA BOURGEOISIE AND THE OVER-INFLATED CHARACTER OF GREEK SOCIETY

If the role of the indigenous oligarchy is relevant to understanding the formalistic character of Greek politics and culture, the diaspora Greek bourgeoisie has contributed to the accentuation of this formalism in a very different way. In fact, the most striking peculiarity of Greek capitalism is the formidable financial power and the crucial role which the Greek merchants living abroad played not only during the War of Independence but also in the post-independence period. It would not be an exaggeration to say that in certain respects the forces which exerted the most central influence in the shaping of the nineteenth-century Greek society lay outside mainland Greece. Whether one looks at the development of Greek nationalism, the development of the Greek economy before and after independence, or the growth of the post-independence political, educational and other cultural institutions, it has always been the contribution of the diaspora Hellenes which was decisive.[29]

Thus it is only in terms of the generous contributions of the diaspora

Greek communities that one can explain the over-inflated character of the Greek educational system, the development of which was completely out of proportion to the limited indigenous resources of the nineteenth-century Greece. For instance, it has been calculated that up to 1870 the ten top donations to education by rich Greeks living abroad were in total much higher than the State's entire education budget.[30] And it is not unrelated to this precocious educational growth that relative to its population Greece today has one of the highest ratios of university graduates in Europe.[31] It is also largely in terms of the formidable growth of the diaspora merchant class before and after independence that one can explain why Greece, up to the Second World War, had the most commercialised economy in the Balkans, with a high degree of urban-isation and an over-inflated service sector not explicable in terms of the relatively weak indigenous merchant class.[32] In other words, in addition to the influence exercised on the Greek social formation by Western imperialism, the Greek diaspora and its strong links with the mainland meant that, *even more than other undeveloped countries, nineteenth-century Greece lacked indigenous sources of growth.* To understand its dynamism and direction therefore, one must look *outside* rather than inside the country's legal boundaries. This influence by remote control, this lack of organic connections between the indigenous social forces and the spectacular developments in crucial areas of social life have, I believe, much to do with the rootless, precarious and formalistic character of Greek institutions.

5   CULTURAL UNDERDEVELOPMENT AND THE ANCIENT GREEK
    HERITAGE

This rootlessness, this lack of indigenous growth left its clear imprint on the cultural level. For not only the political institutions, but also most of the country's dominant ideological-cultural orientations have a Western origin. If one remembers that even the attachment of the modern Greek to his antique past was imported from abroad, as developed by the Europe of the Renaissance and the Enlightenment,[33] one realises the extent to which there is an insufficient organic connection (i.e. a disarticulation) between the dominant culture and the live cultural traditions which grew up spontaneously during the four centuries of Ottoman rule. Just as in the case of all other Western imports, the orientation to and appreciation of classical antiquity, as soon as it had been adopted in Greece, again functioned in a way both different from and less satisfactory than in the West. There, the revival of classical studies was a catalyst and an aspect of the overall complex liberating movement which destroyed the closed medieval community with its scholastic modes of thought and spectacu-larly reasserted the faith in the individual, in scientific thought, in human reason, etc. These humanistic values which the West partly expressed through its rediscovery of the ancient Greek and Latin cultures, were increasingly lost as soon as the preoccupation with the classical heritage was transplanted to Greece. Mainland Greece, under the cultural dominance of the Orthodox Church during the long period of Ottoman rule, never experienced a renaissance and the accompanying socio-political changes.[34] So it is not surprising that when this interest in classical antiquity was transferred to Greece in the late eighteenth and nineteenth century, it played a very different role in the country's social and educational life than in the West.

Consider for instance Adamantios Korais, the main figure of the Greek enlightenment and a diaspora Greek who lived most of his creative life in France. His brilliant work reflects a profound assimilation of the values of political liberalism, humanism and admiration of classical antiquity. His translations and analyses of numerous ancient Greek texts as well as his other writings have contributed more than any other Greek scholar's work to the development of Greek nationalism and the dissemination of French enlightenment culture in mainland Greece. However, his work was distorted by his disciples in Greece who, operating in a socio-cultural context strikingly different from the French, completely discarded his libertarian political and religious ideas, and rejected their master's advocacy of a compromise solution to the language problem. Concerning this latter point, the prominent literary historian Dimaras tells us that:

'It was over language matters that disagreement first arose between the young scholars and Korais' teaching. The vision of the ancient world blinded linguistic theories to any consideration of practical experience or common sense. For the twenty years from about 1833 to 1853, and with Constantine Economou [one of Korais' disciples] as the main protagonist, one sees a gradual turning of the Greek language towards archaism. ... The arguments for this turning were mainly opportunistic: the use of ancient Greek would demonstrate the ancient origins of the new Greeks. This type of argument, consciously or unconsciously, suited both the wise and the foolish, it suited the spirit of the times' [my translation].[35]

It was this type of distorted, barren enlightenment which took root and played the leading role in post-independence Greece at the expense of the living cultural traditions and the language spoken by the people. Of course, it may be argued that the destruction of the traditional, autochthonous culture under the impact of Western ideas is not a specifically Greek experience. Cultural imperialism goes hand in hand with economic imperialism in all peripheral social formations.[36] But what was specific to Greece was the total lack of awareness or any serious resistance to that 'cultural imperialism'. On the cóntrary: the pushing aside of the endogenous culture (songs, dances, poetry, language) was facilitated enormously by the fact that it was seen as the shameful bastardised heritage of four centuries of Ottoman yoke. It was easy, therefore, to attack it and replace it by another cultural tradition which, although dead, was 'really Greek', i.e. nearer the 'glorious ancient heritage'. It is in this manner that we have arrived at the apotheosis of formalism on the cultural level in modern Greece. *Katharevousa*, scholasticism, archeolatry (obsessive preoccupation with and blind admiration of everything 'ancient'), instead of being seen as servile and narrow-minded imitation of a culture far removed from the daily experiences of men and women, came to be seen as indexes of 'Greekness' and patriotic spirit.

6 CONCLUSION

If the above discussion does not provide a full explanation of Greek formalism, I think that it helps a little to clarify further the concept of underdevelopment. On the system level, capitalist underdevelopment (if compared with capitalist development), can be seen as a process of mobilisation and misallocation of economic, political and cultural resources generated by the expansion of western capitalism into the 'third world' — or more precisely by a specific disarticulation between capitalist and non-capitalist modes of production in peripheral social formation. If one looks at the same process from an actor's point of view, one can argue that capitalist underdevelopment refers to the type of capital accumulation whose dynamism is based on a class configuration within which the working classes (urban and rural) are economically more exploited, politically more manipulated/repressed and ideologically more disoriented than in the West.

Seen from this perspective, it has been suggested here that the excessive formalism to be found in many areas of Greek life can be understood as *one* of the results of Greek underdevelopment on the political and cultural levels. From a system point of view, formalism is a manifestation of the serious disarticulation between imported and indigenous politico-ideological institutions; from an actor's point of view it can be seen as an effective politico-ideological weapon with the help of which the ruling classes, in a more or less conscious manner, try to keep the masses 'in their place'.

The objection is often made that the concept of underdevelopment is 'ideological', i.e. that it has a pejorative connotation quite unacceptable in a 'neutral', detached scientific analysis. I think that this argument derived from an attachment to the kind of 'value-free' sociology which, in actual fact, is more value-laden than a frank statement and explanation of such issue-oriented terms as misgrowth, misallocation, etc.

For if one takes into account that terms like underdevelopment or misgrowth do not refer to any absolute and universal notions of 'good' or 'bad' but simply attempt, *in a very limited manner*, to compare and assess the trajectory of Western capitalism with that of 'third-world' capitalism, I see nothing objectionable in the neo-Marxist argument that, in the long term, the majority of the population seem to be more penalised in the latter case than in the former.

There is also the objection that the concept of underdevelopment is so vague that any rigorous definition of the term becomes impossible, especially if the concept is extended to refer to the non-economic levels of a social formation. This defeatist/agnostic attitude to the meaning of underdevelopment is due, I think, to the well-known empiricist habit of trying to define terms in a theoretical vacuum, i.e. outside the theoretical debates within which they assume a precise meaning. My argument in this and in Chapter 2 has been that if the concept of underdevelopment is located within the neo-evolutionist/neo-Marxist debate, not only is it perfectly clear and precise, but it also can continue to provide very useful guidance for understanding the various trajectories and crucial problems that third-world countries are facing today.[37]

Conclusion:
Catching up with the West:
Neo-Evolutionist Ideologies and
Problems of Greek Development

A. Since the fall of the dictatorship in 1974 and the acceleration of the procedures for the full integration of Greece into the European Economic Community, a dominant theme in the press and in political debates has been the country's need for the rapid improvement of its economy and its political and cultural institutions, if it is eventually to reach the level of 'democratic maturity' and social welfare already enjoyed by the advanced social democracies of Western Europe today. This all-pervasive desire to 'catch up' with the West, and especially the step-by-step conception of the process, is strongly reminiscent of the sort of functionalist, neo-evolutionist theories developed by economists and sociologists in the fifties, theories which stated (see Chapter 2) that through the process of world-wide diffusion of capitalism, the economically backward countries will pass through the same states as did the Western industrialised societies, and eventually will achieve all the 'marvels' of Western civilisation. Of course, as we have argued, this naïve evolutionism began to fade out when it became obvious that, instead of the gap between rich and poor countries narrowing, it was becoming wider; also, when it was realised that third-world countries, having entered relatively late into the industrial-isation race, and being forced to accept a dependent, peripheral role in the international division of labour, were following an economic trajectory both different from that of the West and less advantageous for the majority of their peoples. But although on the academic level these neo-evolutionist theories are now completely bankrupt, they still play a very effective role in political ideologies, where they exercise enormous influence and contribute considerably to the maintenance of the *status quo*.

B. This type of neo-evolutionism is not, of course, a phenomenon peculiar to the Greek politico-ideological superstructure. It also operates behind the ideologies of the two superpowers which, to a large extent, set the pattern of political indoctrination and debate in all countries within their 'sphere of influence'.

The ideologies of the United States and the Soviet Union, aside from obvious differences, have two important points in common. The first is that the 'positive' tenets of both seem to be completely incongruent with the socio-economic realities prevailing in these societies. In fact, the one ideology is based on an Adam Smith type of liberal philosophy, which might have had some relevance in nineteenth-century competitive capitalism, but is totally meaningless within the context of today's monopoly capitalism. The other is based on a Marxist philosophy which, however interpreted, is at loggerheads with the monolithic bureaucratic centralism which more than anything else characterises Soviet society.[1]

Because of this ideological vacuum common to both power blocs, the *negative* aspects of each other's dominant ideologies − i.e. the criticism of the opponent's weak points − assume paramount importance. The dominant classes in the Eastern bloc refer constantly to the enormous inequalities and the growing contradictions of capitalism, and those of the West to the rigid totalitarianism of the so-called socialist democracies. And of course any move for radical change within the two camps is considered, on the ideological and political level, as an effort to establish the opposite system. The one side talks incessantly of the dangers of a capitalist reversal, and the other about 'creeping socialism' or the sovietisation of the 'free' Western democracies. The same tactics are being pursued *vis-à-vis* third-world countries. The foreign policy of both superpowers is based on the common fundamental assumption that, with few exceptions, all countries in the world, whatever the state of their economy and the peculiarities of their history and culture, must in the last analysis choose between only two models of development: the Soviet and the Western one. If a country rejects the one, it is considered inevitable that sooner or later it will enter the trajectory of the other.

In other words, the basic common denominator of these two main ideologies is an evolutionist conception of the world and history in which there are basically two development roads, or rather 'ladders': at the top of the one is the United States of America, and of the other the Soviet Union. All the rest of the world's countries, with negligible exceptions, only need to climb these same ladders to get to the same developmental level as those who have already 'made it'.

Needless to say, to the degree that it is believed and accepted, this dualistic evolutionist conception of world development functions as an effective mechanism of control both within these two societies and in their relationship with their client States in the rest of the world. And from this point of view, any development anywhere which could seriously challenge this evolutionist *Weltanschauung* touches at the two superpowers' most sensitive spots. Hence their unanimous hostility to the new trends of

European communism seen most clearly in Mediterranean Europe, including Greece.

There have, of course, been several new ideas and attempts in the past for some 'third' solution, mainly in third-world countries – but such attempts had little chance of success in economies with a low development of the forces of production and a high dependence on metropolitan centres. But when in a country like Italy there is a serious effort from the Left for a programme of social transformation which could combine a pluralistic parliamentary system with a decentralised socialisation (not nationalisation) of the means of production – and when the Left has a serious chance of coming to power peacefully – then the ideological evolutionist strait-jacket of the two superpowers is really threatened. In such an eventuality the subtler means of sabotage would hardly be enough, nor would it be easy to repeat the straightforward undermining which worked so well in Chile and Czechoslovakia. Yet the possible success of a 'socialism with a human face' would have incalculable consequences on a world scale. Unavoidably, it would generate radical rearrangements both in the internal social structures of the two superpowers and in their relations to their satellites. The successful institutionalisation of a genuinely representative socialism would be a living, resounding proof that it is possible indeed to avoid both the vulgar, incessantly unjust aspects of monopoly capitalism and the barbaric bureaucratisation of Soviet 'socialism'. Such a development would uncover the irrational and inhuman aspects of the two supersystems, and thus shake the evolutionist, two-ladder myth – a myth fervently propagated today and serving to hide a very simple truth: that the progress of science and technology has reached the point where a more humane and rational society is not only possible but absolutely necessary for human survival. If today the so-called civilised societies are very far from a society genuinely democratic in the political *and* the economic field, this is due not so much to any utopian character of such a solution, but rather that such a solution poses a threat to the interests of the dominant classes in the two supersystems and to those who follow them all over the world.

C. In this general context, what more specific can be said about the Greek brand of neo-evolutionist ideology which manifests itself in an obsessive desire to imitate and catch up on the country's future Common Market partners? I am not going to deal with the complex problem of explaining the emergence and dominance of such an ideology, nor am I going to assess the chances of its being superseded by an alternative being elaborated by fractions of the rising Greek left.[2] Rather, I would like to stress, in the light of the basic themes developed in this volume, the misleading character of this catching-up theory.

The concept of 'catching-up' makes sense only among countries within a similar socio-economic space which have, for centuries past, followed similar historical trajectories. Greece, whether one likes it or not, belongs historically to a socio-economic and cultural area very different from that of the West. At a time when Western Europe experienced the socio-political transformation which eventually revolutionised the world, Greece was an impoverished province of a declining, quasi-colonial empire (cf. Chapter 1). And when Greece cast off the Ottoman yoke, it did not join the West but rather came to share the fate of its Balkan neighbours who were being savagely and consistently exploited by the political, economic and cultural imperialism of Western Europe (cf. Chapters 1, 5, 7 and 8).

With such a background, the solutions to the country's development problems cannot possibly be found in a mere imitation of the West. Leaving aside the question of whether or not this would be desirable, the plain fact is that 'catching up' (when this is seen as climbing the same evolutionary ladder) is impossible. The only result Greece can achieve by trying to follow the Western trajectory is an imitation of whatever is more superficial and negative in Western culture, it being impossible for Greece at this stage ever to create an analogous infrastructure. In other words, Greece can choose either a developmental strategy different from the Western one, or become what it is already in the process of becoming – an ugly caricature of the West.

More specifically, social inequalities are much greater and are growing at a much faster rate in Greece than in the Western social democracies. As has been argued above (Chapter 7), this is mainly due to the country having followed its own underdevelopment/dependent type of industrial capitalism. Given this very basic fact, it is quite obvious that for Greece to achieve the welfare targets Western societies have achieved already requires very *drastic* curbs of the existing trend to ever-greater inequalities – a trend indissolubly linked with the manner in which Greek capital accumulates. The hypothetic reversal of this powerful trend would, however, jeopardise the model of economic growth (or rather misgrowth) the country has been following for decades now. If the State were to make fundamental changes in the country's structure of income and wealth distribution, this would unavoidably lower profits and put such restrictions on foreign and indigenous capital that Greece would no longer offer the 'favourable climate' for private investments it offers today. In such circumstances, why should capital choose to enter or remain in a politically unstable Greece? Diaspora, foreign and indigenous capital alike would, in a context of increasing freedom of capital movement, prefer the more predictable and secure markets of north-western Europe – thus undermining an economy whose dynamism is primarily based on private initiative.

What, therefore, the neo-evolutionist Greek ideology is concealing is that the welfare State, a basic presupposition of a stable and open parliamentary system, is incompatible with the model of dependent industrialisation being pursued by Greece; and that this dilemma between rapid capital accumulation and relative social justice was not experienced in the West in the form and to the extent that underdeveloped countries are experiencing it today.

D. This does not mean, of course, that the only remaining solution is a turn-about to the Eastern model of capital accumulation. The Greek Left had a serious chance of following this road in 1944, but such a possibility no longer exists today; if for no other reason than that the class structure of post-war Greece is no fertile ground for the *revolutionary* mobilisation of the masses (cf. Chapter 6, section 3).

What seems certain to me is that any effective solution to the country's vital problems cannot be sought in ready-made formulae to be found in either the East or the West. An effective solution — i.e. a solution which puts high priority on the political and economic autonomy of the majority of the Greek people — must reject the neo-evolutionist myths so prevalent today and base itself instead on a serious analysis of the peculiarities and the specific forms of underdevelopment the Greek social formation has undergone. Such a solution, which will be certainly attacked by both the Right and the traditional Left, can only be implemented when political forces have emerged with the knowledge and the will to open up new roads and tackle the developmental problems of the country afresh.

It is worth mentioning once more that the road to autonomous development does not consist of a series of evolutionary steps which one country after the other can follow gradually and steadily. It is a road full of potholes and impasses, but also one offering secret short cuts which, when found and followed, can make 'late-comers' into 'pioneers'. Just as some technological breakthrough can subsequently turn into an impasse when new technologies are discovered, so can the welfare advance of Western social democracies be superseded when economic and political developments demand new solutions that the late-comers can follow more easily. One should always bear in mind that the working classes in most Western European countries (except France) have been so much integrated into the consumptionist conformism of the social democratic *status quo* that a radical move away from their narrow-minded 'economism' and towards new solutions (e.g. genuine industrial democracy) is much more difficult for them than for the Mediterranean workers who have not and cannot advance very far in a social-democratic direction. In fact, although it is too early yet for justified optimism, in the Mediterranean semi-periphery[3] one clearly sees the incipient emergence of political forces which, in the long term, could challenge the economic and ideological tutelage of the two superpowers by creating a new social order.

Just as nineteenth-century economically backward Germany had to find new solutions and eventually shot ahead of the technologically advanced England,[4] so there is no reason why dependent Mediterranean Europe should not find itself ahead of both East and West in terms of social justice and political liberty. I believe that the development of Greece is not a question of imitating or catching up with the West; it is a question of transcending the contradictions of both peripheral and metropolitan capitalism by finding and following new developemental strategies.

Notes

CHAPTER 1

1. For a discussion of the terms 'social formation', 'mode of production', 'capitalism', see Chapter 2, as well as footnotes 22, 101, 132 below.

2. Apart from the State lands and sultanic lands (*emlâki hümayun* and *has hümayun*), there were lands owned by religious and other welfare institutions (*vakf*) as well as two types of private land: the *mülk* lands (of unlimited ownership), and the *erazi-i-miriye* lands where right of ownership was attached to the use of the land — cf. D. A. Zakinthinos, *The Turkish rule* (in Greek), Athens 1953, pp. 8 ff.

3. L. S. Stavrianos, *The Balkans since 1453*, Holt, Rinehart & Winston, New York 1958, pp. 122 ff.

4. It was usual for prisoners of war to be reduced to serfdom. Also, the institution was strong in areas which had been forcefully colonised, or where Byzantine rural relationships had survived. Cf. A. Vakalopoulos, *History of the New Hellenism*, vol. II, 1453—1669, Salonica 1964, pp. 17 ff. On the other hand it is quite true that, given the lower status of the conquered Christian subjects, the free peasants had fewer political rights than their counterparts in Europe. For instance, even 'free' peasants were not allowed to move without permission. Cf. Vakalopoulos, op. cit., p. 20.

5. Cf. P. Anderson, *Lineages of the Absolutist State*, New Left Publications, London 1974, pp. 397 ff.

6. European absolutism must be seen above all as an aristocratic reaction to the long-drawn-out, feudal crisis' — cf. Anderson, op. cit., p. 3. The 'aristo-cratisation' of the monarchical State reached its apogee in Prussia — cf. H. Rosenberg, *Bureaucracy, aristocracy and autocracy: the Prussian experience 1660—1815*, Cambridge, Mass., 1966.

7. The decline of the Ottoman State from the middle or end of the sixteenth-century to its final disintegration in the twentieth-century must not, of course, be seen as a continuous and unilinear process. There were periods of regener-

ation and reform which, however, succeeded for only a short period in halting the long-term declining trend.

8. For an excellent survey of economic, political and social developments in the sixteenth-century Mediterranean world (European as well as Ottoman), cf. F. Braudel, *La Mediterannée et le monde mediterranéen à l'époque de Philippe II*, 2 vols, Armand-Collin, Paris 1966.

9. Emmanuel Wallerstein, *The modern world system: capitalist agriculture and the origins of the European world economy in the sixteenth century*, Academic Press Inc., New York and London 1974.

10. On the capitulatory privileges cf. G. P. Rausas, *Les régimes des capitulations dans l'empire Ottoman*, 2 vols, Paris 1902; and N. Sousa, *The capitulatory regime of* Turkey, Baltimore 1933.

11. Cf. L. S. Stavrianos, op. cit., pp. 124 ff., and also N. Psiroukis, *The history of colonialism* (in Greek), Epikerotita, Athens 1974, pp. 292 ff. Given the relatively low volume of trade between the Ottoman empire and the West in the sixteenth century, Psisourkis exaggerates the distorting effects that external trade had on the structure of the Ottoman economy during this early period. For instance, according to R. Davis, 'considering the size and resources of the Turkish empire, these [commercial] relations were not on a very large scale and they cannot have had great importance for the Ottoman economy as a whole' (*Aleppo and the Devonshire Square*, Macmillan, London 1967, p. 27). It was only during the end of the eighteenth and the beginning of the nineteenth century, with the development of industrial capitalism in the West, that the Ottoman economy was much more drastically affected and disorganised by western imperialism (cf. below). Before that period, the failure, for instance, of the Ottoman economy to develop on a large scale any manufacturing 'proto-capitalist' enterprises outside the guild system must be sought in internal rather than external factors (cf. H. Inalcik, 'Capital formation in the Ottoman Empire', *Jrnl of Economic History*, vol. XXIX, March 1969, pp. 213 ff.).

12. Cf. N. Stavrianos, *The Balkans since 1453*, Holt, Rinehart & Winston, New York 1958, pp. 139 ff.

13. For instance, the extension of cereal cultivation and the creation of big landed property often meant the forced expropriation of small owners (cf. V. Kremmidas, *Introduction to the history of modern Greek society 1700—1821*, Exantas, Athens 1976, pp. 149 ff.). Moreover, Turkish landlords, during the galloping inflation caused by the influx of precious metals into sixteenth-century Europe, forced their peasants to pay their rents in kind rather than in money. Thus the general rise of prices did not at all profit the direct producers who, to escape the growing landlord exploitation, increasingly left their lands for the mountainous areas or to go abroad. Cf. Vergopoulos, *op. cit.*, pp. 50 ff.; cf. also Vakalopoulos, op. cit., pp. 87 ff.

14. A decree of 1530 stipulates, among other things, the conditions under which a timariot's son could inherit his father's timar (only when the latter had died in battle) — cf. Braudel, op. cit. vol. II, p. 65.

15. On these very significant developments, cf. B. A. Cvetkova, 'L'évolution du régime feodal turc de la fin du XVIe siècle jusqu'au milieu du XVIII siècle', in *Etudes historiques* [de l'Académie des Sciences de Bulgarie] *à l'occasion du* XIe *Congrès International des Sciences Historiques*, Stockholm, August 1960; cf. also the same author's 'Sur certaines reformes du régime foncier du temps de

Méhemed II', in *Journal of Economic and Social History of the Orient*, 1963; H. Inalcik, 'Land reforms in Turkish history', in *Muslim World*, July 1955, pp. 221–8; T. Stoianovich, 'Land tenure and related sectors of the Balkan economy 1600–1800', *Journal of Economic History* 1953, pp. 398–411.

16. Stavrianos, op. cit., pp. 138 ff. This dominance must not be seen in purely numerical terms. Thus, as far as the Greek lands were concerned, even when it was fully developed, the chiflik system only engaged a small proportion of the agricultural labour force – according to Vergopoulos (op. cit., p. 41) not more than 15-18 per cent. The dominance of the chiflik must rather be seen in terms of its prevalence in the most dynamic sectors of the agricultural economy.

17. Cf. P. Leon, *Economies et sociétés pre-industrielles*, vol. II, 1650–1780, Armand-Collin, Paris 1970, pp. 73 ff.

18. Cf. G. I. Bratianou, *Etudes byzantines d'histoire économique et sociale*, Paris 1938, p. 244. However it would not be correct to equate Europe's 'second serfdom' completely with the condition of the Ottoman peasantry in the seventeenth and eighteenth centuries. Until the *Tanzimat* reforms of the nineteenth century, the weak Ottoman State tolerated but never gave *de jure* recognition to big landed private property. Thus, for instance, there is no equivalent in the Ottoman system to the 1762 Russian Manifesto by which the State quite formally abandoned the Russian serfs to the mercy of their overlords (cf. Leon, op. cit., p. 340).

19. As far as Greece is concerned, cf. Vakalopoulos, op. cit., vol. III, pp. 241 ff., and vol. IV, pp. 342 ff.; and T. Kandiloros, *The Peloponnesian Armotoli 1500–1821*, Athens 1924.

20. Cf. S. Asdrahas, 'The economy', in *History of the Greek nation, vol. II: Hellenism under foreign rule 1669–1821*, pp. 165 ff.

21. Cf. G. Postel-Vinay, *La rente foncière dans la capitalisme agricole*, Maspèro, Paris 1973.

22. Capitalism, here and in the rest of the book, is defined in its narrow sense: it refers to a mode of production characterised by the use of wage labour and therefore by the divorce of the direct producers from their means of production. From the point of view of the above definition, the integration of an economy into a world capitalist market, and/or the commercialisation of some of its sectors, do not automatically make this economy capitalist. Moreover, in so far as in a concrete social formation one finds more than one mode of production, a social formation shall be called capitalist only when the capitalist mode of production becomes dominant within it. This dominance, as will be argued below, has specific consequences on the ways in which the economy articulates with the political and ideological superstructure. Cf. on this point the relevant discussion in my Chapter 2, as well as M. Dobb, *Studies in the development of capitalism*, International Publishers, New York 1968, pp. 1–32. For a debate on the meaning of capitalism and the relevance of diverging definitions in explaining the transition from feudalism to capitalism in Western Europe, cf. R. Hilton (ed.), *The transition from feudalism to capitalism*, New Left Books, London 1976.

23. On the repopulation and city-colonisation policies of the Ottoman State, cf. Omer-Lufti Barkan, 'Les déportations comme une méthode de peuplement et de colonisation dans l'empire Ottoman', in *Revue de la Faculté des Sciences*

Economiques de l'Université d'Istanbul, XI, 1953; and the same author's 'Quelques observations sur l'organisation économique et sociale des villes Ottomanes des XVI et XVII siècles', in *Receuils de la Société Jean Bodin pour l'histoire comparative des institutions*, VI. 2, Brussels 1956.

24. Cf. V. Kremmidas, *The commerce of the Peloponnese during the 18th century: 1715–1792* (in Greek), Athens 1972, p. 53; also cf. P. Masson, *Histoire du commerce français dans le Levant au XVIIe siecle*, Paris 1896.

25. Cf. N. Sousa, op. cit., and A. C. Wood, *A history of the Levant Company*, London 1935; A. Hornicker, 'Anglo-French rivalry in the Levant from 1583 to 1672', in *Jrnl of Modern History*, Dec 1946, pp. 289–305; M. Epstein, *Early history of the Levant Company*, London 1908.

26. Apart from the Greeks, the Jews and Armenians also played very important roles in the Ottoman economy. Bulgarian, Serbian and other Orthodox merchants became commercially active much later and never managed to become as important as the Greeks – cf. Part. III, Chapter 5.

27. T. Stoianovich, 'The conquering Balkan Orthodox merchant', in *Jrnl of Economic History* 1960, pp. 241–2. Cf. also R. Mautran, *Istanbul dans la seconde moitié du XVII siècle: Essai d'histoire institutionelle, économique et sociale*, Paris 1962, p. 56.

28. G. Leon, 'The Greek merchant marine: 1453–1850', in *Greek Merchant Marine*, pub. by the National Bank of Greece (in Greek), Athens 1972, pp. 19–22; cf. also Zakinthinos, 'Corsaires et pirates dans les mers grèques au temps de la domination turque', in *L'Hellenisme contemporaire*, 10, 1939.

29. A good indication of the former's rise was the imposition of port taxes for foreign ships by the Venetians in 1601. This measure aimed mainly at hitting Venice's Greek competitors who were beginning to play an important role in the Adriatic trade. Another indication was the rapid development of Greek communities in the major Italian cities. For instance, Ancona was a large distribution centre dealing with textiles destined for the Ottoman empire and receiving various agricultural products from the Balkans and the Black Sea (leather, wax, grain). In the middle of the sixteenth century, Ancona had 200 Greek trading establishments. Similar developments occurred in Livorno, Venice, Genoa and other places. (Cf. G. Leon, op. cit., pp. 16–17.).

30. Contrary to the general belief that the Kuchuk Kairnarji agreement had clauses which explicitly granted trading privileges to the Orthodox merchants of the empire (cf. for instance Stavrianos, op. cit., p. 192), it was in fact only later agreements which did so – for instance that of 1783. It was the historian Yiannis Yianoulopoulos who drew my attention to this important point.

31. Cf. T. Stoianovich, 'The conquering Balkan Orthodox merchant', op. cit., pp. 269–73.

32. Cf. N. Mouzelis and M. Attalides, 'Greece', in M. Scotford-Archer and S. Giner (eds), *Contemporary Europe*, Weidenfeld & Nicolson, London, 1973.

33. This was reinforced by the well-known practice of wealthy Greeks donating a considerable part of their fortune to the Church, a custom which in a slightly different form still exists today. Interestingly, there is no contradiction in the minds of these Christians between this kind of philanthropy and the usually dubious manner by which this wealth was acquired, e.g. piracy or brigandage. This can be explained in terms of some salient characteristics of the Greek Orthodox Church, which are as valid today as they were a few centuries ago.

One of the most distinctive features of Greek Orthodoxy is its extreme formalism. At the risk of oversimplification, one could argue that from the point of view of the Orthodox believer faith has very little to do with 'internalised' moral principles. There is very little soul-searching, or the sort of 'inner loneliness' of the individual *vis-à-vis* God such as Weber found in the Protestant believer. For the Greek Orthodox, to be a good Christian means primarily to follow as strictly as possible the conventional rules governing Church attendance, fasting etc. Also, it must be taken into account that the Church enjoyed large temporal powers, and that despite its corruption and exploitation it contributed more than any other body to the maintenance of the Greek language, culture and national identity during the four centuries of Turkish occupation. From the point of view of the believer, the Patriarch was not only a spiritual leader, he was also the ethnarch, the leader of the Greek nation. It is not surprising that even for a modern Greek, religion nd nationalism are inextricably linked: to be a good Christian is to be a good patriot, and vice versa. Thus one can argue that the 'formalistic' and secular character of the Greek Orthodox Church was relevant to the development of Greek commerce. Indeed, the Orthodox economic 'ethic', if not favouring economic activities in the direct and active manner of the Protestant ethic, at least did not hinder them, as did some other worldly types of religion. For the general position of the Church under the Ottoman empire, cf. T. H. Papadopoulos, *Studies and documents relating to the history of the Greek Church and people under Turkish domination*, Brussels 1952; and G. E. Arnakis, 'The Greek Church of Constantinople and the Ottoman empire', in *Jrnl of Modern History*, 1952, pp. 235–50.

34. The size of these illegal wheat operations is indicated by the fact that, even in times of famine, approximately 40 per cent of Ottoman wheat went abroad. Many of the uprisings in big Ottoman urban centres were directly linked with the resulting lack of wheat. Cf. G. Leon, op. cit., 32; an; N. Svoronos, *Le commerce de Salonique au XVIIIe siecle*, Paris 1956.

35. Cf. G. Leon, op. cit., p. 42; and C. Evelpides, 'Economic history of Greece', in *Encyclopaedia ILIOS*, vol. 'Greece', pp. 4419 ff. For the dominant position of Greek merchants in the developing land trade within the Balkans and the rest of Europe, cf. Stoianovitch, op. cit.

36. Cf. G. Leon, op. cit., pp. 30 and 41.

37. Ibid., pp. 41–2.

38. V. Kremmidas, *Introduction to the history of modern Greek society*, op. cit., p. 140.

39. In June 1807, the Marseilles Chamber of Commerce informed the French Minister of the Interior, 'We would be happy, Monseigneur, if we could, as you ask, send your Excellency each month a bulletin on the state of French commerce in the Levant, but this commerce does not exist'; cited by Stavrianos, op. cit., p. 276.

40. G. Leon, op. cit., p. 43.

41. Kremmidas, op. cit., p. 143.

42. Ibid., p. 146.

43. Moskof, C., *The national and social consciousness in Greece: 1830–1909* (in Greek), Salonica 1972, pp. 83 ff.

44. One of the first to express this point of view was the Frenchman François

Boulanger, *Ambelakia ou les associations et les municipalités Hélleniques*, Paris 1875. After him, Greek scholars like C. Paparrigopoulos, G. Filaretos, D. Kalitsounakis, K. Koukkides, T. Georgakis and many others have accepted the cooperative character of Ambelakia. Cf. for instance, T. Georgakis, *The cooperatives in Greece*, Patras 1932, and K. Koukkides, *The spirit of cooperation among modern Greeks in Ambelakia* (in Greek), Athens 1948; for a discussion of the various theories on Ambelakia, cf. P. S. Avdelides, *The agricultural cooperative movement in Greece* (in Greek), Papazisis, Athens 1975, pp. 21 ff.

On the other hand, more recent writers do not see Ambelakia as a genuine cooperative, but: (*a*) as a simple commercial company (J. Kordatos, *Ambelakia and the 'cooperation' myth*, (in Greek), Athens 1955); (*b*) as an organisation resembling more the town guilds of eighteenth-century Greece (John Tsouderos, *The agricultural cooperatives* (in Greek), Athens 1960); (*c*) as an association with some of the characteristics of a cooperative but which, given the pre-capitalistic character of eighteenth-century Greece, could not achieve full and genuine cooperative form (P. S. Avdelides, op. cit., p. 32); (*d*) as the world's first profit-sharing industrial organisation (K. Leontidis, 'Ambelakia', in *Agricultural Economy*, no. 9, 1957).

Although in the shipbuilding industry the organisation of production did not take a similar form, it is well established for instance that the ships' crews did not receive wages. With the shipowner being at the same time a merchant, the crew members were renumerated by participating in the profits resulting from the sale of the merchandise transported. Cf. Kremmidas, op. cit., pp. 175 ff.

45. Cf. J. Kordatos, op. cit.; Kremmidas finds a similar tendency in the shipbuilding industries, op. cit., p. 181.

46. For instance, 'the cooperative distributed free corn to its poorer members and maintained schools, a hospital, and a relief fund'. Stavrianos, op. cit., p. 276. On the other hand, in contrast to the rules of the guild system, there were no restrictions on entrance into the organisation – cf. Avdelides, *op. cit.*, pp. 31–2.

47. Cf. M. Dobb, *Studies in the development of capitalism*, pp. 123 ff.

48. For the case of England, there is a divergence of opinion on the extent to which this concentration of production was due to the 'external' intervention of merchant capital rather than to the 'internal' development of the small producer into a capitalist (cf. Takahashi, 'A contribution to the discussion', in R. Hilton, op. cit.). Concerning the late eighteenth-century Greek industrial development, the problem has not, as far as I know, been examined systematically by Greek historians. But I think that there is no doubt in either case that merchant capital did play some role (if not the leading one) in the process of the emergence of capital in the sphere of production.

49. The persistence of strong communal institutions in pre-independence Greece was partly due to Turkish 'indirect' rule of government as well as to the fact that, despite class differences, all Christian subjects were drawn together by a feeling of solidarity and were equally threatened by the arbitrariness of the Ottoman State. Cf. D. Daniilides, *Modern Greek society and economy*, Athens 1934.

50. Cf. R. Davis, op. cit., pp. 27–9.

51. The sultanic administration made several attempts to implement a policy for the development of industry, but did not succeed. For instance, already in 1703 the Grand Vizier Ramis Mohamed Pasha worked out a plan for the improvement of industry and the founding of new textile enterprises in Salonica, Adrianople, and Constantinople. Mohamed Pasha soon fell, and the project 'to establish cloth and silk fabric manufactures in the States of the Grand Seigneur fell with him', according to the French ambassador, who had definite instructions to hinder any attempts at creating textile competitors in Turkey. Cf. Stoianovich, 'The conquering Balkan Orthodox merchant', op. cit., pp. 259–83.

52. It is also at this stage that the contradiction between the Ottoman economy, distortedly commercialised by the industrialisation of the West and the traditional sultanic political superstructure, reached its extreme form – cf. Kremmidas, op. cit., pp. 13 ff.

53. Ibid., p. 201.

54. Stavrianos, op. cit., pp. 144 ff. Cf. also his 'Antecedents of the Balkan revolution of the 19th century', in *Jrnl of Modern History* 1959, pp. 335–72.

55. For instance, most of the members of the *Philiki Hetairia*, the secret revolutionary society which played a crucial role in initiating the 1821 insurrection, were merchants. See C. W. Crawley, 'John Capodistria and the Greeks before 1821', in *Cambridge Historical Journal*, 1952. Many merchants, however, including the shipping magnates of Hydra, were initially opposed to the revolution. Moreover, commerce in the Peloponnese was controlled by local landowners who also at first opposed any violent uprising. See M. Sakellariou, *The Peloponnese during the second Ottoman rule* (in Greek), Athens 1939. Yet merchants, especially some of those living abroad, supported the revolution because of (*a*) the increasing lawlessness during the declining years of the Ottoman empire which had been hindering commerce, and (*b*) the growing contact between Greek traders and the West. See Stavrianos, *The Balkans since 1453*, op. cit., pp. 335–42. Cf. also J. Kordatos, *The social significance of the 1821 revolution* (in Greek), Epikerotita, Athens 1972. The role that the Greek bourgeoisie played during and after the War of Independence is a highly debatable point among Greek historians, and social scientists, cf. below. Chapter 3, section 3.

56. For the crucial role played by the Greek diaspora bourgeoisie not only during the War of Independence but also in the post-independence period, cf. N. Psiroukis, *The phenomenon of the modern Greek settlement* (in Greek), Epikerotita, Athens 1974; and C. Tsoukalas, *Dépendance et réproduction: le rôle de l'appareil scolaire dans une formation transterritoriale*, University of Paris, unpub. thesis, 1975.

57. N. Svoronos, *Histoire de la Grèce moderne*, Paris 1953, pp. 30 ff.

58. For the role played by the Church, the Phanariotes and the landowning class during the revolution, cf. D. Tsakonas, *The sociology of modern Greek culture* (in Greek), Athens 1968, pp. 99–103. For a comparison with other Balkan countries, cf. T. Stoianovich, 'The social foundations of Balkan politics', in C. and B. Jelavich, *The Balkans in transition*, Berkeley 1963, pp. 297–345; and L. S. Stavrianos, *The Balkans 1815–1914*, New York 1963, pp. 17 ff.

59. To be more precise, the class war had started long before the 1821 revolution. Already towards the end of the eighteenth century, with the general deterio-

ration of peasant conditions and the development of large-scale banditry, the Turkish authorities, in full collaboration with the Greek notables (*kotsabassides*), set out to exterminate the Greek 'primitive rebels' (the *Klephts*) who at that time provided the only foci of national resistance against the Ottoman yoke. This combined effort was so successful that during the first decade of the nineteenth century most Klephts were exterminated or chased outside the Ottoman territories (mainly to the Ionian islands). This, according to the historian C. Stamatopoulos, was a serious factor retarding the outbreak of the Greek revolutionary movement (cf. his *The internal struggle before and after the 1821 revolution*, in Greek, Kalvos, Athens 1971, vol. I, pp. 54—69). With the re-emergence of the Klepht movement before and during the revolution, the split between the Greek notables and the military chieftains reappeared and took on violent form in 1824. After the formers' victory during this first round of the civil war, all subsequent internal struggles were fought out between the dominant classes (Stamatopoulos, op. cit., pp. 340 ff.).

60. For an account of social fragmentation and the interrelations between kinship, regional and class differences in the early nineteenth century, cf. J. Petropoulos, *Politics and Statecraft in the Kingdom of Greece: 1833—1843*, Princeton University Press, New Jersey 1968; and N. Diamandouros, *Political modernisation, social conflict and cultural cleavage in the formation of the modern Greek State, 1821—1828*, unpub. Ph.D. thesis, Columbia University 1972.

61. The term 'Westernisers' and 'traditionalists' are used by Diamandouros, op. cit., in his analysis of the antagonisms among the dominant classes during the later phases of the civil war. Although these terms present certain theoretical difficulties (see my Chapters 2 and 3), I find them useful in this specific context.

62. Diamandouros, op. cit., pp. 160—98.

63. Thus, for instance, the first Greek constitutions were inspired by the French example; and although Capodistria and later King Otho, in their efforts to combat the political autonomy of regional potentates, tried to implement an absolutist model of government, their efforts were ultimately frustrated.

64. Cf. V. Filias, *Society and power in Greece 1830—1909* (in Greek), Makrionitis, Athens 1974, Part I, cf. also below Chapter 8, section 3.

65. The national lands amounted to 35 per cent of all cultivated land, cf. Vergopolous, op. cit., p. 82.

66. Cf. J. Petropoulos, op. cit., pp. 236—38.

67. Cf. Vergopoulos, op. cit., pp. 80 ff.

68. In fact, even before the large-scale distribution of national lands in 1871 (cf. below), a large portion of these lands had come into the hands of small peasant cultivators. Aside from the 1835 law, another means of bringing this about was that those working on the national lands had the right to claim the ownership of their plot if they had carried out permanent improvements. However, we do not know the extent to which this right was actually invoked (see Foreign Office Papers 83, vol. 341).

69. Cf. Vergopoulos, op. cit., pp. 92—138.

70. This is the view of N. Vernicos, *L'évolution et les structures de la production agricole en Grèce*, Dossier de Recherche, Université de Paris VIII, 1973. On the other hand, Moskof, op. cit., thinks that after the 1871 land reform only

one-third of the peasants acquired land. Vergopoulos, op. cit., p. 86, supports Vernicos' calculations.

71. Premier Koumoundouros (1867–78) initiated a mildly protectionist policy, but only for industrial products locally produced. He also tried to protect the Peloponnesian currant growers but not the big chiflik owners growing wheat – cf. Vergopoulos, op. cit., pp. 85 ff.

72. Cf. S. Gregoriadis, *Economic history of modern Greece* (in Greek), Athens 1975, pp. 24 ff.

73. There were major shipyards in Galaxidi, Syros, and Piraeus. For instance, from 1827 until 1834, more than 260 ships were built in Syros alone. Cf. Leon, op. cit., p. 47.

74. G. Leon, op. cit., pp. 47–8.

75. Cf. A. Mansolas, *Survey of the steam-operated industrial establishments in Greece* (in Greek), Athens 1876.

76. The lack of an efficient land-transport system was an especial hardship in regions without access to the sea. So it was quite common for surplus produce of some province to be left to rot, while there was great demand for it in another, not so many miles away. Cf. Evelpides, op. cit., p. 1425.

77. G. Dertilis, *Social change and military intervention in politics: Greece 1881–1928*, unpub. Ph.D. thesis, University of Sheffield 1976, Table VIII.

78. Cf. G. Dertilis, op. cit., chapter A/2, p. 19.

79. The long-term policy of the Othonian monarchy was to eliminate the powers of the various regional oligarchies and create a society of small peasants ruled by a centralised monarchical bureaucracy. Cf. P. Pipinelis, *The monarchy in Greece* (in Greek), Athens 1932.

80. See also below, Chapters 6 and 8.

81. For the extent of kinship and clientelist political networks during the early rule of King Otho, cf. J. Petropoulos, op. cit.; for a more general analysis of Greek political clientelism, cf. K. P. Legg, *Politics in modern Greece*, Stanford University Press, Calif. 1969.

82. G. Dertilis, op. cit., Table XIV.

83. On the relationship between the diaspora bourgeoisie and Greek politics see the excellent analysis of G. Dertilis, op. cit., Chapters A/3 and C/4.

84. Cf. Stavrianos, op. cit., pp. 413–544; see also my Chapter 5.

85. D. Stephanides calculated that between 1879 and 1893 the influx of foreign capital into Greece under various forms (State loans, private investments etc.) amounted to the considerable sum of 750 million gold francs. Figures taken from M. Nikolinakos, *Studies on Greek capitalism* (in Greek), Nea Sinora, Athens 1976, p. 38.

86. Stavrianos, op. cit., pp. 416–17. One also finds significant differences in the influx of diaspora capital. Whereas during the previous period (1830–80) diaspora wealth was channelled into donations to the State and into remittances to village relatives, after 1880 the influx was not only much greater, but it was directed into finance, transport, shipping and the purchase of chiflik lands. Cf. Dertilis, op. cit:, Chapter A/2, pp. 19–20.

87. On railway construction in the Balkans and the Middle East, *cf.* H. Feis, *Europe, the world's banker 1870–1914*, (new edition) New York 1961.

88. Stavrianos, op. cit., p. 420.

89. Moreover, the internal demand for locally produced products increased spec-

tacularly during the last decade under consideration (1912—22) because virtually for the whole of this period Greece was in a permanent state of war (the Balkan wars, World War I, the Graeco-Turkish war). This stimulated not only agricultural and industrial production, but also the shipping business. Cf. A. Andreadis (ed.), *Les effets économiques et sociaux de la guerre en Grèce*, Paris 1928; cf. also his *The Greek war and post-war economy* (in Greek), Athens 1927.

90. Until 1880, Greece's railway network covered only 11 kilometres and the road network 620 km. By 1909, due mainly to Trikoupis' efforts, the former had been extended to 1614 km. and the latter to 2128 km. (S. Gregoriadis, op. cit., p. 28.)

91. In 1884 the wheat tariff was multiplied by five, and that for industrial products by three. Cf. Vergopoulos, op. cit., p. 119.

92. Cf. J. Eftaxias, *The State and the National Bank* (in Greek), Athens 1914; also D. Zografos, *History of the founding of the National Bank*, 2 vols, Athens 1925.

93. Cf. Evelpides, op. cit., pp. 1427 ff.

94. Cf. Vergopoulos, op. cit., pp. 92—106.

95. The hiring of labour was not unknown of course, but it played a subsidiary role; it was more common in Attica and Argolida. Cf. Evelpides, op. cit., p. 1422.

96. They were used in the raising of livestock. On the state of Greek agriculture before and after the agrarian reforms, *cf.* B. Alivisatos, *La réforme agraire en Grèce*, Paris 1932; and also his *Agricultural Greece and her development* (in Greek), Athens 1939.

97. It is only in the post Warld War II period that Greece became self-sufficient in wheat. But this achievement did not greatly help the balance of payments which was deteriorating steadily as a result of the dependent type of industrialisation still being followed in Greece. For foreign trade statistics, cf: G. Dertilis, op. cit., ch. 13, TablesVII/VIII.

98. Cf. A. Sideris, *The agrarian policy of Greece during the last century, 1833—1933*, Athens 1933; cf. also D. Stephanides, *Agrarian policy*, Athens 1948; X. Zolotas, *Agrarian policy* (in Greek), Athens 1933; D. Zografos, *History of Greek agriculture*, 3 vols, Athens 1923, and his *History of the currant*, Athens 1930.

99. Figures taken from the 1920 industrial census and cited in G. Dertilis, op. cit., Tables X and XI. 'Industrial establishments' in this and the following statistics are considered to be those employing more than five workers.

100. Shipping too managed to overcome the 'steam crisis' and to develop quite rapidly, thanks to the activities of the diaspora bourgeoisie which brought old steamships from England and leased them to Greek captains. Thus, in 1915 the Greek merchant marine already had 475 steamships with a total of 893,656 tons. Cf. Stavrianos, op. cit., p. 480.

101. Thus, out of the 2905 industrial establishments mentioned above, only 492 employed more than 25 workers — cf. Dertilis, op. cit., Tables X and XI. Of course, in actual research it is extremely difficult to draw a clear-cut line between capitalist and non-capitalist enterprises. For instance, at what point in its recruitment of wage labour does an economic unit become capitalist? For Marx, 'capitalist production only then really begins when each individual

capitalist employs simultaneously a comparatively large number of labourers; when consequently the labour process is carried on on an extensive scale and yields relatively large quantities of products. A greater number of labourers working together, at the same time, in one place (or, if you will, in the same field of labour), in order to produce the same sort of commodity under the mastership of one capitalist, constitutes both historically and logically the starting-point of capitalist production.' (*Capital*, International Publishers, New York 1967, vol. I, p. 322.) Lenin adopts a similar definition although he specifies more precisely what he means by 'large' numbers: 'When the handicraftman turns into a *real capitalist employing from 15 to 30 wage workers*, the part played by family labour in his workshop declines and becomes quite insignificant.' (*The development of capitalism in Russia*, Collected Works, vol. III, Lawrence & Wishart, London 1964, p. 351 — italics mine.) Although much theoretical work is needed on this point, for the purposes of the present study Lenin's specification is accepted as a rough guide for deciding how many firms should be considered 'capitalist' in the Greek context.

102. See Chapter 5, section 2.
103. Cf. G. Dertilis, op. cit., ch. B/4.
104. The Greek bankruptcy was also due to conjunctural elements — e.g. the currant crisis, cf. Chapter 5, section 2.
105. In fact, after the currant crisis there was a massive migratory movement to the United States, which was only stopped with the abrupt change in USA immigration policy after 1921. There is a striking difference between this type of emigration and those during the Ottoman period. In the latter case the migrants were oriented towards clerical and mercantile activities in the flourishing Greek diaspora communities in Russia, Rumania and Egypt; in the former, they usually left Greece to join the bottom ranks of the American working class.
106. It has also been calculated for the years between 1899 and 1911 that 200,000 people emigrated from Greece. Cf. Evelpides, op. cit., p. 1427.
107. In the sense that the traditional political elites (the *palaiokomatikoi*) gave way to the 'new' men: lawyers, doctors, and *nouveaux riches* merchants. Cf. K. Legg, *Politics in modern Greece*, Stanford 1969, ch. 5.
108. Cf. for instance J. Kordatos, *History of modern Greece* (in Greek), Aion, Athens 1958. For a detailed discussion of these points, see below Chapter 3, section 2.
109. On this point cf. G. Dertilis, op. cit., ch. B/5.
110. Cf. Vergopoulos, op. cit., pp. 99 ff. G. Dertilis (op. cit.) rightly, I think, criticises Vergopoulos for having exaggerated the antagonisms between chiflik landlords and bourgeois interests.
111. On the monarchy issue, cf. below Chapter 6.
112. For a recent and balanced account of the Asia Minor adventure, cf. M. Llewellyn-Smith, *The Ionian vision*, London 1975.
113. A. Pallis has calculated that the total number of refugees who entered Greece after 1922 (including the Greek refugees from Russia and Bulgaria) was more than 1.5 million. Cf. 'Les effets de la guerre sur la population de la Grèce', in A. Andreadis (ed.), *Les effets économiques et sociaux de la guerre en Grèce*, op. cit., p. 135.

114. The destruction of the flourishing Asia Minor Greek communities, according to Constantine Tsoukalas (op. cit.), brought another fundamental change in the Greek social formation. Befor 1922, the economic and cultural links between these diaspora communities and mainland Greece had been so varied and strong that, according to the author, they constituted an integral part of the Greek social formation. This 'trans-territorial' character of the Greek social formation disappeared after 1922 and, for the first time therefore there was coincidence between the Greek nation-State and the Greek social formation. It is also at this point that the diaspora capital ceased to have a special impact on mainland Greece and began to behave like any other foreign capital.

    Although this is an interesting formulation, I think that using the social-formation concept in this way creates serious theoretical difficulties which Tsoukalas did not work out. For instance, if ony tries to examine the 'political instance' of such a social formation, what political institutions would correspond to an infrastructure which extends over two-nation States? Or, in so far as the Greek communities in the USA, or in West Germany, today have an important impact on the Greek economy, why not consider them also as parts of the present Greek social formation? In other words, at what point do diaspora communities cease being part of a social formation? These problems, I think, indicate that the concept of a social formation which is so crucial in Althusserian Marxism today (cf. below, Chapter 2) needs further theoretical elaboration.

115. By virtue of a provision in the 1911 Constitution and the 1917 land reform decrees.

116. Stephanides, op. cit., p. 107.

117. Between 1915 and 1931, wheat production went up from 565,626 tons to 775,386 tons, and that of tobacco from 12,702 to 43,215 tons. All the above figures are provided by Zolotas (op. cit.), and cited in Nikolinakos, op. cit., p. 44.

118. This statement is less true about the refugees who, in contrast to the non-refugees, benefited from some rudimentary assistance. Cf. Nikolinakos, op. cit., p. 45.

119. Cf. Evelpides, *The agriculture of Greece*, Athens 1944, pp. 26 ff.

120. Cf. Vergopoulos, op. cit., pp. 149 ff.

121. As far as entrepreneurial skills are concerned, the crucial contribution of Asia Minor refugees can be seen by the fact that even in 1961, 25 per cent of Greek industrialists had come from outside, most of them from Turkey. Cf. A. Alexander, *Greek Industrialists*, Research Monograph Series, Centre of Planning and Economic Research, Athens 1964, p. 128.

122. Some of them had managed to transfer part of their money outside Turkey, whereas others brought it with them, together with their jewellery and other valuables. Cf. Dertilis, op. cit., ch. E.

123. Cf. Nikolinakos, op. cit., p. 55.

124. Thus, for instance, of the 131 insurance companies operating in Greece in 1929, only fifteen were Greek. Moreover, in the same period the tobacco trade was largely controlled by foreign capitalists. In terms of nationality, 48 per cent of the foreign capital was English, 31 per cent American, and 12 per cent Belgian. Cf. Nikolinakos, op. cit., p. 56.

125. In addition to all these favourable factors, industrialisation was helped after

1922 by the devaluation of the drachma and a series of other governmental decrees for the support and development of industry. Cf. A Sideris, 'Economic history of Greece', in *Economic and Accounting Encyclopaedia*, vol. IV, pp 148 ff.

126. Gregoriadis, op. cit., p. 48.

127. This trend was to be highly accentuated after the Second World War. Cf. Chapter 7, section 2B.

128. The most important of them were the group of companies controlled by the National Bank, the Commercial Bank, the Bodossakis-Athanassiadis Group etc.

129. Given the luxury nature of the main Greek exports and the relatively inelastic international demand for such products, Greek exporters became increasingly dependent on their foreign buyers. Cf. M. Serafetinidi, *The breakdown of parliamentary institutions in Greece*, unfinished thesis, London School of Economics 1976. ch. 6.

130. See below, Chapter 2, section 2B.

131. See below, Chapter 7, section 2B.

132. In contrast to the capitalist mode of production, simple commodity production implies: (*a*) individual private ownership of the means of production; (*b*) individual private appropriation of the products of labour and their disposal through the market. (Cf. S. Cook, 'Value, Price and Simple Commodity Production', *Jrnl of Peasant Studies*, vol. 3, no. 4, p. 398.)

From the point of view of the above definition and for the purposes of this study, privately-owned economic units, whether in industry or agriculture, using family labour (or firms in which family labour outweighs wage labour), are considered as belonging to the simple commodity category. Of course, as already mentioned (cf. above, note 103), it is extremely difficult to distinguish the borderline between simple commodity and capitalist enterprises. Lenin, for instance, stresses the infinite variations and gradations between capitalist and pre-capitalist modes of production in his study of the Russian social formation (*The development of capitalism in Russia*, op. cit., ch. 3 and ff.). There is no doubt that within the Marxist literature there is a serious theoretical gap concerning such borderline cases. Moreover, as far as Greece is concerned, the existing statistics on the number and size of enterprises create additional difficulties because they ignore any focus on relations of production. However, if such difficulties do not allow a precise delineation of the boundaries between the capitalist and the simple commodity sector, I think that the rough categorisation attempted here is sufficient to point the salient features of Greek underdevelopment.

133. For a detailed analysis of these mechanisms, in so far as they link small commodity agricultural production to industry, cf. Vergopoulos, op. cit., pp. 176 ff. For a more theoretical treatment of these transfers. cf. S. Amin and C. Vergopoulos, *La question paysanne et le capitalisme*, Anthropos, Paris 1974; see also my Chapter 4, and especially Chapter 7, section 2.

134. There are no serious studies of income distribution in Greece. For some inter-war figures concerning the evolution of upper-class incomes, cf. Dertilis, op. cit., ch. B, Table XII. For post-war figures, cf. M. Malios, *The present phase of capitalist development in Greece* (in Greek), Athens 1975, pp. 139 and 141; D. Karageorgas, 'The distribution of tax burden by income groups in Greece', in *Economic Journal*, June 1973.

135. Cf. Vergopoulos, op. cit., pp. 238 ff.
136. See below, Chapter 2, section 2; and Chapter 7, section 3C.
137. As economic and political developments in the post-war period are treated in some detail in Chapter 7, I shall be very brief in the last part of this chapter so as to avoid repetitions.
138. For a detailed analysis of the post-war growth of the Greek economy, cf. N. Vernicos, *L'économie de la Grèce 1950—1970*, unpub. thesis, University of Paris VIII, 2 vols, 1976.
139. The average growth rate in the fifties was 6 per cent. Cf. *National Accounts of Greece 1948—70* (in Greek), pp. 120—1.
140. Gregoriadis, op. cit., pp. 70—8. Cf. also Vernicos, op. cit.; G. Coutsoumaris, *The morphology of Greek industry*, Athens 1963; H. Ellis *et al.*, *Industrial capital in the development of the Greek economy* (in Greek), Centre of Economic Research, Athens 1965; E. Kartakis, *Le Développement industriel de la Grèce*, Lausanne 1970.
141. Cf. D. Psilos, *Capital market in Greece*, Centre of Economic Research, Athens 1964; p. 194; cf. also M. Serafetinidi, op. cit., ch. 1.
142. For more details on this point see Chapter 7, section 2B.
143. For the transition from the one type of conflict to the other, see Chapter 6, sections 2 and 3.
144. See below, Chapter 5.
145. See below, Chapter 8, section 2.
146. For these developments, cf. the recent study by A. Elefantis, *The promise of the impossible revolution: the Greek Communist Party in the inter-war period*, Olkos, Athens 1976.
147. Cf. G. Katiphoris, *The Barbarians' Legislation*, Athens 1975; and R. Coundouros, *Law and the obstruction of social change: a case study of laws for the security of the prevailing social order in Greece*, unpub. M.Phil. thesis, Brunel University 1974.
148. See below, Chapter 6, sections 2 and 3.
149. This is not to deny the role that the monarchy issue played during as well as after the civil war period. But looking at it from a broad historical perspective clearly shows this issue to have been much more central in the dynamics of the inter-war rather than post-war politics. The focal issue during and after the civil war was surely less a question of the monarchy's survival and more that of the bourgeois order as a whole.
150. From this point of view, the quasi-parliamentary and highly repressive governments after the civil war, the seven-year dictatorship which followed them, and the post-dictatorial presidential regime of Karamanlis can be seen as three attempted solutions — containing varying dosages of repression — by which the Greek dominant classes have tried to deal with the 'threat from below'. Given the model of capital accumulation which Greece has been following since 1922, this threat cannot but increase as the ever more marginalised urban and rural working classes seek a more active and autonomous participation in politics to redress the enormous inequalities generated by Greek capitalism (cf. below, Chapter 7).
151. Althusserian Marxism stresses the point that in pre-capitalist social formations the economy, although determining the superstructure in the last instance (by indicating which institutional sphere shall be dominant) is nevertheless not

dominant in relation to the political and ideological spheres. It is only in capitalist social formations that the economy is both determining in the last instance and dominant (cf. L. Althusser, *For Marx*, Allen Lane, London 1969; also his *Reading Capital*, New Left Books, London 1970; P. Hirst and B. Hindess, *Pre-capitalist economic formations*, Routledge & Kegan Paul, London 1975). Although the idea of 'determination in the last instance' and, to a lesser extent, that of the dominance of one instance over another present complicated theoretical problems (cf. below Chapter 2, especially note 53), I think the Althusserians' attempt to theoretically work out the relationship between economic and politico-ideological structures in capitalist and pre-capitalist social formations is a useful one.

152. Cf. A. Giddens, *The Class Structure of Advanced Societies*, Hutchinson, London 1973.

153. Despite the fact that bourgeois parties remain personalistic up to the present day, there are fundamental differences between their present organisation and that in the nineteenth century. In the latter case, for instance, local oligarchs had such a degree of control over their voters and enjoyed such an autonomy *vis-à-vis* national party leaders, that the party, on the national level, was nothing more than an extremely loose coalition of provincial political 'barons'. Whereas with Venizelos onwards, although the major parties continued to be held together through strong personalities, their national organisation became much stronger as orientations and allegiances started shifting from the local to the national level. This strengthening of national party organisation meant, of course, a change in the structure of patronage. Even in the rural areas, it meant that national issues and broad economic developments could more easily cut through clientelistic networks and traditional, particularistic ties. (For the relation between patronage and class analysis cf. Chapter 3, section 2C.) But it is worth repeating that given the persistence of personalistic politics, these more direct linkages between class structure and political practices did not lead, as in the West, to the effective articulation and promotion of broad class interests (cf. Chapter 8, especially footnote 28).

154. Hence the massive emigration of Greek workers to western Europe. Cf. M. Nikolinakos, *Capitalism and migration* (in Greek), Papazisis, Athens 1973.

155. Whereas in 1938 manufacturing output amounted to 85.6 per cent of all industrial output, it declined to 79.7 per cent in 1948–9, and to 73 per cent during the 1959–60 period. Cf. G. Coutsoumaris, op. cit. p. 55.

156. Taken from G. Giannaros, 'Foreign capital in the Greek economy', in E. Illiou et al., *Multinational monopolies* (in Greek), Athens 1973, p. 404; cf. also G. Petrochilos, *The role of foreign capital in the Greek economy*, unfinished Ph.D. thesis, University of Birmingham.

157. There was also increasing collaboration between Greek and foreign capital in joint ventures. Cf. Petrochilos, op. cit.; for a theoretical treatment on the nature of this new capitalist penetration, cf. N. Poulantzas, *Les classes sociales dans le capitalisme d'aujourd'hui*, Seuil, Paris 1974; and as far as Greece is concerned, his *Le crise des dictatures; Portugal, Grèce, Espagne*, Seuil, Paris 1975.

158. For figures on all these points, see below Chapter 2, section 2; and Chapter 7, section 2.

CHAPTER 2

1. E. E. Hagen, *On the theory of social change*, Dorsey Press, Homewood, Ill., 1962; D. C. McLeland, *The achieving society*, D. Van Nostrand, Princeton, N. J., 1961; W. W Rostow, *The stages of economic growth*, Cambridge University Press 1962; D. Lerner, *The passing of traditional societies*, Glencoe, Ill., 1958; Eisenstadt, *Modernisation: protest and change*, Prentice-Hall, Englewood Cliffs, 1965; N. Smelser, *Social change in the Industrial Revolution*, Routledge, London 1959; T. Parsons, *Societies: Evolutionary and Comparative Perspectives*, Prentice-Hall, Englewood Cliffs 1966; R. Bellah, *Tokugawa Religion*, Free Press, Chicago, 1957.

2. I decided to give more attention to the methodological/metatheoretical critiques of neo-Marxism, as they have not been much discussed in the literature of the sociology of development.

3. For a presentation of the neo-evolutionist thesis, cf. W. W. Rostow, *The stages of economic growth*, op. cit. For an early critique of neo-evolutionist theories, cf. A. Gunder Frank, 'Sociology of development and the underdevelopment of soiology', *Catalyst* no. 3, University of Buffalo 1967; cf. also H. Bernstein, 'Modernisation theory and the sociological study of development', *Journal of Development Studies*, vol. VII, 1971.

4. Some representative works of this school are: P. Baran, *The political economy of growth*, Monthly Review Press, New York 1957; A. Gunder Frank, *Capitalism and underdevelopment in Latin America: Historical studies of Chile and Brazil*, Monthly Review Press, New York 1969; C. Furtado, *Development and underdevelopment*, University of California Press, Berkeley, Cal. 1964; F. H. Cardoso, *Sociologie du développement en Amérique Latine*, Anthropos, Paris 1969; S. Amin, *L'accumulation á l'échelle mondiale*, Anthropos, Paris 1970. Of course, the general label of neo-Marxism covers a variety of theoretical orientations and sub-schools, and it is not possible to deal with such differentiations here. For an article which does so for Latin America, cf. P. O'Brien, 'A critique of Latin American theories of dependency', in I. Oxaal *et al.*, *Beyond the sociology of development*, Routledge, London 1975, pp. 7—27; cf. also A. Forster-Carter, 'Neo-Marxist approaches to development and underdevelopment', in E. de Kadt and G. Williams (eds), *Sociology and Development*, Tavistock, London 1974; and T. Dos Santos, 'The crisis of development theory and the problem of dependence in Latin America', in H. Bernstein (ed.), *Underdevelopment and Development*, Penguin, London 1973.   Finally, the label neo-Marxist (rather than simply Marxist) is justified, I think, by the fact that this group of writers has elaborated a body of theories which differ both substantively and methodologically from the writings of Marx, and of writers like Lenin and Rosa Luxemburg, who used Marx's methodology for a systematic study of Western imperialism. For instance, on the substantive level, Marx expected that in colonial countries the capitalist mode of production would operate in more or less the same way as it had done in the West. From this point of view Western colonialism, by spreading capitalism the world over, would have as an unintentional consequence the industrialisation of the third world. This evolutionist perspective, as will be argued below, is dramatically opposed to the neo-Marxist position. As for the methodological differences between Marx and neo-Marxists, these will be discussed in the last section of

this chapter.

5. For a systematic presentation of this thesis, see the works of P. Baran and A. Gunder Frank, op. cit.

6. For introductory works in this area of study, cf. L. Rhodes (ed.), *Imperialism and underdevelopment: A reader*, Monthly Review, New York 1970; and Anouar Abdel-Malek (ed.), *Sociologie de l'impérialisme*, Anthropos, Paris 1971; R. J. Owen and R. B. Sutcliffe (eds), *Studies in the theory of imperialism*, Longman, London 1972. For a theory which explicitly ascribes more weight to external factors of underdevelopment, cf. T. Szentes, *The political economy of underdevelopment*, Budapest 1971; see also the influential work of A. Emmanuel, *Unequal exchange*, New Left Books, London 1972.

7. For an excellent work which focuses more on the relationship between underdevelopment and internal class relationships, see G. Arrighi, *The political economy of Rhodesia*, Mouton, The Hague 1967.

8. I have tried to develop in greater detail such differences in 'Modernisation, development and the peasant', *Development and Change*, vol. IV, 1972–73, pp. 73–88; cf. also Chapter 3 below.

9. The concept of 'action' and 'actor' does not refer here to the restrictive and often reductionist meaning which social phenomenologists ascribe to the term. It refers not only to 'typical' actors (the student, the peasant etc.), but to collectivities or groups (students, peasants) in so far as they are actually or potentially capable of taking action (e.g. in elaborating policies). In other words, I do not consider it a reification to speak of an organisation, a class or any other collectivity as a whole in decision-making terms. (For a debate on this point, cf. D. Silverman, 'Formal organisation or industrial sociology', *Sociology* 1968, pp. 226 ff., and my criticism of Silverman's position, 'Silverman on organisation', *Sociology* 1969, p. 112.)

10. An excellent illustration of this approach is B. Moore, *The social origins of dictatorship and democracy*, Penguin Press, London 1967. A more recent work in the same tradition is E. Wallerstein, *The modern world system: capitalist agriculture in 16th-century Europe*, New York 1974. For a class analysis which focuses more on third-world countries, cf. G. Arrighi, op. cit., and G. Arrighi and J. Saul, *Essays on the political economy of Africa*, London 1973. Of course, the use of class analysis will have varying degrees of success. Since serious class analysis requires profound historical knowledge of the countries examined, it is not surprising that some neo-Marxist writers often substitute effective analysis with prefabricated formulas which are applied dogmatically and indiscriminately to all third-world countries – formulas referring to the fundamental 'tendential laws' of capitalism, the inexorable contraditions of imperialism, the inevitability of the world revolution of the proletariat etc. (For instance, it seems to me that Frank's work is *in part* neglectful of proper class analysis and dogmatic in the above sense. For other examples concerning the Greek case, cf. Chapter 3.)

11. For a further elaboration of this point, cf. Nicos Mouzelis, 'System and social integration', *British Jrnl of Sociology*, vol. XXV(4).

12. An illustration of this approach is Smelser's seven-stage model of structural/ functional differentiation as applied in the analysis of the English Industrial Revolution (*Social change in the Industrial Revolution*, op. cit.). For instance, in stage one, 'dissatisfactions' emerge with the existing economic arrangements

and in subsequent stages certain 'ideas' appear which, eventually, if and when specified and implemented, resolve the dissatisfactions. During all this complex process one never knows *who* is dissatisfied, *whose* ideas emerge and are implemented, *who* profits from the solutions etc. It is as if a *deus ex machina* called Social System were creating problems and then generating processes which solved them. Of course, Smelser cannot avoid mentioning classes altogether in his voluminous study. But whenever classes do make their timid appearance, they do so *despite* rather than because of his conceptual framework. (For a more systematic discussion of the above points, *cf.* Chapter 3.) For an analysis of the same period from the opposite perspective, cf. E. P. Thompson, *The making of the English working class*, Penguin, London 1963.

13. Whereas in 1938 manufacturing output amounted to 85.6 per cent of all industrial output, it declined to 79.7 per cent in 1948–49, and to 73 per cent during the 1959–60 period (cf. G. Coutsoumaris, *The morphology of Greek industry*, Athens 1963, p. 55).

14. In the fifties, the average annual rate of growth was around 6 per cent (cf. *National Accounts of Greece, 1948–70, in Greek, pp. 121–22*).

15. On this point see D. Psilos, *Capital market in Greece*, Centre of Economic Research, Athens 1964, pp. 23–43.

16. It is not surprising, therefore, that during this period the major banking establishments in Greece had great difficulties and often failed to dispose of the 15 per cent of their funds that the State obliged them to advance for the development of the industrial sector (cf. Psilos, op. cit., ch. 14). For more information on this point cf. below, Chapter 7.

17. Between 1953 and 1969 the total amount of foreign investments *approved* was $1232.4 million; while in just one year (1969) $2504 million went to the gross formation of fixed capital in the Greek economy. Cf. N. Vernicos, *L'économie de la Grèce 1950–1970*, unpub. doctoral thesis, University of Paris VIII, 1975, vol. I, p. 372. For a general account of the role of foreign capital in Greece, cf. T. Jannitsis, *Private Auslandskapitalien im Industrialisierungsprozess Griechenlands (1953–70)*, Doctoral thesis, Free University of Berlin, 1974.

18. Thus, whereas in the period 1948–50 light industry represented 77.5 per cent of the total manufacturing output, it went down to 60.9 per cent in 1963–66, and to 55.1 per cent in 1967–70. (Cf. B. Nefeloudis, *Demythisation with numbers*, in Greek, Athens 1973, p. 146.) This very important shift is clearly reflected in the changing structure of the Greek export trade. Whereas in 1960 agricultural products constituted 80 per cent of the country's exports, the percentage went down to 54 per cent in 1966, and to 42 per cent in 1968, as Greece was gradually able to export industrial goods.

19. For a detailed analysis of this growth see Vernicos, op. cit., vol. I; and E. Kartakis, *Le Développement industriel de la Grèce*, Lausanne 1970.

20. Cf. for instance B. Warren, 'Imperialism and capitalist industrialisation', *New Left Review*, no. 81.

21. For Marx's position on this issue, cf. S. Avineri, *K. Marx on colonialism and modernisation*, Doubleday, New York 1968.

Although Lenin, to some extent, accepted Marx's position on this point (for instance, he thought that the metropolis exporting capital to the colony helped the latter more than it helped the former), his 'law of unequal development' of capitalism was in certain ways an early formulation of the neo-Marxist, anti-evolutionist thesis. His argument that, in contrast to England, pre-capitalist modes of production were not destroyed in Russia but subordinated to capitalism, comes very near to what the neo-Marxists argue about the structure of third-world underdeveloped economies. (Cf. V. I. Lenin, *The development of capitalism in Russia*, Collected works, vol. III. Lawrence & Wishart, London 1964; and H. Lefebvre, *Pour connaître la pensée de Lenine*, Bordos, Paris 1957, pp. 221 ff.)

22. Cf. for instance the reply to Warren's article by J. Petras, McMichael and Rhodes, "Imperialism and the contradictions of development', *New Left Review*. no. 85: the fact that many underdeveloped countries try to industrialise, but in an 'enclave' and dependent manner, was pointed out years ago by such neo-Marxist writers as C. Furtado and S. Amin, op. cit.

23. By 'enclave' I do not, of course, mean that there are no links between the technologically advanced and the other sectors of the economy, but that the existing links are negative ones. Cf. for instance, C. Furtado, *Development and underdevelopment*, op. cit., and his *Diagnosis of the Brazilian crisis*, California University Press 1965; for a clear and systematic account of some fundamental differences between Western industrialisation and third-world underdevelopment, cf. P. Bairoch, *Revolution industrielle et sous-développement*, Mouton, Paris 1974.

24. Cf. Coutsoumaris, op. cit., p. 37.

25. *KEBA* [Centre for the Development of Small-scale Industrial Enterprises], *Statistical field investigation of small and medium industry in Greece* (in Greek), Athens 1972, vol. II, p. 12. For a discussion of the reasons which inhibit the growth of small enterprises in Greece, cf. Kartakis, op. cit., pp. 20 ff.

26. Cited in G. Photopoulos, 'The Dependence of the Greek economy on foreign capital' (in Greek), *Economicos Tahidromos*, no. 1107, p. 12.

27. For various measures of productivity by size of manufacturing establishments, see *KEBA*, op. cit., ch. V.

28. For instance, in 1950 the total number of agricultural establishments was 1,006,973. Of these, 28.5 per cent were smaller than one hectare, and 68.4 per cent cultivated an area between 1 and 10 hectares. At the same time the average cultivated surface per exploitation was 3.59 hectares and the average number of persons employed 3.57. Both these averages were further reduced in 1961 and 1971. Cf. C. Vergopoulos, *The agrarian problem in Greece* (in Greek), Athens 1975, p. 189. Given this type of land fragmentation, it is not surprising to find that in 1950 independent cultivators and their working family-members constituted 92.39 per cent of the agricultural labour force. (Vergopoulos, *op. cit.*, p. 198.)

29. Cf. OECD, *Agricultural policies in 1966: Europe, North America, Japan*, Paris 1967, pp. 24–8; cf. also OECD, *Agricultural Development in southern Europe*, Paris 1969; and below, Chapter 4, section 3B.

30. On the definition of capitalist and simple commodity production in relation to the size of the enterprise, cf. Chapter 1, notes 101 and 131.

31. For instance, according to a relatively recent estimate, 40 per cent of the lowest Greek income groups receive 9.5 per cent of the national income (after deduction of taxes and social security contributions), whereas the 17 per cent belonging to the top income brackets receive 58 per cent. Cf. D. Karageorgas, 'The distribution of the tax burden by income groups in Greece', *Economic*

Journal, June 1973. These inequalities are much greater than in the West. In England, for instance, the top 20 per cent of the population receive approximately 35 per cent of the national income and the bottom 40 per cent only 19 per cent (cited in Photopoulos, op. cit., p. 9.)

The huge Greek inequalities become understandable if one takes into account that whereas the national income doubled between 1954 and 1965, profits tripled and banking profits, between 1966 and 1971 alone, quadrupled. (Figures taken from M. Malios, *The present phase of capitalist development in Greece*, in Greek, Athens 1975, pp. 139 and 141.) And, as the relative share of big capital increases, the relative share of all other income decreases. For instance, in 1951 agricultural per-capita income was 83.3 per cent of the average national income; it dropped to 60.3 per cent in 1962, and 51.1 per cent in 1971. (*Cf.* N. Vernicos, *Greece facing the 'eighties*, Athens 1975, p. 116.)

32. For more information on this point as well as on the relevance of the growing inequalities to political developments in Greece, cf. below, Chapter 7.

33. Cf. for instance Anibal Quijano Obregon, 'The marginal role of the economy and the marginalised labour force', *Economy and Society*, vol. III, no. 4.

34. For a systematic analysis of such mechanisms linking Greek agriculture to the capitalist-industrial sector, cf. C. Vergopoulos, *The agrarian problem in Greece: The issue of the social incorporation of agriculture* (in Greek), Athens 1975.

35. This is not to deny a general rise in the standard of living of the whole population with the very high growth rates of the GNP during the last two decades; but in *relative* terms the share in the growing national income of most income groups is deteriorating as the share of big capital is increasing. Cf. below, Chapter 7, section 3C.

36. For instance, the index of industrial production increased four times more than the index of industrial employment during the 1951—71 period. And among all industrial sectors, the manufacturing sector showed the lowest labour absorption capacity for that same period. (Figures taken from Photopoulos, op. cit., p. 37.)

37. Cf. G. Coutsoumaris, op. cit., pp. 266 ff. For more recent data, cf. *KEBA*, op. cit., vol. II, ch. 3.

38. Whereas between 1952 and 1961 the value of Greek exports was 42 per cent of that of the country's imports, this dropped to 36 per cent during the 1962—71 period (cited in Photopoulos, op. cit., p. 9).

39. Thus 'nearly half of the 30 million pounds invested in French railways in the late 1840's came from a group of British financiers . . . But when the industrial revolution was in full swing, foreign capital soon withdrew, usually after diminished activity for a decade or two . . . When the industrial revolution had run its course, the western countries of the European Continent themselves became increasingly important exporters of capital,' I. T. Berend and G. Ranki, *Economic development in east-central Europe in the 19th and 20th centuries*, Columbia University Press, New York 1974, p. 94.

40. Cf. L. S. Stavrianos, *The Balkans since 1453*, New York 1958, pp. 413 ff.; cf. also Berend and Ranki, op. cit., pp. 105 ff.

41. Cf. E. J. Tsouderos, *Le Rélèvement économique de la Grèce*, Berger-Levrault, Paris 1920. For an account of Greece's financial position in the nineteenth century, cf. A. Levandis, *The Greek foreign debt and the Great Powers 1821—1898*, New York 1944.

42. Cf. below, Chapter 7.
43. L. Althusser, *For Marx*, Lane, London 1969; also his *Reading Capital*, New Left Books, London, 1970. For an introduction to his thought, cf. M. Glucksmann, *Structuralist analysis in contemporary social thought*, Routledge, London 1974; for recent changes in his initial positions, *cf.* L. Althusser, *Elements d'auto-critique*, Hachette, Paris 1974. For the epistemological foundations of Althusserian Marxism, cf. G. Bachelard, *Le materialisme rational*, Paris 1963; and also his *Formation de l'esprit scientifique*, Paris 1967.
44. For a critique of neo-Marxist theories along these lines, cf. for instance, J. Taylor, 'Neo-Marxism and underdevelopment: A sociological phantasy', *Jrnl of Contemporary Asia*, vol. III, 1974; a similar critique is to be found in the reader edited by I. Oxaal, T. Barnett and D. Booth, *Beyond the sociology of development*, Routledge, London 1975; cf. also Lorraine Culley, 'Economic development in neo-Marxist theory', in B. Hindess (ed.), *Sociological theories of the economy*, to be published by Macmillan.
45. For a general introduction to this theoretical tradition, cf. M. Bloch (ed.), *Marxist analysis and social anthropology*, Malaby Press, London 1975; see also M. Godelier, *Horizons, trajets marxistes en anthropologie*, Maspèro, Paris 1975; for some representative works, cf. C. Meillassoux, *Anthropologie économique des Gouro de Côte d'Ivoire*, Mouton, Paris, 3rd ed. 1974; see also his 'From Reproduction to production : A Marxist approach to economic anthropology', *Economy and Society*, vol. I, pp. 93–105; E. Terray, *Le Marxisme devant les sociétés 'primitives'*, Maspèro, Paris 1969; and his *L'organisation sociale des Dida*, Annales de l'Université d'Albidjan, series F, vol. I(2); P. P. Rey, *Colonialisme, néo-colonialisme et transition au capitalisme*, Maspèro, Paris 1971; see also P. P. Rey and G. Dupré, 'Reflections on the pertinence of a theory on the history of Exchange', *Economy and Society*, vol. II, no. 2.
46. The classical work on dualism is J. H. Boeke's *Economics and economic policy of dual societies*, New York 1953; see also his 'Capitalist development in Indonesia and Uganda: a contrast', in UNESCO, *Social change and economic development*, Paris 1963. For an introduction and bibliography on dualistic theories, cf. G. E. Meier (ed.), *Leading issues in economic development*, Oxford University Press 1970, pp. 125–288.
47. See for instance R. Stavenhagen, 'Seven erroneous theses about Latin America', in L. H. Horowitz *et al.*, *Latin American radicalism*, Vintage Books, New York 1969, pp. 102–17.
48. Cf. Amin, op. cit.; see also his more recent work *Le Développement inégal*, Minuit, Paris 1973.
49. The argument here is not that one should completely reject the centre-periphery dichotomy. It can be useful, but only when it has been theoretically worked out. And for this to happen, as I will argue below, the mode of production and the social formation concepts are necessary.
50. E. Laclau, 'Feudalism and capitalism in Latin America', *New Left Review* no. 67, May-June 1971. For a convenient summary of criticisms of Frank's theories, cf. D. Booth, 'André Gunder Frank: an introduction and appreciation', in *Beyond the sociology of development*, op. cit., pp. 50–86; and also N. Long, 'Structural dependency, modes of production and economic brokerage in rural Peru', in *Beyond the sociology of development*, op. cit., pp. 253–82.
51. The existence of an elaborate theory on such concepts does not mean that

there are no disagreements among the writers who work within this tradition. For instance, some of them use a 'broad' definition of the mode of production concept which includes ideological and political elements (Terray, Poulantzas), whereas others exclude from the definition 'superstructural' elements (Balibar) or even the concept of 'relations of production' (Meillassoux). For a critique of Meillassoux's usage of the mode of production concept, cf. E. Terray, *Le Marxisme devant la sociétés primitives*, op. cit.; for a similar debate between Balibar and Poulantzas, cf. N. Poulantzas, 'The capitalist State: a reply to Miliband and Laclau', *New Left Review*, no. 95, p. 78; for a clear, middle-of-the-road definition of the concept, cf. M. Godelier, 'Qu'est-ce que définir une formation économique et sociale: l'example des Incas', in *La Pensée*, Sep–Oct 1971.

As I believe that a lot of theoretical and empirical work must still be done before such concepts acquire a more definite and precise meaning, I have intentionally avoided giving explicit definitions, hoping that their meaning will become clear by the way they are used, especially in Chapters 1, 7 and 8.

52. For a recent critique of the empiricist character of modern sociology, cf. D. Willer and J. Willer, *Systematic empiricism: critique of a pseudo-science*, Englewood Cliffs, N.J., 1973; cf. also P. Hirst, *Durkheim, Bernard and epistemology*, Routledge, London 1975.

53. Also, the point that it is only in capitalist social formations that the economy is both dominant and 'determining in the last instance', whereas in pre-capitalist social formations it is political or ideological instances which are dominant – this is an idea the utility of which I tried to show in the previous chapter. This is not to say that Althusser's position on these matters does not create theoretical difficulties. First of all, the idea of the economy always being 'determining in the last instance' seems to me more a clever face-saving formula than a serious theoretical statement abot the relationships between infra- and superstructure. I think that the utility of the formula is ritualistic rather than theoretical. It allows those Marxists who want to be faithful to their master's work to accept the obvious fact that in some cases non-economic institutions play the dominant role in the structuring and change of a whole social formation, without their having to abandon any of the sacrosanct elements of historic materialism (i.e. that the economy is *always* the most important instance). For the idea of 'determination in the last instance' (i.e. the idea that the economy, even when not dominant, determines which instance will become dominant in a social formation), is theoretically harmless as far as research is concerned. As a tool of analysis it provides no guidance whatsoever, either positive or misleading, for the examination of concrete social formations.

Another weak point in Althusser's formulation of the relationship between the economy and the superstructure is the opaque, 'untheorised' way in which he talks about the links or articulations between instances. What precisely is the nature of these articulations? What exactly does he mean when he talks about 'structures producing effects' or determining other structures? What is the logical or theoretical status of concepts such as *relative autonomy* or *dominance* when referring to relationships between instances? So when speaking of the dominance of one class over another, how is this dominance different from the dominance of one structure or instance over another? These theoretical gaps can easily lead to a reification of structures or to excessive formalism. As I will try to argue below, some of these theoretical difficulties stem from the fact that Althusser reduces classes in particular and collective actors in general to mere 'bearers of structures', and thus falls victim to a special type of reductionism: one which makes collective actors into the passive product of a hierarchy of 'structures'.

54. L. Lublinskaya, *French absolutism: the crucial phase: 1620–1629*, Cambridge University Press, 1968.

55. For instance, the arguments of M. Dobb, who views capitalism and feudalism in terms of modes of production, are much more convincing than those of Sweezy, who defines feudalism in exchange terms (lack of markets etc.). Cf. R. Hilton (ed.), *The transition from feudalism to capitalism*, New Left Books, London 1976. For a critique of theories of the economy which focus on the sphere of distribution and neglect the sphere of production, cf. A. Jenkins, 'Substantivism as a Comparative Theory of Economic Forms', in B. Hindess (ed.), op. cit.

56. Cf. G. Labica, 'Quatre observations sur le concept de mode de production et de formation économique de la société', *La Pensée*, Sep–Oct 1971, pp. 88ff.; the anti-evolutionist implication of the mode of production concept is repeatedly emphasised by B. Hindess and P. Hirst, *Pre-capitalist modes of production*, Routledge, London 1975.

57. C. D. Scott, 'Peasants, proleterianisation and the articulation of modes of production', in *Jrnl of Peasant Studies*, Apr 1976, p. 323.

58. For some writers, simple commodity production does not constitute a *mode of production* at all. For instance, according to R. Meek, *Studies in the labour theory of value* (Lawrence & Wishart, London 1956), Marx uses the concept of simple commodity production as an analytical tool in order to highlight the properties of the capitalist mode of production. For other writers (cf. O. Lange, *Political economy*, vol. I, Macmillan, New York 1963), simple commodity production, although never dominant in a social formation, does constitute a specific mode to be found in almost all contemporary social formations. In this study, the latter position is accepted. For a discussion on this point, cf. S. Cook, 'Value, Price and Simple Commodity Production', *Jrnl of Peasant Studies*, July 1976.

59. In the language of development economics this type of negative linkage is often expressed in terms of the 'backwash' effects of the 'modern' sector to the rest of the economy being stronger than the 'spread' effects (cf. G. Myrdal, *Economic Theory and Underdeveloped Regions*, Duckworth, London, 1957, pp. 13 ff.). For the lack of strong 'spread' effects between the capitalist and the simple commodity sectors in Greece cf. Chapter 1, section 5 and Chapter 4, section 2.

60. Ignacy Sachs has expressed a similar idea when he states that 'the specificity of the third-world problematic can be defined as the *coexistence of anachronisms* inside the systems under study on the one hand [i.e. the third-world countries], and between them and the industrialised countries on the other – where the latter are characterised not only by greater development of their forces of production, but *mainly by the greater homogeneity of their relations of production*' [translation and italics mine]: *La découverte du tiers monde*, Flammarion, Paris 1972, p. 124. For a similar definition of underdevelopment, cf. C. Kay, *Development and Underdevelopment: a Marxist analysis*, Macmillan,

London 1975.

61. N. Poulantzas, *La crise des dictatures: Portugal, Grèce, Espagne*, Maspèro, Paris 1975, p. 15; and C. Vergopoulos, op. cit., introduction.

62. For the concept of disarticulation, cf. S. Amin, *L'accumulation à l'échelle mondiale*, op. cit., p. 321.

63. To mention an obvious example: because of the 'enclave' character of capitalist Greek industry (and the role that foreign capital plays within it), any rapid industrialisation implies automatically a dramatic increase of imports, an increase by no means neutralised by import substitution savings or by an increase in industrial exports (cf. Chapter 7, section 3). This means a very specific type of deterioration in the balance of payments situation. For a discussion of the specificity of dependence in Latin American countries, cf. T. Dos Santos, 'The crisis of development theory and the problem of dependence in Latin America', in H. Bernstein (ed.), *Underdevelopment and Development*, op. cit.

64. Ibid., p. 17. On this point, cf. below, Chapter 4, section 3. Poulantzas seems to be bothered by he fact that the concepts of underdevelopment, as well as its opposite, that of development, imply the existence of some sort of 'economic development *neutral* in itself, with a uniform outcome, which cannot but be positive' (*La crise des dictatures*, op. cit., p. 20). It is true that neo-evolutionist theories often use the term development and modernisation in such a 'neutral' manner, i.e. without any reference to its capitalist or non-capitalist character. However, this is certainly not true in neo-Marxist theories. Terms take their precise meaning when seen within a specific theoretical tradition. When Frank, Furtado or Stavenhagen use the term underdevelopment, they clearly imply *capitalist* underdevelopment. I leave aside the complicated problem of whether or not one can speak of non-capitalist underdevelopment (e.g. 'disarticulations' within a planned economy which enhance its dependence on other planned economies). But whatever position one takes on this issue, it is easy to avoid the alleged 'neutrality' of the term development/underdevelopment by adding the adjective 'capitalist' when referring to free-market economies.

As far as the 'positive' connotation of the term development is concerned, it is perfectly true that neo-Marxist theories, as I have repeatedly stressed, consider the capitalist trajectory of the West more 'positive' than the capitalist trajectory of third-world countries (in the precise sense that in the latter case the problem of mass poverty, unemployment and dependence remains unsolved). I see nothing wrong with this type of obvious comparison. Moreover, when Poulantzas talks about the *dependent* industrialisation of countries like Greece, Spain or Portugal, there is also the 'positive' implication that Western industrialisation was less dependent, more autonomous.

Another objection to the term underdevelopment was put forward by C. Bettelheim, who argues that 'those who use the term "underdeveloped countries" admit implicitly or explicitly that these countries are simply at a later stage of evolutionary development, and therefore that, in order to develop, they should follow the same path as the so-called developed countries' (*Planification et croissance accélérée*, Maspèro, Paris 1967, p. 27; my translation). This evolutionist fallacy is primarily held by writers who use the term 'developing' countries. As I have repeatedly said above, the term underdeveloped countries, as used by all neo-Marxists (Furtado, Frank, Baran, Amin,

Cardoso, Casanova, Arrighi, etc.), implies *exactly the opposite*: that third-world countries are following an economic trajectory radically different from the Western one; and that underdevelopment is not an 'original' stage characteristic of 'traditional' societies, but a condition induced by Western imperialism (cf. S. Gunder Frank, op. cit.). Of course, from an Althusserian point of view, it can be argued that the term underdevelopment is not 'scientific' or not 'theorised' properly, since it has been constructed from theories which do not strictly follow the methodology of *Das Kapital*. (Cf. for instance J. Taylor, op. cit. and L. Culley, op. cit.) But in so far as no serious theories exist as yet which deal explicitly with third-world capitalist social formations in 'rigorous' Marxist terms, any replacement of the concept of underdevelopment by some other ('deformed', 'dependent' capitalism etc.) will be even more atheoretical and *ad hoc*. Finally, it is interesting to note that the study of third-world capital accumulation which, in my view, most closely follows the type of analysis underlying Marx's *Capital* (G. Kay's *Development and Underdevelopment: a Marxist analysis*, London 1975) does use the concept of underdevelopment for examining the structure of peripheral capitalism.

What is finally important is not whether one should use the term 'under-developed', 'dependent' or 'peripheral' when referring to the socio-economic conditions of third-world countries. The important thing is not the word as such, but the methodological and other theoretical implications often attached to certain terms. That is why it is always essential to locate concepts within specific thoretical debates — for it is only these debates which can clarify their meanings.

65. As Lockwood has pointed out, one of the strengths of Marx's theory of change is his successful attempt to show how system contradictions (e.g. between forces nd relations of production, between modes of production, between infra- and superstructure) can, *in certain conditions*, lead to class conflict and change. See D. Lockwood, 'Social integration and system integration', in G. K. Zollschan and W. Hirsch (eds), *Exploration in social change*, Routledge, London 1964, pp. 244–56; see also N. Mouzelis, 'Social and system integration: some reflections on a fundamental distinction', op. cit.

66. For an elaboration of this very useful distinction, cf. N. Poulantzas, *Political power and social classes*, New Left Books, London 1975, pp. 85 ff. See also M. Castells, *La question urbaine*, Maspèro, Paris 1972. It should be emphasised that the distinction between structure (system) and practice (action) is an analytic one. To use Poulantzas' expression, it does not refer to 'ontologically different domains' but to two different ways of looking at the same social processes.

67. Gunder Frank's work is a good example of an atheoretical, *ad hoc* treatment of class. The difficulties of using class analysis without the mode of production concept have been pointed out by Lorraine Culley in her critique of the work of Frank, Baran and Sweezy (cf. her 'Economic development in neo-Marxist theory', in B. Hindess, (ed.), *Sociological Theories of the Economy*, op. cit.

Although I would agree with her on this point, I consider as totally unjustified her dismissal of all development theories (including neo-Marxist ones) as teleological. This blanket accusation, which is shared by most authors in the volume mentioned above, is based on the notion that all theories which rank societies or any social form along a continuum (constructed either by the use of such well-known dichotomies as traditional-modern, religious-secular etc., or by the formulation of some general trend such as that of a structural differentiation, rationalisation, industrialisation), are built on a teleological error. This error, according to the author, lies in the instances along the continuum being necessarily portrayed as expressions, manifestations of an 'inner principle' (modernity, rationality), this principle being the 'essence' of the phenomenon under consideration. This attack on development theories, and on sociology in general, is formulated in more theoretical terms by Barry Hindess ('Humanism and teleology in sociological theory', in the same volume). According to Hindess, 'to postulate any form of teleology is to postulate a principle of ranking, in terms of which the forms in the hierarchy may be ordered. The principle itself may take many forms .. An example which is particularly prevalent in sociology is provided by those teleologies which light upon some alleged feature of the present as their ranking principle: for example the teleologies of modernisation, development, or industrialisation . . . in which societies are ranked according to their divergence from the alleged features of "modern society", "industrial society", "structural differentiated" society or whatever' (p. 28). According to this position, even if theories of industrial-isation, development, etc. do not postulate any historical necessity or any 'iron laws' of the passage from one point in the continuum to the next, they are at least minimally teleological since they 'combine an essentialist conception of distinct forms with a principle of temporal order' (ibid., p. 39).

The first point to make is that neo-Marxist theories, as already discussed, are not teleological even in Hindess' 'minimal sense'. For the development-underdevelopment dichotomy has a clearly anti-evolutionist connotation, it cannot be used as a means of ranking societies along a continuum in the same sense as the traditional-modern or developing-developed dichotomies do (cf. above, section 1). But apart from this, even for development theories outside the neo-Marxist school, the 'essentialist' accusation seems to me quite unjusti-fied. For it is perfectly well possible to construct typologies and rank societies or any other social form without being teleological in either the 'minimal' or the 'maximal' sense. For mere ranking which is used by most social thinkers, including Marx and Lenin, has neither essentialist connotations nor does it imply any evolutionist necessity. For instance, I fail to see why the ranking, for comparative or any other reasons, of societies according to their degree of industrialisation (cf. e.g., A. Gerschenkron, *Economic backwardness in histori-cal perspective*, Praeger, London 1962), or of industrial organisations according to their degree of technological complexity (cf. J. Woodward, *Industrial organisation*, London 1965), entails the fallacy of portraying such societies or organisations as the essentialist emanations of the 'inner principle' of industri-alism or technological complexity. One may well criticise this type of ranking in a variety of ways, but not in teleological terms.

To conclude this argument, I think that the problem of teleology (in its weak or strong sense) becomes relevant, as far as a theory of change is concerned, not at the stage of typological construction or ranking, but when one tries to *explain* change, i.e. to identify the mechanisms which lead from one point of the continuum to the next. More generally, it seems to me that the whole issue of 'essentialism' or 'expressive causality' may be a serious concern for Althusser the philosopher, still struggling with the ghost of Hegel; but that it is merely a red herring in the context of present-day development theories, whether of the Marxist or non-Marxist variety.

68. On this point, cf. I. Roxborough, 'Dependency theory in the sociology of development', *West African Journal of Sociology and Political Science*, vol. I, no. 2, Jan 1976.

69. Cf. E. Sereni, 'De Marx à Lenine: la catégorie de "formation économique et sociale",' *La Pensée*, Sep—Oct 1971; Poulantzas argues in a similar vein when he writes: 'If we confine ourselves to modes of production alone, examining them in a pure and abstract fashion, we find that each of them involves two classes — the exploiting class which is politically and ideologically dominant and the exploited class which is politically and ideologically dominated: masters and slaves in the slave mode of production, lords and serfs in the feudal mode of production, bourgeois and workers in the capitalist mode of production. But a concrete society (a social formation) *involves more* than two classes, in so far as it is composed of various modes and forms of production.' ('On social classes', *New Left Review*, Mar—Apr 1973, p. 33.)

70. For a clear discussion of the ways in which the basic invariant elements (workers, means of production, non-workers etc.) combine in various modes of production, cf. E. Balibar, 'Sur les concepts fondamentaux du matérialisme historique', in L. Althusser and E. Balibar, *Lire le Capital*, vol. II, Maspèro, Paris 1973. pp. 112—51.

71. Cf. his *Pouvoir Politique et Classes Sociales*, Maspèro, Paris 1968; also his *Les Classes Sociales dans le Capitalisme aujourd'hui*, Seuil, Paris 1974.

72. Cf. N. Poulantzas, 'The Capitalist State: A reply to Miliband and Laclau', *New Left Review*, Jan—Feb 1976.

73. *Pouvoir Politique* . . . . , op. cit., p. 66.

74. *Lire le Capital*, vol. II, op. cit., p. 146 (my translation).

75. *Les Classes Sociales* . . . . . , op. cit., p. 19.

76. Ibid. p. 17.

77. *Ibid.*, p. 32.

78. Cf. for instance in the same tradition the more recent work of G. Carchedi, 'On the economic identification of the new middle class', *Economy and Society*, Feb 1975, and E. O. Wright, 'Class Boundaries in Advanced Capitalist Societies', *New Left Review*, Jan—Aug 1976.

79. Cf. for instance M. Castells, *Luttes urbaines*, Maspèro, Paris 1973; Lublinskaya, op. cit.; N. Poulantzas, in his *Fascisme et dictature* (Maspèro, Paris 1970) manages to portray classes more autonomously. But this is not because of his or Althusser's metatheory, but rather in spite of it.

80. *Horizons, trajets marxistes en anthropologie*, Maspèro, Paris 1973, pp. 13—82.

81. The translation of Godelier's terms into Parsonian language is mine. Despite the close affinity between Parsonian functionalism and Althusserian Marxism (*in so far as the problem of collective actors is concerned*), Althusser would be horrified at the idea that some of his fundamental methatheoretical positions come close to 'bourgeois' functionalist sociology.

One could object, of course, that an attempt at translating Althusserian Marxism into Parsonian functionalism is illegitimate in so far as a third paradigm transcending the above does not exist and that therefore it is theoretically impossible to compare or establish any sort of link between the two. This position, discernible in attenuated form in Kuhn's early work, starts out from the dubious assumption that competing paradigms in any one field of study are totally disconnected from each other, exhibiting a high degree of individual internal unity and coherence. Although it is not possible to discuss this epistemological problem here at any length, if one closely examines the dominant paradigms, at least in the social sciences, it becomes obvious immediately that they are not totally self-contained, that they interpenetrate each other in various ways. Therefore, as A. Giddens has recently pointed out, one should stop considering 'meaning frames as discrete, self-contained universes and substitute as starting point that all paradigms are meditated by others' (*New rules of sociological method*, Hutchinson, London 1976, p. 144).

With this in mind, I do not consider it illegitimate to use in one and the same volume, depending on the problem under consideration, concepts derived from different paradigms (e.g. the concept of 'society' and that of a 'social formation'). I believe generally that in the present state of the social sciences one should try to break the barriers between the Marxist and non-Marxist social sciences; and a precondition for this is the striking of a balance between two extreme, equally unacceptable positions. These are, on the one hand, the conceptual purism of some Marxist writers (i.e. their single-minded determination never to 'contaminate' the Marxist discourse with 'bourgeois' and therefore 'reactionary' concepts); and on the other hand, the *ad hoc* eclecticism characteristic of the writings of some non-Marxist sociologists — consider for instance the arbitrary manner in which the concept of alienation is used in industrial sociology today, cf. R. Blauner, *Alienation and Freedom* (Chicago University Press, Chicago 1964).

82. Godelier, *Horizons* . . . , op. cit., p. 67.
83. Ibid., p. 68.
84. Ibid., p. 74.
85. Ibid., p. 72 (translation and parenthesis mine).
86. Cf. for instance R. Dore, 'Function and cause', *American Sociological Review*, 1961; and R. K. Merton, *Social theory and social structure*, Social Press, Glencoe 1963, pp. 60—4. Godelier is quite explicit about his ascription of causal effects to functions, as cf. his *Horizons* . . . . . , op. cit., p. 44. Of course I am not implying that all structuralist analysis falls into this type of teleological trap. Neither do I deny that there are also basic differences between the structural functionalism of conventional anthropology, and that of Marxist anthropology. But there is no doubt in my mind that neither of these structuralisms, in so far as they portray actors as mere products of structures, can deal properly with problems of causation and change.
87. For an early formulation on the importance of actors in social causation, cf. R. M. McIver, *Social causation*, Harper, New York, 1942. From the Marxist side, Lukàcs' *History and Class Consciousness*, by portraying the proletariat as a collective historical subject makes a similar point. However, by postulating the possibility of an 'absolute class consciousness' and by entrusting the proletariat with a unique mission in history, his analysis becomes teleological and metaphysical. As P. Connerton has pointed out, Lukàcs 'brought once more into focus the potentiality of human agency and then went on again to displace it' (cf. 'The Collective historical subject: Reflections on Lukàcs' history and class consciousness', *British Journal of Sociology*, June 1974, p. 176). But there is no reason why one could not treat classes as collective historical agents while

accepting historical contingency and, therefore, rejecting Lukàcs' metaphysics. In fact, I fully agree with Connerton, who argues that a critical theorist who 'wished to distinguish what is living from what is dead in Lukàcs' work would need to elaborate its historical dynamic while exorcising its metaphysical spook' (ibid., p. 177).

88. Cf. *Capital*, International Publishers, New York 1968, vol. I, part VIII, pp. 713–74.

89. Cf. L. Althusser and E. Balibar, op. cit., pp. 178 ff; cf. also Sereni, op. cit.; C. Luporini, 'Reality and historicity: economy and dialectics in Marxism', *Economy and Society*, vol. IV, no. 2, pp. 206–31; M. Godelier, *Rationalité et irrationalité en économie*, Maspèro, Paris 1966, part II.

90. 'Sur les concepts fondamentaux du matérialisme historique', op. cit., pp. 178 ff.

91. Ibid., pp. 217–25.

92. For such a critique of Balibar's position, cf. P. Hirst and B. Hindess, *Pre-capitalist Economic Formations*, Routledge, London 1975; pp. 263 ff. They rightly stress that, by underemphasising the importance of class struggle, both Althusser and Balibar have failed to deal properly with the transition problem. But despite Hirst and Hindess' constant reference to the 'class struggle', this concept plays little more than a decorative role in their book; the relationship between the conditions of existence, reproduction or destruction of a mode and the class struggle remains untheorised. All they have to say about this crucial relationship is that the dominant mode of production sets certain limits to the *possible* forms that the class struggle can take. What actually happens within these limits and, more important, what the relationships are between concrete class struggles and the transformation of these limits (i.e. the transformation of modes of production) is a matter which, according to the authors, entirely depends on the conjuncture of each specific situation and cannot, therefore, be theorised. Thus in the place of Balibar's structuralist teleological formulations, one has a theoretical vacuum which necessarily leads to an *ad hoc*, empiricist treatment of class (cf. T. Asad and H. Wolpe, 'Concepts of modes of production', *Economy and Society*, Nov 1976). In other words, I do think that the real alternative to Althusser's passive treatment of class (i.e. to his one-sided emphasis on the structure → practice relationship), is not a relapse into empiricism, but the theorisation of the relationship in the *opposite direction* as well, from practices to structures. By this I do not, of course, advocate the fabrication of ready-made formulas or predictions giving instant solutions or answers to specific class struggles. I simply suggest the construction of conceptual tools (of 'generalities II', in Althusser's language) which could sensitise the student to the fact that there is a two-way dialectical relationship between structures and practices: that structures (modes of production, class 'places') set limits to class struggles but also that the latter reproduce *and* transform, in the long term, these structural limits.

To conclude, I would argue that despite serious differences among Marxists under Althusser's sway, none of them, to my knowledge, has managed to break out of the theoretical cul-de-sac of his ultra-structuralism, especially on the metatheoretical level; nobody has yet produced adequate conceptual tools for the study of transition. It is not, therefore, surprising that, apart from entirely negative criticisms, they have not succeeded in replacing neo-Marxism with a more constructive approach to the study of peripheral social formations.

93. 'System and social integration', *op. cit.*, pp. 247 ff.

94. For another unsuccessful attempt to solve the problem of transition within a strictly structuralist framework, cf. the voluminous work of Ives Barel, *La réproduction sociale: systèmes vivants, invariance et changement*, Anthropos, Paris 1973. Closer to the sociology of development literature, one should also mention in this context Alavi's *ad hoc* conceptualisation of a 'colonial mode of production', specific to the type of transitional condition characterising third-world countries (cf. his 'India and the colonial mode of production', *Socialist Register*, 1975).

95. Concerning 'structural indeterminancy' during transition periods, a very good illustration is provided by Lublinskaya's work (*cf.* her *French absolutism: the crucial phase 1620—1629*, Cambridge University Press, Cambridge 1968; also her 'Popular masses and absolutism', *Economy and Society*, vol. II, no. 3). In trying to explain the numerous popular uprisings in France during the first half of the seventeenth century, Lublinskaya, together with many other historians, points out that these uprisings took extremely variable forms — so much so that it is not possible to explain them either in terms of the development of class-consciousness among the masses, or in terms of any stable class alliances. According to Lublinskaya, this fluid and 'fuzzy' social situation was due to the fact that the seventeenth-century French social formation was in the middle of its transition from feudalism to capitalism. In non-transitional periods, with the clear-cut dominance of a certain mode of production, class alliances are more stable, and it is therefore easier to link in a more or less straightforward way social unrest to the dominant structures of production. In transitional periods, on the other hand, when the old dominant mode is disintegrating and the new one has not yet established its dominance, structural constraints are looser, and it becomes much more difficult to 'deduce' social conflict and unrest from a purely structuralist analysis of modes of production. As I have already pointed out, it is particularly in the study of such transitional cases that a logico-deductive approach seems less satisfactory than a historico-genetic one.

Finally, it is worth suggesting in this context that the idea of structural indeterminancy during transition periods might be linked to the point made by development economists that in underdeveloped countries, contrary to the developed ones, functional relations between variables are often discontinuous. 'These discontinuities may take either of two forms. If A is a function of B, instead of a smooth curve relating the two variables, there may be a sudden jump in the value of B at a critical value of A; or the functions may have sharp points. Both the first and second derivatives may have positive signs within one range of A and negative signs in another value of A.' (B. Higgins, *Economic Development*, Constable, London 1959.) It is my contention that if one tries to go beyond the mere establishment of such discontinuous curves, if one tries to *explain* them, class analysis is necessary.

96. K. Marx, *Pre-capitalist economic formations*, Lawrence & Wishart, London 1964; for a collection of texts by Marx, Engels and Lenin on the subject, cf. Centre d'Etudes et de Recherches Marxistes, *Sur les sociétés précapitalistes*, Editions Sociales, Paris 1973.

97. E. Hobsbawm, *Industry and empire*, Penguin, London 1968; F. Braudel, *La méditerranée et le monde méditerranéen a l'époque de Philippe II*, Armand-

Collin, Paris 1966; P. Anderson, *Passages from antiquity to feudalism*, and *Lineages of the absolute State*, New Left Books, London 1974; Lublinskaya, op. cit.

98. R. Bendix, *Work and authority in industry*, Wiley, New York 1956; B. Moore, op. cit., and E. Wallerstein, *The modern world system: Capitalist agriculture in 16th-century Europe*, New York 1974. Of course, there are significant differences between these writers. For instance, Wallerstein, leaving aside some serious empirical fallacies in his work, pays more attention to systemic constraints than B. Moore and in that sense his work achieves a better balance between a system and an action approach. But that these authors have a very great deal in common becomes obvious if one compares their writings with those which overemphasise the systemic approach.

99. Cf. C. Tsoukalas, 'Dépendance et réproduction: le rôle de l'appareil scolaire dans une formation trans-territoriale (Université de Paris 1975, unpub. thesis); cf. also below, Chapter 4, section 1, and Chapter 9.

100. Cf. N. Mouzelis and M. Attalides, 'Greece', in M. Scotford Archer and S. Giner (eds), *Contemporary Europe*, Weidenfeld & Nicolson, London 1973, part I.

101. For Greek examples of such studies, cf. Chapter 3.

102. Cf. P. Streeten, 'The use and abuse of models of development planning', in K. Martin and J. Knapp (eds), *The teaching of development economics*, Frank Cass, London 1966.

CHAPTER 3

1. As a serious definition of the concept of class would imply a systematic reference to various class theories, I shall not try to define in rigorous terms what I mean by class. However, I hope that the relevant meanings and the crucial differences between the concepts of class and stratum will emerge clearly from the discussion of the various problems involved. For a serious analysis of class theories, cf. A. Giddens, *The class structure of the advanced societies*, Hutchinson, London 1973; G. Gurvitch, *Le concept de classes sociales de Marx à nos jours*, Centre de documentation Universitaire, Paris, France, 1954; N. Poulantzas, *Pouvoir politique et classes sociales*, Maspèro, Paris, 1968.

2. By *metatheory* or *paradigm* I mean those conceptualisations that do not refer directly to a set of empirically testable hypotheses on a specific problem area, but rather 'map out the problem area and thus prepare the ground for its empirical investigation' – cf. S. F. Nadel, *The theory of social structure*, vol. I, Routledge, London 1962.

3. This is particularly true of Marx's more 'historical' works like his *Class struggle in France 1848–1850* or *The civil war in France* and of those Marxists who follow and emphasise the less mechanistic, more voluntaristic elements of Marx's thought – e.g. Lukács, Ossowski. Other Marxist schools portray classes, and collective actors in general, in a less 'voluntaristic' fashion, i.e. as mere products of structures. For a critique of the Althusserian school along such lines, cf. R. Miliband, 'Poulantzas and the capitalist state', *New Left Review*, Nov–Dec 1973, pp. 86 ff.; cf. also my Chapters 2 and 4.

4. For a discussion of a division in sociology along such lines, cf. A. Dawe, 'The two sociologies', *British Jrnl of Sociology* XXI(2), 1970, pp. 207–18; A.

Gouldner, *The coming crisis of western sociology*, Heinemann, London 1970, D. Lockwood, 'Social integration and system integration', in G. K. Zollschan and W. Hirsch (eds), *Explorations in social change*, Routledge, London 1964, pp. 244–51; and N. Mouzelis, 'Social and system integration: some reflections on a fundamental distinction', *British Jrnl of Sociology*, XXV(4) 1974, pp. 395–409.

5. T. Parsons (*The social system*, Routledge, London 1951) distinguishes four major sub-systems corresponding to the four functional problems that any system has to solve: the adaptation, goal achievement, integration, and latency sub-systems.

6. Cf. Lockwood, op. cit., p. 246.

7. N. Smelser, *Social change in the Industrial Revolution, 1770–1840*, 2 vols, Routledge, London 1960.

8. For a criticism of functionalist role-analysis along such lines, cf. A. V. Cicourel, 'Basic and normative rules in the negotiation of status and role', in H. P. Dreitzel (ed.), *Recent Sociology*, no. 2, Collier-Macmillan, London 1970, pp. 4–48; see also P. Filmer et al., *New directions in sociological theory*, Collier-Macmillan, London 1972, pp. 57–76.

9. In fact such critics – whether influenced by symbolic interactionism, phenomenology or ethnomethodology – point out that even when actors comply faithfully with role expectations, they do not do so in an automaton-like manner. Social action and interaction is not a mere following of norms. Every encounter is a symbolic construction, a negotiation in meanings, an intricate and risky game in which role expectations are only one of the elements that players take into account in relating to each other; cf. for instance E. Goffman, *The presentation of self in everyday life*, Anchor Books, New York 1959.

10. As far as explanation is concerned, functionalism does not go further than pointing out that there is a connection between stratificational phenomena in general and the existence of social needs – i.e. that the unequal distribution of rewards seems to be a prerequisite for the functioning of all social systems (cf. for instance K. Davis and W. E. Moore, 'Some principles of stratification', *American Sociological Review* 10(2), 1945, pp. 242–49). Leaving aside the ideological and teleological connotations of such an explanation, it certainly does not tell us very much about variations in social inequality, neither does it provide us with tools for the study of the development of inequalities in specific contexts.

11. Op. cit., pp. 107–17.

12. J. Dimaki, *Towards a Greek sociology of education*, 2 vols (in Greek), National Centre of Social Studies, Athens 1974.

13. Ibid., vol. I, pp. 80–109.

14. Ibid., vol. I, pp. 127–30.

15. Ibid., vol. I, pp. 118–39.

16. C. Tsoukalas, *Dépendance et réproduction: le rôle de l'appareil scolaire dans une formation trans-territoriale*, Université de Paris I (Sorbonne), unpub. thesis 1975.

17. Ibid., vol. II, Part II, ch. 2; and also below Chapter 8, section 4.

18. Cf. for instance C. Moustaka, *The internal migrant*, Social Sciences Centre, Athens 1964. For an inventory of studies on Greek migration, cf. E. Vlachos, *An annotated bibliography on Greek migration*, mimeographed, Social Sciences

Centre, Monographs on Migration, Athens 1966. See also E. Dimitras and E. Vlachos, *Sociological surveys on Greek emigrants*, Centre of Social Research, Athens 1971.

19. C. Safilios-Rothschild, 'Socio-psychological factors affecting fertility in urban Greece: a preliminary report', *Jrnl of Marriage and Family* 31(3), 1969; see also her 'Attitudes of Greek spouses towards marital infidelity' in G. Nenback (ed.), *The dynamics of extramarital relations*, Prentice-Hall, 1969.

20. G. E. Kourvetaris, 'Professional self-images and political perspectives in the Greek military', *American Sociological Review* 36, 1971, pp. 1043–57.

21. K. P. Legg, *Politics in modern Greece*, Part III, Stanford University Press, Stanford, Cal. 1969.

22. For a very systematic and extensive review of sociological writings on Greece, see E. Vlachos, *Modern Greek society: continuity and change. An annotated classification of selected sources*, Special Monograph series, Department of Sociology and Anthropology, Colorado State University, 1969.

23. For a systematic discussion of this problem see N. Mouzelis, 'Social and system integration', op. cit.

24. Cf. N. Mouzelis, 'Modernisation, development and the peasant', *Development and Change* IV (3), 1972–73, pp. 73–6.

25. A. P. Alexander, *Greek industrialists*, Centre of Planning and Economic Research, Athens 1964.

26. A. A. Pepelasis, 'Agriculture in a restrictive environment: the case of Greece', *Economic Geography* 36, 1960, pp. 145–57; cf. also his 'The legal system and economic development of Greece', *Jrnl of Economic History* XIX(2), pp. 173–98.

27. More precisely, according to Kourvetaris (op. cit., pp. 1050 ff.) the self-image of the Greek officer is a mixture of traditional (heroic) and modern (specialist-managerial) values. For a study of the Greek family in terms of structural-functional differentiation, see D. Bardis, 'The changing family in modern Greece', *Sociology and Social Research* 40, 1955, pp. 19–23.

28. Legg, *Politics of Modern Greece*, op. cit.

29. Cf. for instance F. H. Cardoso, *Sociologie du développement en Amérique Latine*, Anthropos, Paris 1969; R. Stavenhagen, *Les classes sociales dans les sociétés agraires*, Anthropos, Paris 1969; S. Amin, *L'accumulation à l'échelle mondiale*, Anthropos, Paris 1970; G. Arrighi, *The political economy of Rhodesia*, Mouton, The Hague 1967; P. Baran, *The political economy of growth*, Monthly Review Press, New York and London 1957. For an excellent analysis of various roads to the development of industrialised countries, cf. B. Moore, *The social origins of dictatorship and democracy*, Allen Lane, London 1967.

30. J. Kordatos, *History of modern Greece*, 5 vols. (in Greek), Aion Publishing House, Athens 1958; also his *Introduction to the history of Greek capitalism*, Athens 1930; N. Psiroukis, *The Asia Minor catastrophe* (in Greek), Athens 1974; G. Skliros, *The contemporary problems of Hellenism* (in Greek) Alexandria 1919. See also J. Zevgos, *Short study of modern Greek history* (in Greek), Pezos Logos, Athens 1945. One should mention here three recent significant works in the same tradition: C. Moskof, *National and social consciousness in Greece 1830–1909* (in Greek), Neo Poria, Salonica 1972; and V. Filias, *Society and power in Greece 1800–1864* (in Greek), Makrionitis,

Athens 1974; C. Vergopoulos, *The Agrarian Problem in Greece* (in Greek),
Exantos, 1975.

31. J. Kordatos, *The social significance of the 1821 revolution* (in Greek),
Epikairotita, Athens 1972. Of course, not all merchants supported the revolution. For instance, the shipping magnates of Hydra and the Peloponnesian
notables in control of local commerce were initially against any violent
uprising. (cf. M. Sakellariou, *The Peloponnese during the second Ottoman rule*,
in Greek, Athens 1939.)

32. Filias, op. cit., part I.

33. Filias, op. cit., part II.

34. N. Diamandouros, *Political modernisation, social conflict and cultural cleavage
in the formation of the modern Greek State 1821–1928*, Ph.D. dissertation,
Columbia University, New York 1972. Diamandouros is influenced by functionalist theories of modernisation; however, his training as a historian,
fortunately, takes him beyond this framework to a serious consideration of
actors. For more on the class analysis of the 1821 revolutionary period, cf.
Chapter 1, sections 2 and 3, and Chapter 8, section 3.

35. However, it is worth mentioning in this context that a certain conceptual
clarification of terms like 'feudal', 'bourgeois', 'modern', etc., is necessary for
the debate on the class nature of the 1821 revolution to become more fruitful.
For instance B. Kremmidas in a recent publication (*Introduction to the History
of Modern Greek Society: 1700–1891* in Greek, Exantas, Athens, 1976)
criticises Filias for considering pre-revolutionary Greece as a 'feudal' society.
According to him, taking into account the considerable developments in the
economy of eighteenth-century Greece, at that time it was already a capitalist
country. Kremmidas arrives at this misleading conclusion because, as G. Frank
does in another context (cf. Chapter 2), he defines capitalism in the sphere of
distribution. Thus for Kremmidas, given that in the eighteenth-century Greece
was integrated into the world capitalist market, it necessarily was a capitalist
society! (Op. cit., p. 197.) If on the other hand one defines capitalism in terms
of relations of production, it becomes quite obvious that despite some
'proto-capitalist' developments in eighteenth-century Greek industry, the capitalist mode of production became dominant in the Greek social formation
much later (cf. Chapter 1, sections 1 to 5).

36. Of course, together with the social stratification approach, the theory of
structural-functional differentiation has its place in sociology, especially in the
study of development. But it is simply a convenient tool for the description of
certain fundamental trends. It can never in itself explain such trends. An
example from Greek history will make this point clear. If one considers the
development of Greek institutional forms over a long period of time, one can
clearly discern a process of increasing differentiation between religious and
political institutions. Thus, when Greece was under Turkish occupation, the
Greek Orthodox Church constituted the main link between the Sultan and his
Greek subjects. In that sense, the Church, although subjected to strict central
control, not only had a high degree of autonomy in religious and cultural
matters, it also acquired a large number of political functions. Indeed, together
with local Greek notables, the Church was responsible for the running of all
municipal affairs.
    After the Greek national uprising of 1821 and the establishment of the

modern Greek State, there was a clear differentiation between religious and political functions. Almost all of the political functions that had previously been exercised by the Church organisation were shifted to the newly established State. Therefore, after independence, political roles and religious roles were much more clearly differentiated on every level (village community, region, nation). But *social differentiation took a specific form*: religious roles and institutions were subjugated to political roles and institutions. If one tries now to explain this specific type of differentiation, one must necessarily move from the system to the social level of analysis, from institutions to classes. Among other factors, one has to examine the role that the traditional ruling groups played during the nationalist War of Independence. Among them, the high clergy was initially hostile to any idea of overthrowing Turkish rule, under which it occupied such a dominant position (cf. above Chapter 1, section 2). By taking into account the weak role of the high clergy during the nationalist uprising, one understands why the holders of political power managed quite soon after independence (*a*) to establish the autonomy of the autochtonous Church *vis-à-vis* the Patriarchate, and (*b*) to put the religious authorities under the direct control of the State. As a matter of fact, the 1833 ecclesiastical constitution of the autonomous Greek Orthodox Church, influenced by the German Protestant tradition, put the Church under the absolute control of the State (see F. A. Frazer, *The Orthodox Church and independent Greece*, Cambridge University Press 1969). Its subordinate position has not changed much since that time; even today, through the Ministry of Religious Affairs, the Church is more or less run as an administrative branch of the State.

37. It is quite well established by now that Marx's stage-typology (ancient mode of production, feudal, capitalist etc.) was not meant to be a deterministic, unilinear theory of development (cf. for instance S. Avineri, *The social and political thought of K. Marx*, Cambridge University Press 1968).

   Although Marx often thinks in terms of stages (e.g. when he considers that third-world countries will, through the spread of capitalism, sooner or later become industrialised), his construction of stages should be seen as an attempt to identify *general evolutionary* trends rather than temporally *specific* lines of evolutionary change. (For the crucial distinction between general and specific evolution, see M. D. Sahlins and E. R. Service (eds), *Evolution and culture*, University of Michigan Press, Ann Arbor, Mich., 1960.)

38. For instance, I think that, as Filias rightly argues, Kordatos and Skliros overemphasise the bourgeois character of the 1821 Greek revolution. This is largely due to an uncritical application and crude interpretation of Marx's stage theory in the context of Greece.

39. N. Psiroukis, *Fascism and the 4th of August* (in Greek), Athens 1974.

40. For example, G. Lambrinos considers the 1843 'revolution' as a glorious movement of the 'people' against the reactionary establishment and the throne (*The monarchy in Greece*, in Greek, pp. 35–6). In fact, as both the conservative historian P. Pipinelis (*The monarchy in Greece*, in Greek, Athens 1932) and Filias (op. cit.) point out, the great mass of the people had nothing to do with he events of September 1843. The so-called 'revolution' of 1843 was a purely intra-elite conflict between oligarchical factions and the throne.

41. See, for instance, L. Althusser and E. Balibar, *Reading Capital*, New Left Review Publications, London 1970, cf. also Chapters 1 and 2 above.

42. For more information on the 1909 coup, cf. below, Chapter 6, section 2.

43. For an account of this penetration, see L. S. Stavrianos, *The Balkans since 1453*, part V, Rinehart & Winston, New York 1958.

44. Cf. V. Papacosmas, *The Greek military revolt of 1909*, unpub. thesis, Indiana University, Bloomington, Ind., 1970, pp. 55 ff.

45. As a matter of fact, various associations, operating as pressure groups and attempting to influence public opinion through their newspapers, had appeared in the 1880s, and already there were attempts to organise trade unions from 1895 on.

46. On this point cf. G. Dertilis, op. cit.

47. For the concept of 'hegemony', see A. Gramsci, *Prison notebooks*, Lawrence & Wishart, London 1971, pp. 53 ff.

48. C. Furtado, 'Sous-développement et dépendance', *Temps Modernes*, Oct 1974.

49. Luciano Li Causi, 'Anthropology and Ideology: the case of patronage in Mediterranean Societies', *Radical Science Journal*, no. 1, 1975.

50. For the concept of mobilisation cf. R. Bendix, *Nation-Building and Citizenship*, Action Books, New York 1969; and P. Nettl, *Political Mobilisation*, Faber, London 1967.

51. A third possibility is the case where the working classes (urban or rural) are neither 'contained' within pre-existing bourgeois parties as in inter-war Greece, not politically organised in a more or less autonomous position as in inter-war Bulgaria — but are mobilised from above by charismatic/ populist leaders who manage, through paternalistic and quasi-corporatist policies, to keep working-class organisations under the strong tutelage of the State (e.g. Peron in Argentina, Vargas in Brazil — cf. J. M. Malloy, ed., *Authoritarianism and Corporatism in Latin America*, University of Pittsburg Press, 1977). In all three cases, of course, clientelism persists, but it takes different forms — forms which are radically different from the 'oligarchic' clientelism prevailing before the dominance of the capitalist mode of production and the ensuing entrance of the masses into politics.

Of course these three different modes of 'bringing in' the masses into the political process are not mutually exclusive. In any concrete situation, not only is there a mixture of the three (with one being dominant) but it is also possible for a political system to shift from one dominant mode of integration to another. Thus given the closer relationship between class locations and political practices once the capitalist mode of production prevails, populist/corporatist controls (as in the Brazilian case) or the confinement of the masses through bourgeois parties (as in the inter-war Greek case) can easily become ineffective, as relatively autonomous working-class parties become important. Of course, when their importance reaches the point of threatening the *status quo* they are forcibly suppressed. Thus dictatorial attempts to depoliticise, i.e. to exclude the masses from active politics, seems to be common in all three types of political system.

The above generalisations are not, of course, presented as a 'general theory' of politics in underdeveloped countries. They are highly tentative suggestions which, if properly worked out, can be useful in the study of politics in *some* underdeveloped countries. It is beyond the scope of this chapter to identify the type of societies to which such generalisations are relevant — or, even more important, to analyse the linkage between the timing and style of capitalist underdevelopment and the mode of integration of the working masses into the political process.

52. Cf. Legg, *The Politics of Modern Greece*, op. cit., Parts I and II.

53. Cf. above Chapter 1, section 5E and below Chapter 8, section 3.

54. Cf. his *Politics and Statecraft in the Kingdom of Greece*, Princeton University Press, Princeton, N.J., 1968.

55. D. Lerner, *The passing of traditional society*, Macmillan, London 1964. For a similar approach to the study of peasants during modernisation, see E. M. Rogers, *Modernisation among peasants: the impact of communication*, Holt, Rinehart & Winston, New York 1969. For a criticism of the framework underlying the above works, see N. Mouzelis, 'Modernisation, development and the peasant', *Development and Change* IV (3), 1972–73, pp. 73–88.

56. See below, Chapter 5.

57. From this point of view the concept of class, if properly used, can constitute a very effective link between the action and the system approaches.

58. For the concepts of horizontal and vertical coalitions, see E. Wolf, *Peasants*, Prentice-Hall, Englewood Cliff, N.J., 1966, pp. 81–6; for a treatment of such problems in terms of class (and more generally action), see R. Stavenhagen, *Les classes sociales dans les sociétés agraires*, Anthropos, Paris 1969; R. Stavenhagen (ed.), *Agrarian problems and peasant movements in Latin America*, Anchor Books, New York 1970; E. E. Malefakis, *Agrarian reform and peasant revolution in Spain*, part II, Yale University Press, Newhaven, Conn., 1970.

59. Cf. below Ch. 5. 'Modernisation, development and the peasant', op. cit.

60. V. Filias, op. cit.

61. Two well-known examples in this tradition are J. K. Campbell, *Honour, family and patronage*, Clarendon Press, Oxford 1964; and E. Friedl, *Vasilika: a village in modern Greece*, Holt, Rinehart & Winston, New York 1962.

62. For an example of this type of generalisation see E. M. Rogers, op. cit.

63. An exception to this is M. J. Lineton, *Mina: present and past. Depopulation in a village in Mani*, unpub. thesis, University of Kent 1971. The author, in the second part of his dissertation, examines village problems in the light of an analysis of the underdeveloped structure of Greek society. Such an emphasis on the whole does not necessarily lead away from village studies, but it might suggest new ways of looking at village communities.

64. R. Fox, 'Realm and region in the anthropology of complex societies', mimeographed paper.

65. For two very suggestive studies focusing on village-city links, see E. Friedl, 'The role of kinship in the transmission of of national culture to rural villages in mainland Greece' *American Anthropologist* 61, 1959, pp. 30–8; and the same author's 'Lagging emulation in post-peasant society', *American Anthropologist* 66, 1964, pp. 569–80.

66. Cf. Fox, op. cit., pp. 4 ff.

67. For an example of such a broad framework adopted by an anthropologist, see E. Wolf, *Peasant revolutions in the 20th century*, Faber, London 1971.

68. The alternating importance of class and region (or broad kinship coalitions) as a basis of social cleavage during the early years of the Greek uprising (1821–7) is examined by J. Petropoulos, *Politics and Statecraft in the Kingdom of Greece 1833–1843*, chs 1–2, Princeton University Press, Princeton, N.J., 1968; see also N. Diamandouros, op. cit.

69. Ibid., pp. 210 ff., Poulantzas has a similar view of the 'totality' of the concept. According to him, it is impossible to define class by limiting one's focus of analysis in the economic sphere. The concept of class is inextricably linked with the totality of a social formation, with the mode of articulation of its various spheres (economic, political, ideological). Cf. his *Pouvoir politique et classes sociales*, op. cit., and his article 'On social classes' in *New Left Review*, Apr 1973, pp. 27—55. Taking into account the 'totality' of the concept of class, it becomes obvious that analysis in terms of classes is a special case of action analysis (i.e. one can deal with actors, even economic ones, without necessarily dealing with classes).

70. After all, Marx himself was one of the first social scientists to use questionnaires and the survey method of analysis in order to get information on workers' conditions in industry — cf. R. Blauner, 'Work satisfaction and industrial trends in modern society', in R. Bendix et al. (eds), *Class, status and power*, Free Press, New York 1965.

71. For a discussion of the ahistorical character of both functionalism and its critics, cf. Herminio Martins, 'Time and Theory in Sociology', in John Rex (ed.), *Approaches to Sociology: An Introduction to Major Trends in British Sociology*, 1974, pp. 246—94.

72. Cf. B. Moore, op. cit.; and R. Bendix, *Work and authority in industry*, Wiley, New York 1956; and his *Nation-building and citizenship*, Anchor Books, New York 1969; and E. Wallerstein, *The modern world system: capitalist agriculture in 16th-century* Europe, New York 1974.

73. I have in mind those of C. Moskof, V. Filias, C. Vergopoulos, C. Tsoukalas, op. cit., and A. Elefantis, *The promise of the impossible revolution: the Greek Communist party in the inter-war period* (in Greek), Athens, 1976.

74. Cf. for instance G. Bachelard, *La formation de l'esprit scientifique*, Paris 1967; L. Althusser, *For Marx*, op. cit., and R. B. Braithwaite, *Scientific explanation*, London 1964.

75. Cf. on this point Willer and Willer, op. cit.

76. For such a problematic, cf. C. Vergopoulos, op. cit.

77. Cf. R. B. Braithwaite, op. cit., pp. 76—8, and G. Ryle, *Dilemmas*, London 1962, pp. 82—92.

78. The older generation of social science professors, who did their studies abroad during the inter-war period, mostly attended German universities.

79. For an example of such a work on modern Greece, cf. J. Petropoulos, op. cit.

CHAPTER 4

1. Anthropos, Paris 1974.

2. Exantas, Athens 1975 (in Greek). It will appear in French translation by the end of 1977.

3. L. Althusser, *Reading Capital*, London 1970, and *For Marx*, London 1969.

4. E. Terray, *Le Marxisme devant les sociétés primitives: deux études*, Maspèro, Paris 1969; C. Meillassoux, 'From reproduction to production. A Marxist approach to economic anthropology', *Economy and Society*, vol. I, no. 1; G. Dupré and P. P. Rey, 'Reflections on the pertinence of a theory of the history of exchange', *Economy and Society*, vol. II, no. 2, pp. 131—63; M. Godelier,

'Objet et méthode de l'anthropologie économique', *L'Homme* vol. V, 1965. For an application of the concept of mode of production to the development of agriculture, cf. G. Postel-Vinay, *La rente fonciére dans le capitalisme agricole*, Paris 1974; and P. P. Rey, *Les alliances des classes*, Maspèro, Paris 1973.

5. Although in Amin's contribution one can discern the influence of the two theoretical trends mentioned above, his major writings on the underdevelopment of third-world countries (e.g. *L'accumulation à l'échelle mondiale*, Anthropos, Paris 1970) follow the neo-Marxist school of development — a school of which Althusserians are very critical. For an Althusserian critique of neo-Marxist theories of development, cf. J. Taylor, 'Neo-Marxism and under-development', *Jrnl of Contemporary Asia*, vol. III, 1974.

6. Cf. A. Chaianov, *On the theory of peasant economy* (edited by D. Thorner *et al.*), Inwin, Homewood, Ill., 1966. See also D. Mitrany, *Marx against the peasant: a study in social dogmatism*, Weidenfeld & Nicolson, London 1951.

7. Cf. Amin-Vergopoulos, op. cit., p. 263.

8. Cf. for instance V. Filias, *Society and power in Greece 1800—1864* (in Greek), Athens 1974; and C. Moskof, *National and social consciousness in Greece 1830—1909* (in Greek), Salonica 1972.

9. For a critique of writings on modern Greece along such lines, cf. above, Chapter 3.

10. K. D. Karavidas, *Agrotika* (in Greek), Athens 1931.

11. Cf. for instance A. Sideris, *The agricultural policy of Greece 1833—1933*, Athens 1933.

12. Cf. for instance K. Thompson, *Land fragmentation in Greece*, Centre of Planning and Economic Research, Athens 1963.

13. Cf. David and Judith Willer, *Systematic empiricism: critique of a pseudo-science*, Prentice-Hall, Englewood Cliffs, N.J., 1973.

14. Cf. Vergopoulos, op. cit., pp. 208—10.

15. Concerning the number of tractors, Vergopoulos uses the classical statistical trick for aggrandising certain economic variables: starting from a period when the number of tractors was very small (the end of the civil war), it is easy to show enormous rates of increase for subsequent periods (p. 209). The same type of computation is used in order to prove that industrialisation under Koumoundouros (in the 1860s) was faster than under Trikoupis (in the 1870s) — cf. p. 132. Moreover, contrary to Vergopoulos' general argument, wheat cultivation remained stable in Greece between 1910 and 1936. (Cf. G. Dertilis, op. cit., Table V.) Of course, as far as post-war agricultural productivity is concerned, it is very difficult to generalise. In present-day Greek agriculture there are significant productivity differences according to regions, types of cultivation etc. But in the absence of serious and systematic research on such differences and looking at the overall picture, I think one can say that, due to extreme land fragmentation, inadequate State assistance and low agricultural incomes, there are huge productivity differentials between agriculture and capital-intensive industry — as well as between Greek and Western European agricultures.

16. Cf. OECD, *Agricultural Statistics 1953—1969*, Paris 1969, pp. 52—3; cf. also OECD, *Agricultural development in southern Europe*, Paris 1969, p. 22.

17. Cf. OECD, *Agricultural policies in 1966: Europe, North America, Japan*, Paris 1967, pp. 24—8.

18. C. Furtado, *Development and underdevelopment*, University of California Press, Berkeley 1964.
19. For statistics on this point, cf. Chapter 2, section 2B.
20. Amin himself, in one of his recent books, emphasises the much greater productivity differentials between technologically advanced and backward sectors of peripheral social formations. (*Le Développement inégal*, ed. Minuit, Paris 1973, p. 187.)
21. Cf. S. Amin, *L'accumulation . . .*, op. cit., pp. 373—76. For a recent analysis of underdevelopment in terms of the articulation of modes of production, cf. J. Kay, *Development and underdevelopment: a Marxist analysis*, London 1975.
22. Vergopoulos, op. cit., p. 17.
23. Cf. G. Photopoulos, 'The dependence of the Greek economy on foreign capital' (in Greek), *Economicos Tahidromos*, July 1975; and M. Malios, *The present phase of capitalist development in Greece* (in Greek), Athens 1975. Cf. also my Chapters 2 and 7.
24. In fact, Vergopoulos, influenced by a group of French researchers studying the development of agriculture in modern France, tried in a rather uncritical manner to apply some of their ideas to the case of Greece. Cf. particularly C. Servolin, 'L'absorption de l'agriculture dans le mode de production capitaliste', in Y. Tavernier, M. Gervais and C. Servolin, *L'univers politique des paysans*, Paris 1972; cf. also H. Mendras, *Les paysans et la modernisation de l'agriculture*, Paris 1958.
25. G. Hermet, 'L'Espagne', in H. Mendras and Y. Tavernier (eds), *Terre, paysans et politique*, vol. II, Futuribles, Paris 1970, pp. 45—75; cf. also E. Malefakis, *Agrarian reform and peasant revolution in Spain*, Yale University Press, Newhaven and London 1970.
26. Cf. I. T. Berend and G. Ranki, *Economic development in east-central Europe in the 19th and 20th century*, Columbia University Press, New York and London 1974; cf. also E. Wallerstein, *The modern world system: capitalist agriculture and the origins of the European world-economy in the 16th century*, Academic Press, New York and London 1974, chs 2 and 6.
27. This is a chance Eastern European peasants never had, since there was never an equivalent power vacuum in Eastern Europe. Cf. P. Anderson, *Lineages of the Absolutist State*, New Left Publications, London 1974.
28. Cf. W. E. Moore, *Economic demography of eastern and southern Europe*, London 1945, pp. 77—91 and 230—52.
29. Amin-Vergopoulos, op. cit., p. 226.
30. For a critique of Althusserian Marxism along such lines, cf. E. Laclau, 'The specificity of the political: the Poulantzas-Miliband debate', *Economy and Society*, vol. IV, no. 1, pp. 87—110; and R. Miliband, 'Poulantzas and the capitalist State', *New Left Review*, Nov—Dec 1974, pp. 86 ff., cf. also above, Chapter 2.
31. Cf. D. Lockwood, 'Social and system integration', in G. Zollschan and W. Hirsch (eds), *Exploration in social change*, Routledge, London, pp. 244—56; and N. Mouzelis, 'Social and system integration: some reflections on a fundamental distinction', *British Jrnl of Sociology*, vol. XXV(4), pp. 395—409.
32. For a structural explanation of the failure of the Greek peasantry to organise itself politically during the inter-war period, cf. below, Chapter 5.

CHAPTER 5

1. For an account of similarities in Balkan societies, see L. S. Stavrianos, *The Balkans since 1453*, New York 1958, especially pp. 96–116, 137–53, 198–214, 413–24; Hugh Seton-Watson, *Eastern Europe between the Wars 1918–1941*, Cambridge 1945; N. Iorga, *Le charactère commun des institutions de Sud-Est de l'Europe*, Paris 1929, p. 138.

2. For statistics on railway, road and sea transport during the inter-war years in the Balkans, cf. P.E.P., *Economic development in S.E. Europe*, London 1945, pp. 60–79.

3. Cf. Stavrianos, op. cit., p. 417; cf. also A. J. May, 'Trans-Balkan railway schemes', *Jrnl of Modern History*, Dec 1938, pp. 496–527.

4. It was calculated that in 1932 the total foreign debt per head of population was 378 Swiss francs for Greece, and 188 for Bulgaria (cf. Royal Institute of International Affairs, *The Balkan States*, London 1936).

5. Cf. Stavrianos, op. cit., p. 445.

6. Cf. E. J. Tsouderos, *Le rélèvement économique de la Grèce*, Berger-Levrault, Paris 1920. For an account of Greece's financial position in the nineteenth century, cf. A. Levandis, *The Greek foreign debt and the Great Powers 1821–1898*, New York, 1944.

7. A good indication of this is the predominance of an indirect system of taxation in all Balkan countries before and during the inter-war period; cf. A. Angelo-poulos, 'Les finances publiques d'états Balkaniques', *Les Balkans*, vol. II Sep 1933, pp. 629 ff.; Royal Institute of International Affairs, *The Balkan States*, London 1936, p. 50.

8. For the inter-war agrarian reforms in the Balkans, cf. D. Mitrany, *Marx against the peasant*, 1951; C. Evelpides, *Les états Balkaniques*, Paris 1930; for a short survey of land tenure systems in various Balkan countries during the inter-war period, cf. W. E. Moore, *Economic demography of eastern and southern Europe*, Geneva 1945, pp. 210–67.

9. Cf. W. E. Moore, op. cit., pp. 250–1; J. D. Bell, *The agrarian movement in Bulgaria*, unpub. thesis, Princeton University 1970, ch. 1.

10. Cf. D. Mitrany, op. cit.; O. S. Morgan (ed.), *Agricultural systems of Middle Europe*, New York 1933; Evelpidi, op. cit.; A. Sideris, *The agricultural Policy of Greece 1833–1933* (in Greek), Athens 1934.

11. Cf. W. E. Moore, op. cit., pp. 17–28.

12. Cf. W. E. Moore, op. cit., pp. 63 and 71–2. For a more optimistic calculation of labour surplus, cf. N. Spulber, *The economics of communist Eastern Europe*, pp. 275–6. For statistics on number of people per 100 hectares of cultivated land, cf. J. Tomasevich, *Peasants, politics and economic development in Yugoslavia*, Stanford 1955, p. 309.

13. Cf. Stavrianos, op. cit., pp. 599 ff.; N. Spulber, op. cit.; A. Gerschenkron, *Economic backwardness in historical perspective*, New York 1962, pp. 198–234; P.E.P., op. cit., pp. 39–140.

14. Cf. above, Chapter 2, sections 2 and 3.

15. Cf. Chapter 2 and Chapter 7, section 2.

16. For an analysis of Balkan peasant ideology, cf. Branko Peselz, *Peasant movements in south-eastern Europe*, unpub. thesis, Georgetown University 1950; G. M. Dimitrov, 'Agrarianism', in F. Gross, *European ideologies*, New York 1948;

and Mitrany, op. cit.

17. For a detailed history of Bulgaria's agrarian party, cf. J. D. Bell, *The agrarian movement in Bulgaria*, op. cit.; cf. also M. Oren, *Revolution administered: agrarianism and communism in Bulgaria*, Baltimore 1973; A. Omelianov, 'A Bulgarian experiment', in P. A. Sorokin *et al.*, *A systematic source book in rural society*, vol. II, Minneapolis 1931.

18. For a short history of the Greek Agrarian Party, cf. D. Pournaras, *The history of the agrarian movement in Greece*, Athens 1931.

19. For a very good historical account of the development of the Balkan merchant classes, cf. T. Stoianovich, 'The conquering Balkan Orthodox merchant', in *Jrnl. of Economic History*, 1960, pp. 269—73; cf. also above, Chapter 1, section 1.

20. Bulgarian and other Slav merchants started to challenge Greek commercial supremacy in the eastern Balkans only after the treaty of Adrianople in 1829. By this treaty the Danubian principalities were allowed to engage in international trade.

21. Not only the Aegean coast but even the coastal areas around the Black Sea were predominantly inhabited by Greek, Jewish and Armenian people, cf. Stoianovich, op. cit., p. 310.

22. Ibid., p. 311.

23. Greece's cultural hegemony in the eighteenth-century Balkans was not only due to its powerful merchant class. The position of the Greek Orthodox Church was another contributing factor. Before the establishment of autocephalous Slav nationalist Churches, the Greek Patriarchate in Constantinople administered the religious lives of all Orthodox Christians, Greek or non-Greek. All important ecclesiastical positions were monopolised by Greeks, the Greek liturgy was imposed in all churches, and Greek was made the language of instruction at schools; cf. Stavrianos, op. cit., pp. 368 ff.; cf. also N. Iorga, op. cit.

24. The Greek War of Independence (1821—27) brought a temporary halt to the commercial activities of the Greek merchant class. But this setback — at least as far as the Mediterranean trade was concerned — was overcome and trade flourished again after independence. As far as overland inter-Balkan trade is concerned, due to the emergence of Balkan nationalism and other unfavourable conditions, this declined more or less permanently at the beginning of the nineteenth century; cf. Stoianovich, op. cit., p. 312.

25. The term *modernisation* is used here in rather a specific way. It refers mainly to the 'process by which an underdeveloped region changes in response to inputs (ideology, behavioural codes, commodities and institutional models) from already established industrialised centres; a process which is based on that region's continued dependence on the urban-industrial metropolis.' In contrast to this, *development* refers to the process by which an underdeveloped region attempts to acquire an autonomous and diversified industrial economy on its own terms; cf. P. Schneider et al., 'Modernisation and development', in *Comparative Studies in Society and History*, June 1972, p. 340.

26. Cf. above, Chapter 1, section 2.

27. Cf. Stavrianos, op. cit., pp. 364 ff.

28. A turning-point in the cultural relationships between Greece and Bulgaria was the establishment of an autonomous Bulgarian Church in 1870 which put an end to the religious hegemony of the Greek Patriarchate in Constantinople; cf.

E. S. Karpathios, 'Bulgaria, Church', in *Great Hellenic Encyclopaedia*, vol. VII, pp. 672–82.

29. This difference is even reflected in the Bulgarian nationalist ideologies which have a rather defensive character: for instance, Father Paisii, who wrote the first Bulgarian history, makes a continuous effort to convince his readers that Bulgarians are 'as good as or even better' than Greeks. There is also an attempt to contrast Bulgaria's rural virtues with evil Greek urbanism (cf. M. Pundeff, 'Bulgarian nationalism', in P. Sugar and I. J. Lederer (eds), *Nationalism in eastern Europe*, Washington 1969, p. 102).

30. Cf. P.E.P., op. cit., p. 129; and T. Deldycke et al., The Working *population and its structure*, Brussels 1968.

31. Cf. K. D. Karavidas, *Agrotika* (in Greek), Athens 1931, pp. 125–36 and 201–68.

32. On the Zadruga family system, cf. P. E. Mosely, 'The peasant family: the Zadruga or communal joint-family in the Balkans and its recent evolution', in C. F. Ware (ed.), *The cultural approach to history*, New York 1940, pp. 95–108. For a contrast of Greek and Bulgarian family institutions during the inter-war period, cf. Karavidas, op. cit., pp. 201–68.

33. D. Daniilides, *Modern Greek society and economy* (in Greek) Athens 1934, pp. 126–42.

34. D. Mitrany, op. cit., pp. 118–19.

35. Cf. for instance, E. Wolf, *Peasant wars of the twentieth century*, London 1971, pp. 276–302; cf. also H. Alavi, 'Peasants and revolution', in R. Miliband and J. Saville (eds), *The Socialist Register*, London 1965, pp. 290 ff.

36. On the foreign origin of the Bulgarian bourgeoisie, cf. Stoianovich, op. cit.,; cf. also N. Pasic, 'Factors in the formation of nations in the Balkans and among the southern Slavs', *International Social Science Jrnl*, 1971, no. 3, pp. 419 ff.

37. Cf. Karavidas, op. cit., pp. 125–6.

38. N. Iorga, 'The French Revolution and south-eastern Europe', in S. Fischer-Galati (ed.), *Man, State and Society in Eastern European History*, New York 1970, p. 131.

39. Cf. K. G. Popoff, *La Bulgarie économique*, Sofia 1920, pp. 83–134.

40. Cf. Petko Kunin, *The agrarian and peasant problem in Bulgaria* (in Bulgarian), Sofia 1971, ch. 1.

41. P. Kunin, op. cit., p. 61 ff.

42. Cf. J. Kordatos, *Pages from the agrarian movement of Greece* (in Greek), Athens, 1964, pp. 143 ff.

43. Cf. D. N. Afendakis, *Agricultural credit in Turkey, Bulgaria, Yugoslavia and Greece* (in Greek), Athens, n.d.; C. Evelpides, 'La coopération aux pays Balkaniques dans le domaine du credit agricole', *Les Balkans*, vol. IV, pp. 732–46; K. Popoff, *Aspects of the creation and development of the cooperative movement in Bulgaria* (in Bulgarian), Sofia 1924.

44. Gerschenkron, op. cit. p. 222.

45. T. Shanin, *The awkward class*, London 1927, part II.

46.

Properties		1897		1908	
		No. of properties	%	No. of properties	%
Very small	(under 20 decares)	363,646	45.48	424,898	45.52
Small	(20—100 decares)	334,384	41.83	386,728	41.44
Medium	(100—300 decares)	92,509	11.57	111,632	11.96
Big	(300—1000 decares)	8,101	1.01	9,173	0.98
Very big	(over 1000 decares)	948	0.11	936	0.10
	TOTAL	799,588	100.00	933,367	100.00

From K. G. Popoff, op. cit., p. 97.

47. Cf. W. E. Moore, op. cit., pp. 77—91 and 250—52.
48. Cf. A. D. Sideris, op. cit., G. Servatis and C. Pertounzi, 'The agricultural policy of Greece', in O. S. Morgan (ed.), *Agricultural systems of middle Europe*, New York 1933, pp. 137—200; C. Evelpidi, op. cit., pp. 89 ff.
49. Cf. for instance, S. M. Lipset, *Agrarian socialism*, New York 1950; E. Wolf, 'On peasant rebellions', in T. Shanin (ed.), *Peasants and peasant societies*, London 1971, pp. 264—74.
50. Figures taken from M. J. Lineton, *Mina present and past — depopulation in a village in Mani, southern Greece*, unpub. thesis, University of Kent 1971, p. 276; cf. also C. Moustaka, *The internal migrant*, Social Sciences Centre Monograph, Athens 1964; S. Hazoglou, 'Internal migration' (in Greek), in *Spoudai*, no. 4, 1965—66; J. Baxevannis, 'Population, internal migration and urbanisation in Greece', *Balkan Studies*, no. 6, 1965, pp. 83—98.
51. For the relatively high percentage of peasants' sons in higher education in Greece, cf. J. Lambiri-Dimaki, 'Les chances d'accès à l'enseignement en Grece', in R. Castel and J. Passeron, *Education, développement et démocratie*, Paris 1967.
52. Lineton, op. cit., p. 175.
53. Cf. I. Stefanov, 'Socio-economic changes and internal migration in Bulgaria', in B. W. Frijling (ed.), *Social change in Europe*, Leiden 1973, p. 40. According to the last pre-Second World War census, Bulgarians living in localities with over 20,000 inhabitants numbered only 12.7 per cent of the total population (cf. P.E.P., op. cit., p. 81). Even as late as 1955 the percentage was only 15.3 (cf. Russett, *World Handbook of political and social indicators*, Newhaven 1964, p. 52).
54. Cf. article on 'Greece' in *Great Greek Encyclopaedia*, p. 234; cf. also H. P. Fairchild, *Greek immigration to the United States*, Newhaven 1911; A. Krikos, *Greek emigration to the New World* (in Greek); T. Saloutos, *The Greeks in the United States*, Cambridge, Mass., 1964.
55. Cf. J. Roucek, 'Les Boulgares d'Amerique', *Balkans*, vol. IX, pp. 55—70.
56. Apart from agrarianism, communism was also a very significant political force in inter-war Bulgaria; cf. J. Rotschild, *The Communist Party of Bulgaria 1883—1936*, New York 1959; D. G. Jackson, *Comintern and peasant in east Europe*, New York 1966; R. V. Burks, *The dynamics of Communism in eastern Europe*, Princeton 1961; Hugh Seton-Watson, *The eastern European revolution*,

London 1950.

57. Cf. A. Angelopoulos, op. cit., pp. 674—9.

58. Cf. J. Petropoulos, *Politics and statecraft in the Kingdom of Greece 1833—1843*, Princeton 1968; *cf.* also J. Campbell and P. Sherrard, *Modern Greece*, London 1968, pp. 83—126.

59. For the early struggles between the State and various local elites, cf. N. Diamandouros, *Political modernisation: social conflict and cultural cleavage in the formation of the modern Greek State 1821—28*, unpub. thesis, Columbia University 1972.

60. E. Dicey, *The peasant State*, London 1894, p. 145.

61. Following Michel's 'Law of Oligarchy' one can of course argue that, considering the bourgeois origins of some of the peasant leaders and the unavoidable corruption which followed their taking of power, the Agrarian Union was not very different from other bourgeois parties. But this position does not take into account the radical policies which the Agrarian Union did in fact pursue both on the international and the national level. For instance, as far as foreign policy is concerned, Stamboliiski completely reversed the militaristic and irredentist policies of all his predecessors, and promoted a policy of peaceful cooperation among all Balkan nations. On the national level he tried to discourage large-scale industrialisation, and sought a path to development which could profit the peasants and safeguard their village communities. It might be objected that a policy which tries to achieve economic growth without the painful disruption of peasant life is utopian (cf. B. Moore, *The social origins of dictatorship and democracy*, London 1967). The important point is that such policies were attempted, and they did pose a real challenge to the traditional Bulgarian establishment.

62. The specific circumstances and reasons for the eventual defeat of the Bulgarian peasant movement are well beyond the scope of this chapter. Here I would simply like to point out that such circumstances and reasons must be studied within the context of the overall, fundamental contradiction between an underdeveloped economy (characterised by the negative articulation of capitalist and non-capitalist modes of production) and imported, Western-type parliamentary institutions.

63. Cf. for instance, A. Stewart, 'Populism: the social roots', in E. Gellner and G. Ionescu (eds), *Populism*, London 1969.

64. For a review of such theories and an interesting formulation, cf. J. B. Allcock, 'Populism: a brief biography', in *Sociology*, Sep 1971, pp. 371—88.

65. Of course, it must be pointed out that being 'drawn in', i.e. greater integration with the centre, by no means implies a more balanced, less painful adaptation to the strains of rapid change. There is no indication that Greek peasants were better off than the Bulgarian ones during the inter-war years (if anything, the opposite). For instance, just before the Second World War, Greece — together with Portugal and Albania — had the lowest calorie consumption rate in Europe: 2300 to 2500 calories per day per inhabitant (*cf.* Stavrianos, op. cit., p. 683).

66. Concerning peasant studies, E. Wolf for example, in examining the revolutionary potential of the peasantry in Russia, Mexico, Cuba, Algeria, China and Vietnam, emphasises geographical and social isolation as factors conducive to peasant mobilisation (*Peasant Wars of the 20th Century*, op. cit., pp.

276—302).

67. For an attempt to produce this type of generalisation about peasants, cf. E. M. Rogers, *Modernisation among peasants: the impact of communication*, New York 1969.

68. Cf. for instance, A. Pearse, 'Peasants and revolution: the case of Bolivia', *Economy and Society*, vol. I, no. 3, pp. 266 ff.

69. More concretely and taking the Stamboliiski argument as an instance, although his charisma tremendously helped the revival of the Agrarian Union after its temporary decline in 1909, it is quite certain that a Greek Stamboliiski would not have found a similarly favourable field for developing his potentialities. Moreover, I do not think that it is accidental that Venizelos, the Greek statesman who in terms of charisma compares with Stamboliiski, did not become the champion of the peasants but of the rising Greek bourgeoisie. As far as the 'defeat at wars' argument goes, this does not explain why the Agrarian Union became the major opposition party in Bulgaria before the Balkan Wars.

CHAPTER 6

1. Cf. above, Chapter 1, sections 2 and 3.

2. For the nature and development of this type of political conflict during the early years of Greek independence, cf. John Petropoulos, *Politics and statecraft in the Kingdom of Greece 1833—1843*, Princeton. N. J., 1968; cf. also N. Diamandouros, *Political modernisation, social conflict and cultural cleavage in the formation of the modern Greek State 1821—1828*, unpub. thesis, Columbia University, 1972.

3. Cf. P. Pipinelis, *Political history of the Greek revolution* (in Greek), Athens 1926. Cf. also his *The monarchy in Greece* (in Greek), Athens 1932; and V. Filias, *Society and power in Greece 1800—1884* (in Greek), Athens 1974.

4. For instance, from 1864 to 1909 Greece had 58 governments (cf. list of Greek governments presented by D. Dakin, *The Unification of Greece 1770—1923*, London 1972, pp. 286 ff.). For similar statistics see article on 'Greek political parties' in *Helios Encyclopaedia*, vol. VII (in Greek).

5. S. Markezinis, *The political history of modern Greece* (in Greek) Athens 1966, vol. II, parts 1 and 2.

6. The fact that during this period the military, while on active service, could occupy key positions in the legislative and executive branches of the State is a clear indication of the lack of differentiation between military and political elites. This practice stopped in 1910.

7. Cf. above Chapter 2, section 4.

8. Cf. L. S. Stavrianos, *The Balkans since 1453*, New York 1965, pp. 413 ff.

9. Concerning these changes, J. Campbell and P. Sherrard write: 'Therefore, the last forty years of the nineteenth century saw a very considerable expansion of the world of professional men and salaried clerks working in financial, commercial and government institutions. These with the great number of small wholesale and retail traders formed the nucleus of a growing urban middle class wearing European clothes, priding themselves on having an education and attitudes similar to their western counterparts.' *Modern Greece*, London 1968,

p. 98. For the comprador aspects of the nineteenth-century Greek bourgeoisie, cf. Filias, op. cit.

10. The fact that the officers who initiated the coup were more concerned with their professional interests than with broader social changes (cf. T. Veremis, *The Greek army in politics*, unpub. thesis, Trinity College, Oxford, 1974, p. 29) does not of course make the coup less bourgeois in its effects. For what matters is not the motivations of the specific officers but the *unintended consequences* of their actions.

11. Cf. V. Papacosmas, *The Greek military revolt of 1909*, unpub. thesis, Indiana University 1970, pp. 55 ff.

12. As a matter of fact, various associations, operating as pressure groups and attempting to influence public opinion through their own newspapers had already appeared in the 1880s; and from 1895 on there were attempts to organise trade unions. All these newly emerging groups contributed considerably to the creation of a favourable climate for the 1909 coup.

13. After the coup, the guilds of Athens organised the first Greek mass rally in support of the Military League. Similar demonstrations took place in various provincial towns (cf. Papacomas, op. cit., pp. 125 ff.

14. Cf. N. Mouzelis and M. Attalides, 'Greece', in S. Giner and M. Archer (eds), *Contemporary Europe*, London 1971, pp. 163 ff.

15. Cf. K. Legg, *Politics in modern Greece*, Stanford, Calif. 1969, Chapter 5.

16. Cf. D. Kitsikis, 'Evolution de l'élite politique Greque', in M. B. Kiray (ed.), *Social stratification and development in the Mediterranean basin*, Paris 1973.

17. Of course, the relative decline of the power position of the throne was a very gradual process. Already the establishment of *dedilomeni* in 1875 (a parliamentary practice which did not allow the King the right to appoint minority governments) to some extent reduced blatant royal interventions in parliamentary politics. The advent of Venizelos, although of course it did not bring the emergence of 'modern' mass parties, saw the development and strengthening of *national* party organisations (e.g. the Liberal Party established offices in various provincial towns). Thus political leaders began to have more control over their members and greater bargaining power *vis-à-vis* the King. With increasing party discipline, the ability of the King to manipulate politicians and elections decreased. (I am, of course, speaking in relative terms.) As the 1965–67 events demonstrated, such an ability did not entirely disappear, but royal manipulation is not as easy in the twentieth century as it had been in the nineteenth. Thus it was very simple for King George in 1868 to dismiss Prime Minister Koumoundouros (who, despite his overwhelming majority in parliament, gave in without protest) over a disagreement on the Cretan question. It was much less easy for King Constantine to get rid of Venizelos in 1915.

18. It is again possible to ascribe the initial disagreement and clash between the King and Venizelos to conjunctural factors: e.g. to personality incompatibilities between these two highly charismatic men. But I think that in this case too one can make out a serious case for a structural explanation of the split — i.e. in terms of the shifting throne-bourgeoisie power relationship. Of course, the extent to which one should assign more weight to conjunctural as against structural factors in an attempt to understand the *dichasmos* is, in the last analysis, a matter for further empirical research.

19. For a detailed chronological list of all 'illegal' military activities from October

1923 until March 1935, cf. Veremis, op. cit., pp. 384—89.

20. For a relatively detailed account, cf. G. Vendiris, *Greece 1910—1920* (in Greek), 2 vols, Athens 1930; and G. Dafnis, *Greece 1923—1940* (in Greek), 2 vols, Athens 1955.

21. Cf. above, Chapter 5.

22. In its extreme form, the *Megali Idea* (the Great Idea) ideology advocated the recapturing of Constantinople and some sort of resuscitation of the Byzantine Empire.

23. Cf. below, Chapter 8, section 1.

24. Although general conscription was introduced in 1880, it was only during the Balkan Wars that numbers increased spectacularly. For statistics on this point, cf. D. Dakin, op. cit., p. 316.

25. In 1917 tuition fees for the Evelpidon School (the top Greek military academy) were abolished. Before then, only wealthy students could afford this type of military education and in the nineteenth century familial property or a good marriage were necessary for maintaining an officer's style of life. Of course, the 'old respectable families stopped sending their children to the Military Academy once the institution became less exclusive and lost its social prestige' (Veremis, op. cit., p. 78). Cf. also Veremis, 'The officer corps in Greece 1912—1936', in *Byzantine and Modern Greek Studies*, vol. II, London 1976, pp. 113—14.

26. The relatively dependent position of the military becomes understandable if one takes into account the historical origins of the modern Greek Army. Contrary to what happened in many newly independent countries, for instance, in Greece there was a lack of continuity between the military forces who participated in the War of Independence against the Turks, and those who constituted the post-independence Greek army. Indeed, with the establishment of the monarchical State in the early nineteenth century, the local military chieftains, who had contributed more than anyone else to the war of liberation, were seen as an obstacle to the creation of a centralised, well-disciplined modern army. They were therefore brushed aside. King Otho, with the help of Bavarian officers and troops, created from he top a new military organisation, controlled by the throne. Cf. I. Makriyannis, *Memoirs* (trans. H. A. Liderdale), London 1966.

27. Cf. G. Dafnis, op. cit., vol. I, pp. 277 ff.

28. Cf. T. Veremis, op. cit., chapters III and XII.

29. There were three main factions in the army: the *amynites* (officers who joined Venizelos' 1916 revolt in Salonica), the *apotaktoi* (royalist officers), and the *paraminantes* (Venizelist officers who did not join Venizelos in Salonica) — cf. T. Veremis, op. cit., pp. 58 ff.

30. The coup was mainly a reaction by an ideologically mixed group of officers (some monarchists, some non-republican Venizelists and some disgruntled republicans) who were opposed to the Military League's 'extremist' policies and growing power. Cf. Dafnis, *Greece between the wars* (in Greek), Athens 1955, vol. I, chapter 2; and Veremis, op. cit., pp. 137—47. Again, if one looks at unsuccessful coups from the republican side (e.g. the 1933 and 1935 attempts to forcefully prevent the pro-royalist populists from coming to power), such military interventions had no popular appeal among a population tired of coups and political instability. A major reason for these interventions was the fear by

Venizelist officers that a populist government might jeopardise their professional interests. Cf. Veremis, op. cit., pp. 213—88.

31. For instance, during the first six months of 1936, as many as 344 strikes took place in various places. This strike wave culminated in the events of 9—10 May in Salonica when 12 demonstrators were killed. (J. Campbell, op. cit., p. 159.)

32. For a historical analysis of the Metaxas coup, cf. K. Koliopoulos, *Britain and Greece 1935—1941*, unpub. thesis, London School of Economics 1972.

33. For a detailed historical analysis of the IDEA group and of the other repressive State agencies during the post civil-war era, see G. Katiphoris, *Greece: the institutionalisation of a defence society*, London, forthcoming; cf. also below, chapter 7, section 1.

34. Cf. K. Legg, op. cit., and J. Menaud, *Les forces politiques en Grèce*, Montreal 1965, ch. 5.

35. Cf. for instance T. Charlier-Yannopoulou, 'A propos de la crise politique Grèque', in *Revue Française de la Science Politique*, vol. 17 no. 1, 1967.

36. For an elaboration of the above points cf. next chapter.

37. By 'active' I mean the type of support that, for instance, the Spanish landowning classes were giving to Franco.

38. Cf. Katiphoris, op. cit.; and below, Chapter 7, section 4.

39. For the inter-war agrarian reforms in the Balkans, cf. D. Mitrany, *Marx against the peasant*, 1951; and C. Evelpides, *Les Etats Balkaniques*, Paris 1930; for a short survey of land systems in various Balkan countries during the inter-war period, cf. W. E. Moore, *Economic demography of eastern and southern Europe*, Geneva 1945; cf. also above Chapter 5.

40. Cf. G. Koutsoumaris, *The morphology of Greek industry*, Athens 1963; E. Kartakis, *Le développement industriel de la Grèce*, Lausanne 1970; cf. also Chapter 2, section 2.

41. Cf. J. Kordatos, *The workers' movement in Greece* (in Greek), Athens 1956; cf. also his *Introduction to the history of Greek capitalism* (in Greek), Athens 1930; and C. Jecchines, *Trade-unionism in Greece*, Chicago 1967.

42. C. Tsoukalas explains the structure and development of Greek urbanisation in terms of the tremendous influence of the diaspora Greek bourgeoisie on the modern Greek State and society. *Cf. Dépendance et réproduction: le rôle de l'appareil scolaire dans une formation trans-territoriale − Le cas de la Grèce*, Doctorat des Lettres, Sorbonne 1975.

43. Finally, in considering the failure of the junta to build up totalitarian organisations for its support, one must take into account that militant nationalism plays an extremely important role in cases of successful fascist mobilisation (Germany, Italy). This type of nationalism is extremely difficult to develop in a context where industrialisation is largely dependent on foreign capital. If one takes into account this point and the fact that successful, foreign capital-led industrialisation takes place at the expense of the rural and urban working classes (see next chapter), it is easy to understand that not only the Greek dictatorship but also many similar regimes in Latin America (Brazil, Argentina, Chile) fail to build mass support and to 'institutionalise' themselves. Cf. J. M. Malloy (ed.), *Authoritarianism and Corporatism in Latin America*, University of Pittsburgh Press, 1977 − especially the articles by D. Chalmers, G. A. O'Donnell, S. D. Baretta and H. E. Douglas.

44. For the transition period (1880−1922), cf. Chapter 1, section 4. By arguing

that the monarchy conflict is typical of the transition period, I do not imply of course, that it played no role during the subsequent period — in fact the 'return of the king' is still a live issue in Greece today. All that I am arguing is that with the dominance of the capitalist mode of production during the four decades after 1922 a new conflict emerged (bourgeoisie versus the masses) which displaced in importance the intra-bourgeois 'throne' issue.

CHAPTER 7

1. In March 1943, July 1943, and April 1944. Cf. G. Karayannis, *1940–1952: The Greek drama*, in Greek, Athens n.d., pp. 105–69.

2. IDEA was founded in Athens in 1944 by the merging of ENA with TRIENA (a right-wing officers' resistance group). The most interesting insider's account of IDEA is given by Karayannis, op. cit., who was himself an IDEA man.

3. For a detailed account see G. Katiphoris, *The Barbarians' legislation* (in Greek), Athens 1975. Cf. also his 'The Colonels' Greece', unpublished manuscript, 1974.

4. S. Gregoriadis, *History of contemporary Greece* (in Greek), Athens 1974, vol. II, pp. 140–219.

5. C. A. Coombs, *Post-war public finance in Greece*, London 1947.

6. Cf. *National Accounts of Greece 1948–70*, pp. 120–1. For a detailed analysis of the growth of the Greek economy, cf. N. Vernicos, *L'économie de la Grèce 1950–1970*, unpub. thesis, University of Paris VIII, vol. I.

7. D. Psilos, *Capital market in Greece*, Centre of Economic Research, Athens 1964, pp. 185–6.

8. For instance, from 1955 to 1969, the assets of the commercial banks increased twenty times. Cf. M. Malios, *The present phase of capitalist development in Greece* (in Greek), Athens 1975.

9. Cf. Psilos, op. cit., ch. 10.

10. For all the above points on the development and structure of finance capital in Greece I am indebted to M. Serafetinidi's analysis in *The Breakdown of Parliamentary Institutions in Greece*, unfinished Ph.D. thesis, London School of Economics, ch. 1.

11. Malios, op. cit., pp. 156 ff.

12. Psilos, op. cit., ch. 14.

13. Cf. H. Ellis *et al.*, *Industrial capital in the development of the Greek economy* (in Greek), Centre of Economic Research, Athens 1965, pp. 197–204.

14. Private investment in agriculture was only 5.9 per cent of total private investment in 1950. It went up to 9.4 per cent in 1960, and down again to 8 per cent in 1970. Cf. Vergopoulos, op. cit., p. 203.

15. Ibid., ch. 4.

16. S. Andreadis, *Greek Shipping* (in Greek), Athens 1964.

17. The rate of ploughing back profits is very low in Greek firms (cf. Psilos, op. cit., p. 245) and, as the Greek stock market is extremely weak, they have no alternative for their short and long-term finance other than the commercial banks (cf. ibid., p. 189). This is another clear indication of the extent to which all Greek firms are dependent on State and finance capital.

18. For statistics on this point cf. above, Chapter 2, note 13.

19. Cf. above, Chapter 1, section 6; and Chapter 2, section 2A.
20. G. Petrochilos, 'The role of foreign capital in the Greek economy', unfinished thesis, University of Birmingham.
21. Vernicos, op. cit., vol. I, p. 372.
22. B. Nefeloudis, *Demythisation with numbers* (in Greek), Athens 1973, p. 146.
23. Cf. Chapter 1, sections 4 and 5.
24. Cf. Malios, op. cit., pp. 136 ff.
25. Cf. Photopoulos, 'The dependence of the Greek economy on foreign capital' (in Greek), *Economicos Tahidromos* no. 17, July 1975, p. 10.
26. Cf. Serafetinidi, op. cit., ch. 4.
27. For some of the reasons which can explain this inability, cf. E. Kartakis, *Le Développement industriel de la Grèce*, Lausanne 1970, pp. 20 ff.
28. Thus in 1961 the State issued 4088 permits for the establishment of new enterprises, and 2536 for the extension of existing ones. Of these only 29 and respectively were of any importance (i.e. were investing more than $30,000). Cf. Ellis *et al.*, op. cit., p. 189.
29. Cf. Serafetinidi, op. cit., ch. 8; cf. also above Chapter 2, note 28.
30. *Statistical Annual of Greece 1971*, p. 378.
31. Cf. D. Karageorgas, 'The distribution of tax burden by income groups in Greece', *Economic Journal*, June 1973.
32. Malios, op. cit., pp. 139 and 141.
33. N. Vernicos, *Greece facing the 'eighties*, Athens 1975, p. 116.
34. Cf. T. Lianos, *Wages and employment* (in Greek), Athens 1975, p. 89.
35. Between 1959 and 1969 the average wage per hour in a low-skilled industry such as beverages increased from 10.1 dr to 23.6 dr, whereas it went up from 10.8 dr to 37.9 dr in the petroleum and coal products industry. (Cf. T. Lianos and K. Prodromides, *Aspects of income distribution in Greece*, Centre of Planning and Economic Research, Athens 1974.)
36. Cf. J. Crockert, *Consumption expenses and incomes in Greece*, Athens 1970, p. 113. More research is needed on this point, but Greece seems to exhibit a trend which has already been noticed in some Latin American countries: namely, the emergence of a relatively affluent middle class (as distinct from the bourgeoisie) which maintains or increases its share in the GNP — at a time when all strata below it see their relative share decreasing. This stratum becomes a major consumer of the newly-founded durable goods industries. For an interesting but theoretically inadequate discussion of this trend, *cf.* P. Salama, 'Vers un nouveau modèle de l'accumulation', in *Critique de l'Economie Politique*, Apr–Sep 1974, pp. 42–9.
37. Nefeloudis, op. cit., p. 96.
38. For an early application of the concept of the mode of production in the analysis of the Greek economy, cf. M. Serafetinidi, op. cit.
39. Empirical evidence on this point is given in an as yet unfinished research project on the development of the patronage system in two Greek provinces during the sixties. Cf. M. Comninos, 'The development of the patronage system in Etolo-Akarnania and Kavala', unfinished thesis, London School of Economics.
40. Cf. S. Gregoriadis, *The history of the dictatorship*, Athens 1975, vol. I, p. 14. This should not be confused with the 'Prometheus' plan used by the same team to take power in April 1967.
41. Cf. Chapter 6, section 3.

42. Cf. S. Gregoriadis, op. cit., vol. I, ch. 2.

43. Cf. Evelpidon Military Academy, *The history of the Evelpidon Academy 1828–1926*, Athens 1962.

44. Cf. General Panourgias' report on the events which led to the coup, presented to Karamanlis in June 1967 (*Acropolis*, 20 Aug, 1974).

45. As already mentioned, the civil war requirements lowered the Military Academy standards of recruitment, and for the first time established a system of free education (under Law 577/22-9-1945). As people of poorer backgrounds could now study at the Academy, there was a distinct difference in class origins between officers who had graduated before and after the war. The top leadership at the time of the coup belonged to the former cohort, while the majority of the low- and middle-ranking officers belonged to the latter. For statistics on the Greek officers' class origin, cf. D. Smokovitis, *A special social group: the Greek armed forces*, unpub. thesis, University of Salonica 1975.

46. This point is emphasised by S. Papaspilopoulos, 'Une économie tributaire du modèle neo-liberal', *Le Monde Diplomatique*, Oct 1974; cf. also by the same author, 'Structures socio-politiques et développement économique en Grèce', *Les Temps Modernes*, no. 276 bis, 1969.

47. Of course, for a full explanation of the Cypriot crisis one should take into account a variety of factors, both on the national and international level, which are beyond the scope of this book. The present explanation is only incompatible with those accounts of the Cyprus problem which do not allow any autonomy to the internal structure of Greece and Cyprus, portraying the colonels as helpless pawns in the power politics of the Great Powers. This type of explanation is not only misleading, it also constitutes a very suitable ideology for exonerating the junta from its responsibility in the creation and handling of the Cyprus affair. For a recent, short, overall account of the Cyprus crisis see Christopher Hitchens, 'Détente and destablisation — report from Cyprus', *New Left Review*, no. 94.

48. Most books on the dictatorship now written by social scientists adopt this explanation. For instance, P. Rodakis, *The colonels' dictatorship: rise and fall* (in Greek), Athens 1974; or John Katris, *The birth of neo-fascism* (in Greek), Geneva 1971. For an extended bibliography of the voluminous literature on the Greek dictatorship, cf. C. Korizis, *The authoritarian regime 1967–1974* (in Greek), Athens 1975.

49. Cf. Gregoriadis, *The history of the dictatorship*, op. cit., vol. I, pp. 45 ff.

50. For instance, a well-publicised myth is that the Greek KYP (Intelligence Service) was for many years directly financed by the CIA and that, therefore, this agency was even formally beyond the control of the Greek State. But as has been pointed out in a recent sombre account of the history of the dictatorship, 'The Greek Central Intelligence Service functions on the basis of special laws. By a series of decrees it is linked to the budget of the Defence Ministry from which it pays its personnel. If it were true that, despite these laws and decrees, it was being financed directly by a foreign agency — the CIA — this would have constituted a colossal scandal entailing a very heavy responsibility for a great number of people. It would have been impossible for such a gross misdemeanour to have been left undiscovered for so many years.' Cf. Gregoriadis, op. cit., vol. I, p. 32.

51. For a similar position on the importance of 'internal factors' cf. N. Poulantzas,

La crise des dictatures: Portugal, Grèce, Espagne, Paris 1975 (English translation, New Left Books, London 1977).

52. See *La crise des dictatures*, op. cit. Poulantzas uses this intra-bourgeois conflict to explain mainly the fall of the dictatorial regimes in Greece and Portugal. M. Nikolinakos (*Resistance and opposition 1967—1974*, in Greek, Athens 1975, pp. 137—40 and 170 ff.) provides a similar explanation of the junta's rise.

53. See, for instance, V. Filias, op. cit.

54. C. Vergopoulos, op. cit., p. 15 (my translation).

CHAPTER 8

1. Of course this clientelistic character was more pronounced during Greece's pre-capitalist period; but it persisted, under a different form, even when, after the dominance of the capitalist mode of production, Greek politics took a more directly class character: cf. Chapter 1, sections 3 and 4, and Chapter 3, section 2C. On the clientelistic character of Greek politics cf. K. P. Legg, *Politics in modern Greece*, Stanford University Press, Stanford Calif., 1969; and J. Menaud, *Les forces politiques en Grèce*, Athens 1966.

2. Venizelos, the great statesman and father of the Greek Liberal party, was the dominant figure in Greek inter-war politics. For a political history of the inter-war period, cf. G. Dafnis, *Greece between the two wars, 1923—1940* (in Greek), 2 vols, Athens 1955; cf. also above, Chapter 6.

3. Cf. A. Sideris, *The agricultural policy of Greece 1833—1933*, Athens 1934; cf. also above, Chapter 5.

4. Although Venizelos was not involved in the military tactics adopted during the late phase of the campaign, it had been mainly his idea and his decision that Greece should acquire extensive territories in Asia Minor, even at the price of ceding already acquired territories in the north of Greece (cf. A. Pallis, *Greece's Anatolian adventures and after*, London 1937, pp. 15 ff). Strangely enough, the only bourgeois politician who assessed correctly the strength of the rising Turkish nationalism and the impossibility of maintaining for long an overseas Greek province with a predominant Turkish population was the future quasi-fascist dictator of Greece, John Metaxas. Cf. M. Llewellyn-Smith, *The Ionian vision*, London 1975; also N. Psiroukis, *The Asia Minor catastrophe* (in Greek), Athens 1964.

5. In addition to the *dichasmos*, another element which filled the ideological gap after the Asia Minor catastrophe was the rising anti-communist ideology — cf. G. Katiphoris, *The Barbarians' legislation* (in Greek), Athens 1975; cf. also A. Elefantis, *The promise of the impossible revolution: the Greek Communist Party during the inter-war period* (in Greek), Athens 1976, ch. 6; cf. also above, Chapter 1, section 5.

6. Given the lack of effective pressure from the student body, most of the relatively radical proposals, formulated by two post-dictatorial, government-appointed committees, for the reform of higher education remained a dead letter.

7. There is a vast literature on the language problem in Greece. For a recent excellent introduction to the subject see E. Moshonas' long introduction to A. Pallis, *Broussos* (in Greek), New Library, Athens 1976. The present Karamanlis

government has just passed a law which establishes *demotiki* as the language to be taught in both primary and secondary schools. It remains to be seen to what extent future governments will accept this fundamental change.

8. For an annotated bibliography on Greek education cf. E. Vlachos, *Modern Greek Society: Continuity and Change*, special mimeographic series, Colorado State University, 1969.

9. Cf. for instance Christos Yiannaras, 'The Circuit', *Vima*, 22 Nov 1975 (in Greek).

10. Cf. for instance F. W. Riggs, *Administration in developing countries: the theory of prismatic society*, Houghton & Mifflin, Boston 1964.

11. Cf. Chapter 2.

12. The incongruency between the autonomous political organisation of the working classes and sustained, inflation-controlled capitalist growth can be seen by the fact that there is not a single Latin American country which, in the post-war period, managed to successfully combat inflation and achieve sustained capitalist growth within a politically competitive framework. The few successful 'stabilisation' programmes were achieved under right-wing authoritarian regimes – cf. Thomas Skidmore, 'The politics of economic stablization in postwar Latin America', in J. Malloy (ed.), *Authoritarianism and capitalism in Latin America*, (University of Pittsburgh Press, Pittsburgh, 1977). Needless to say these 'successful' attempts were achieved at the expense of the working classes. To take the best-known example, the so-called 'Brazilian miracle' achieved by the military regime since it took power in 1964 did not benefit the workers very much: 'in the eight-year period from March 1966 to April 1974 (during which real per capita GNP increased substantially) the real value of the minimum wage averaged only 68.2 percent of its average real value in the period from July 1954 to December 1962', K. S. Mericle, 'Corporatist control of the working class: authoritarian Brazil since 1964', in J. M. Malloy (ed.), op. cit., p. 306; cf. also J. Quartim, *Dictatorship and Armed Struggle in Brazil*, New Left Books, London 1971.

13. Poulantzas has argued that a fundamental prerequisite for the reproduction of capitalism is the political fragmentation of the working class (cf. *Political power and social classes*, New Left Books, London 1973). Although generally speaking this statement holds true for both developed and underdeveloped capitalist formations, it is important to stress that in the reproduction of underdeveloped capitalism this fragmentation is more accentuated. The fact that the western European working classes are politically fragmented and reformist in orientation should not make one neglect the very considerable differences in political autonomy and power between them and their counterparts in underdeveloped countries.

14. For an introduction to eighteenth-century Greek society, cf. the collective work 'History of the Greek nation', vol. XI, *Hellenism under foreign rule 1669–1821* (in Greek), Ekdotiki Athinon, Athens 1975.

15. A classical work on this problem is D. Apter's *Ghana in transition*, New York 1963.

16. Cf. V. Kremmidas, *Introduction to the History of modern Greek society* (in Greek), Exantas, Athens 1976, introduction.

17. Cf. S. Asdrahas, 'The economy', in *Hellenism under foreign rule 1669–1821*, op. cit., pp. 159–98.

18. For the link between the flourishing Greek diaspora communities and Western colonialism, cf. N. Psiroukis, *The phenomenon of the modern Greek diaspora community* (in Greek), Athens 1974.

19. Cf. above, Chapter 1, section 2.

20. Kremmidas, op. cit., pp. 157 ff.

21. Cf. T. Stamatopoulos, *The internal strife before and after the revolution of 1821* (in Greek), 3 vols, Kalvos, Athens 1972, vol. 1, pp. 340 ff.

22. The term 'modernisers' and 'traditionalists' are used by N. Diamandouros, *Political modernisation, social conflict and cultural cleavage in the formation of the modern Greek State 1821—1828*, unpub. thesis, Columbia University 1972.

23. There is a lot of disagreement among Greek social scientists and historians on the 'bourgeois' nature of the Greek revolution and on the form of the State which evolved after it; Chapter 3, section 3.

24. For the early conflicts between the centralising State and the local oligarchies, cf. John Petropoulos, *Politics and Statecraft in the Kingdom of Greece: 1833—1943*, Princeton University Press, N.J., 1968; Stamatopoulos, op. cit.; P. Pipinelis, *The monarchy in Greece 1833—1843* (in Greek), Athens 1932; and his *Political history of the Greek revolution* (in Greek), Athens 1926.

25. Cf. G. Karanikolas, *Rigged elections in Greece* (in Greek), Epikerotita, Athens 1973.

26. From this point of view one can see the constitutional reforms of 1843 and 1864 — both of which curtailed royal power — as successful attempts by the Greek oligarchy to maintain its autonomy *vis-à-vis* the throne. The long period of constitutional stability between 1864 and 1909 can be seen as the result of a balance of forces between throne and oligarchy, a balance which was eventually to be upset by the rise of the new middle classes in the twentieth century (cf. above, Chapter 6). Finally, it must be emphasised once more that this dominance of the traditional oligarchical families had of course very strict limits, prescribed by the political and economic domination exercised over Greece by the foreign powers.

27. For a comparison of the differences between the functioning of parliamentarianism in Western Europe and in Greece, cf. Filias, op. cit.

28. As has been argued already (cf. above, p. 27 and pp. 65ff), the persistence of clientelism does not imply that present-day patronage networks are the same as in the nineteenth century. With increasing urbanisation and industrialisation, clientelism not only underwent fundamental changes (such as a shift from the 'monopolistic' patronage of the local oligarchs to a more flexible, open-ended 'party-oriented' clientelism), but it also became *weakened* as a mode of political integration (in the sense that the development of mass politics and the emergence of 'horizontal' organisations disrupt 'vertical' networks, especially in the cities). This, of course, does not mean, as some functionalist/neo-evolutionist political scientists think, that the weakening of clientelism will lead to the type of political development experienced by Western capitalist societies. What it does lead to is rather an uneasy coexistence of vertical and horizontal political organisations, alternating in importance with the fluctuation in the balance of the political forces at any specific moment (for instance, the victory of the right-wing forces during the Greek civil war reinforced clientelism during the first post-civil war decade). One might generalise and argue that, contrary to what happens in developed capitalist formations (where horizontal principles of

political organisation tend to prevail *irreversibly*), in underdeveloped capitalism – although vertical/clientelistic networks are both transformed and weakened by processes of State and market expansion etc. – they persist and coexist with emerging horizontal organisations which are generally weak and fragile. Thus one major feature of politics in these societies, at least in the urban centres, is the weak institutionalisation of both vertical and horizontal political organisations; this, to a limited extent, explains the notorious political instability of those underdeveloped capitalist countries with either permanent or intermittent parliamentary political institutions.

29. Cf. above, Chapter 1, sections 1 and 2. Even today one cannot understand the functioning of the Greek economy without seriously taking into account the contributions from Greeks living abroad. (I am thinking here not so much of the Greek cosmopolitan class of shipowners but of the thousands of Greek migrants whose considerable remittances are absolutely vital to the country's economy).

30. Tsoukalas, op. cit., part II, ch. 2. At the same time, until the First World War, the flourishing Greek communities abroad, especially those of Asia Minor, exerted a powerful attraction on thousands of Greeks leaving the Greek countryside and islands 'in order to join the growing number of merchants, financiers, commercial representatives, employees, doctors, lawyers etc. who to a large extent constituted the population of such communities' – C. Tsoukalas, 'Higher education in Greece as a mechanism of social reproduction' (in Greek), *Deukalion*, vol. XIII, p. 26 (my translation).

31. For instance, in 1961 the Greek ratio of university graduates to total population was 3.6 per cent, whereas in Spain it was 1.4 per cent, in Italy 2.6 per cent, and West Germany 2.7 per cent, and in Great Britain 3.4 per cent. Cf. OECD, *Projet régional méditerranéen: Grèce*, Paris 1965, p. 61.

32. For instance, before the First World War, Athens was the largest of the Balkan capitals, despite Greece being the second smallest Balkan country in terms of both population and territory. For more data on the relatively advanced state of Greek urbanisation, cf. above, Chapter 6. For the early commercialisation of Greek agriculture, cf. Chapters 5 and 6.

33. Cf. J. Campbell and P. Sherrard, *Modern Greece*, London 1968, pp. 19 ff. It might on the other hand be argued that Western interest in classical antiquity was very much stimulated by the migration of Greek scholars to the West, especially after the fall of Constantinople in 1453. Although nobody can deny this influence, the Renaissance in Western Europe, including the interest in classical antiquity, was – as Burckhardt has very rightly argued – due much more to processes endogenous to Western European societies than to the impact of Greek-Byzantine scholars, which only played a very secondary role. (J. Burckhardt, *The civilisation of the Renaissance in Italy*, Modern Library, New York 1954.)

34. For the cultural situation in Greece during the first two centuries of Ottoman rule, cf. *Hellenism under foreign rule 1453–1669*, op. cit., pp. 356–496.

35. C. Dimaras, 'The Greek enlightenment', in *Hellenism under foreign rule 1669–1821*, op. cit., p. 359.

36. It should be emphasised here that cultural diffusion and the importation of foreign cultural elements can by no means always be identified with cultural underdevelopment. It all depends on the type of relationship between the

lending and the borrowing society, as well as on the manner in which the cultural import is assimilated by the host country. Thus cultural underdevelopment always implies a negative assimilation (negative as defined in section 2B), or a disarticulation between imported and endogenous institutions.

37. Of course, in contrast to economic underdevelopment, a theory of political and cultural underdevelopment is non-existent at the present moment. As far as the politics of third-world countries are concerned, on the level of metatheory, most existing conceptual frameworks are inspired by the functionalist paradigm: cf., for instance, G. Almond and J. Coleman (eds), *The Politics of the Developing Areas*, Princeton University Press, N.J., 1960; J. Lapalombara, *Bureaucracy and Political Development*, Princeton University Press, N.J., 1963; J. L. Finkle and R. Gable (eds), *Political Development and Social Change*, Wiley, New York, 1966. I do believe that Marxist conceptual tools (especially the idea of articulation between modes of production), if properly elaborated, can shed new light and can provide a more rigorous analysis of the political and cultural structure of underdeveloped countries.

CONCLUSION

1. Cf. for instance M. Rubel, *Marx: Critique du marxisme*, Payot, Paris 1974.
2. Among the Greek Left, Andreas Papandreou's socialist party argues that only outside the EEC and NATO can Greece find its own autonomous path to development; whereas the Communist Party of the Interior (the 'Italian-type' CP), although very much aware of the problems of underdevelopment and dependence Greece is facing today, has opted for a strategy of democratic socialism with the help of other progressive forces *within* the Common Market. Although pro-EEC, this strategy does not at all show the gradualist, evolutionist elements of right-wing pro-Market ideologies. My argument here is neither for nor against joining the EEC. It is rather a plea for something which has not yet been done in Greece: to study seriously to what extent the eventual Greek entrance will increase or decrease the country's chances for an autonomous development. This is extremely difficult to assess at a time when a serious split seems to be emerging in the Community between the social democracies of the North and the countries with strong 'Euro-communist' movements (Italy, France).
3. The term is used by E. Wallerstein, *The modern world system: capitalist agriculture in 16th-century Europe*, Academic Press, New York 1974.
4. Cf. E. Hobsbawm, *Industry and Empire*, Penguin, London 1975.

Index